D1217430

LINCOLN THE LIBERAL STATESMAN

LINCOLN
THE LIBERAL STATESMAN

BY

J. G. Randall

DODD, MEAD & COMPANY

NEW YORK

APOLLO EDITION
PRINTED IN THE UNITED STATES OF AMERICA

To Carl Sandburg

ACKNOWLEDGMENTS

Six of the essays in this book have been published, in earlier form, in magazines. For the present purpose they have undergone considerable revision; in some cases there has been such a thorough recasting that the author wished he had started from scratch. This, however, in no way diminishes his indebtedness to the periodicals in which the studies first appeared. Permission for publication here has been freely given; for this generous favor the author is grateful to the *Mississippi Valley Historical Review*, the *Abraham Lincoln Quarterly* (for two essays), the McKinley Publishing Company (publishers of *The Social Studies*, successor to *The Historical Outlook*), the *Yale Review*, and the *South Atlantic Quarterly*. In the annotations page-and-volume references are given to these articles. The first essay—"Moot Points in the Lincoln Story"—and the last—"Lincoln the Liberal States-man"—have not been published previously in any form.

The writer cannot hope adequately to express his appreciation to librarians. Special acknowledgment is due to the impressive resources and helpful servicing of the National Archives, in which government files have been preserved. The Library of Congress has given unfailing assistance. Dr. St. George L. Sioussat of the division of manuscripts has been courteously coöperative, and valuable help has been extended by the divisions concerned with prints and photographic reproduction. The sustaining help of the University of Illinois, through its Library and its University Research Board, has been a most substantial advantage.

Students of Lincoln over many years have had an affectionate regard for Frederick H. Meserve; again, as before, the present author must express his obligation to the kindness of this foremost collector of Lincoln photographs. For access to stores of manuscripts the author is grateful to the Massachusetts Historical Society (valuable on Lincoln as on many other subjects) and to the Harvard Library. He cannot forget the efficiency and friendliness of the New York Public Library; at the opposite end of the country he has relied upon the Henry E. Huntington Library at San Marino, California, with its rich endowment, courteous staff, and distinction in the Lincoln field. In the study of John Bright he has been assisted by Mr. Harold J. Laski and by the ever resourceful British Museum. For the lending of manuscripts in private possession he is grateful to Mr. Harry E. Pratt and Mr. Vernon Munroe.

To one of his former graduate students—Miss Grace Willowick of Chicago—the writer owes by special permission the title of the third essay. This title was used by Miss Willowick for her master's dissertation at the University of Illinois, a study of Lincoln's discouraging prospects in the gloomy summer of 1864. The author also wishes to record his gratitude for stout assistance on the index "assembly line" by graduate students now at the University of Illinois: namely, Josephine L. Harper, Maurice G. Baxter, Theodore Fisch, and Melvin J. Mateyka.

For a period of years Dr. David Donald, research associate at the University of Illinois and former fellow of the Social Science Research Council, has served on University appointment as the author's assistant. Not only in heavy tasks of research and authentication, but also in various other forms of scholarly help, his contribution has been of the highest value, the more so because of his competence in the Lincoln field and his special study of William H. Herndon.

In this volume, as in other ventures, the author's wife, Ruth Painter Randall, has been his constant literary adviser.

J. G. R.

PREFACE

IN APPROACHING the subject of Lincoln and the Civil War one is reminded of Saxe's poem in which six blind men of Indostan—all very learned—investigate the elephant. One by one, after feeling the side, the trunk, the tusks, and so on, each came through with his verdict. The animal was like a wall to the one who touched the side, like a spear to the one who felt the tusk. The third blind man was sure with the squirming trunk in his hands that he was dealing with a snake. The leg convinced the fourth that the creature was like a tree, the ear suggested a fan to the fifth, and the sixth, grasping the tail, knew positively that the elephant was like a rope.

In offering essays on selected phases of the Lincoln theme it is the author's hope that the broad view has not been distorted. Many studies from different angles are necessary if the complexity of Lincoln's task and the conflicting currents of his era are to be even approximately understood. The partial view might emphasize expediency, tragic conflict, wartime abnormality, and excess of presidential power. It is, however, the writer's belief that in the general appraisal Lincoln is to be understood in terms of courageous and undaunted liberalism.

For the conditions which he faced naïve enthusiasm did not suffice. Lincoln is to be seen, not as one who uttered poeticisms about democracy, but (to repeat a phrase below) as a tough-minded liberal realist. His tough-mindedness was not a matter of outward facing truculence—far from it—but of realistic criticism focused upon conditions at home. His attention was upon realities, his approach the opposite of the doctrinnaire. This fact gave added value to the content of his thought or the trend of his philosophy, in which the main emphasis was upon the liberal outlook and credo. That he had a philosophy was the more significant because he did not merely inhabit a world of ideas. Living as he did in a period of frenzy and excess, and being a part of all that he had met, he yet refused to surrender to the cynicism of reaction.

The liberal must have a stout heart. To uphold progressive principles requires not lyrical eloquence or utopian fancy. It demands rather a facing up to hard realities and a moral force that is proof against discouragement. It requires also a discernment that can see through anti-democratic or anti-liberal sophisms.

In Lincoln's mental habit there was a blending of feeling and thought. Hard thinking was needful, but he did not want sentiment to be ignored. Emotional drive was so important that it ought by no means to be headed in the wrong direction, loyalty so vital that it should never be unworthily diverted. The "pillars of the temple of liberty," he once said, are to be "hewn from the solid quarry of sober reason." Yet he also spoke of "mystic chords of memory," of his love for "those old-time men," of "our national fabric, with all its benefits, its memories, and its hopes."

His struggles in tugging with legal problems had developed the habit of logical analysis, yet not without sympathetic understanding. He could reason, but his mind was no mere machine; he could also feel, and at times his feeling was clothed in language of high eloquence and rare beauty. So in the art of government: he could chart an administrative course, but not without the personal touch or the tactful gesture. The quieting of quarrels, the studious avoidance of offense, and the soothing of hurt feelings are factors that run continually through his writings in the presidential period. No man in the whole roster of Presidents gave more constant attention to the human element. That he could combine this personal thoughtfulness with emphasis upon tested thinking and pure reason was one of the striking factors in his genius.

Perhaps more than any other of the nation's statesmen Lincoln embodies what we call the American spirit, just as his tall, rugged form is nearest to the figure of Uncle Sam. His countrymen see in him the qualities they regard as nationally characteristic—that is, characteristic of the nation at its inspired best, from the Declaration of Independence to the Four Freedoms. To fit these national aspirations into anything but a liberal framework is inadequate. It is therefore significant that the Lincoln record justifies the liberal interpretation. It is not necessary to argue that Lincoln was perfect, for he was very human; but because we think of him as a symbol, however unique he was in person, it is of value to become informed in some detail as to the historical validity of the symbolism.

Since Lincoln writing has often proceeded by repetition of familiar stereotypes, the present book (at least considerable parts of it) may have an unexpected quality in terms of surprising conclusions. If this is true, it is a resultant factor, due not to a wish to be different but to the reporting of actual findings. Moot points and misconceptions—or rather a few of them out of the many that could have been chosen—will be examined in the first essay. The second will be concerned with the mid-nineteenth century generation of Americans among whom Lincoln had his being. Some attention will be given here to the mental climate that prevailed in the period of Lincoln's prominence and presidential functioning. It has been thought proper at this point to reëxamine some of the alleged "explanations" of the Civil War, to show how war makers have been too much dignified, and to reconsider overworked generalizations as to "North" versus "South." The blundering of that period—despite factors of exaltation—needs to be recalled.

This second study attempts, though feebly and imperfectly, to examine large questions concerning war in general and its irrational relation to human interests and destiny. The subject itself is vast, belonging as it does to the philosophy of history; the present inquiry is to be regarded only as an endeavor or perhaps a rash effort. To call attention to the importance of the subject is the main purpose. What is needed is a symposium of the best minds on the challenging theme of the "causation" of war. It is a subject beclouded and obscured by much writing with too little thought. We still have not had a sufficient unmasking of war for the stupendous fraud that it is.

The war mind needs to be exposed. The hate, partisan excess, bombast, and corruption of the time belong to the nation's history. If one remembers martial glory he should not forget the foul birds, as Lincoln said, that come forth when war stalks over the land. If against that background the contemplation of Lincoln the humanitarian becomes somewhat of a Greek tragedy, that is part of the essential theme.

Abusive outpourings against Lincoln—prolific even within his own party—are presented in the third essay, in which, however, space has been found for only a minor part of the denunciation and belittling sarcasm which Lincoln endured. That he was "the unpopular Mr. Lincoln" is hard for us now to believe, but the fact is abundantly evident in the record.

In the fourth and fifth essays the Sumter challenge is reëxamined and the emergency use of governmental power over citizens in a democracy is analyzed. In considering these matters it will be evident how circumstances forced Lincoln to do things which were highly distasteful to his choice and preference. That an outstanding opponent of militarism—a peace-minded Springfield lawyer—should have given orders which were followed by the Sumter outbreak and tremendous civil war is one of the tragic ironies of history. That it should be Lincoln who denied civil rights was one of the paradoxes of an irrational era. Lincoln was no war maker by nature; certainly he was the very opposite of the dictator type. Yet duty placed him at a point where he thought it was better to stretch the Constitution than to allow the whole cause, including the Constitution, to be lost.

In the sixth essay not only the friendship of John Bright, but the attitude of the English common people toward the American Union, toward Lincoln and emancipation, is studied. In the seventh the treatment of Lincoln's peace and Wilson's will at least faintly suggest how, after 1865 as after 1918, reaction took the saddle and the program of an enlightened leader was wrecked by dissension, intrigue, obstruction, and partisanship. Many more parallels between the Lincoln and Wilson periods—and their uninspired sequels-could have been pointed out.

The title essay—the last one—is intended to give the main argument of the book. In this study, which is more a point of departure than a journey, the purpose has been to suggest how the younger as well as the more mature Lincoln reacted with a kind of Jeffersonian liberalism to problems and conditions in American society.

The importance of liberal values and democratic principles in our own day has properly led to a reconsideration of those leaders in American history who have kept faith with the liberal cause. These leaders are best to be considered in their own setting. To draw the lesson and moral for present problems is, of course, important, but that would be another book; in these pages the author has sought to avoid too much digression from the Lincoln theme. To explore the thought of a liberal statesman fully enough to understand the interplay of motive and application in his own time is to lay the groundwork for conclusions and solutions in the present age. One cannot say that present factors are the same as those of Lincoln's day, though there are similarities. It can, however, be said that, as reactionaries of a past era resemble reactionaries today, so with liberals. In the frightening pace of modern life conditions change with startling effect, but there is a timelessness about progressive and humanitarian principles which causes men who now hold such views to feel a genuine harmony of understanding with a Jefferson or a Lincoln. If such understanding is assisted even in part by these essays, their imperfections, of which the author is well aware, may possibly be pardoned.

J. G. R.

Urbana, Illinois
March 25, 1947

CONTENTS

CONTENTS

I. MOOT POINTS IN THE
LINCOLN STORY

ANY gardener knows that the productiveness of the good earth is not limited to desirable plants. In the rich soil of American pride and reverence for a great leader one notes the cropping-up of those weeds with which every careful student of Lincoln is painfully familiar. False claims, spurious reminiscences, and fraudulent documents abound and increase. Many of them are hardy perennials. The line is blurred between sound history, unrestrained fiction, and that type of narrative that lies uncertainly between. There is a vogue of the latter type of writing. Even when one has genuine history to present it is sometimes felt necessary to give it out in the form of a "story" or novel. The very word "story" has opposite meanings. It may denote a true account; but it may also be used for a yarn, an unfounded tradition, a tall tale, a bedtime romance, a legend, an innocent fib, a bold lie, a mystery, or a medley of true and false elements.

It might prove useful to stop and analyze some of the concepts that come under the heading "what everybody knows." "Everybody knows" that Washington made a famous declaration against "entangling alliances." The truth is that it was Jefferson (March 4, 1801), not Washington, who used this phrase, and that the voluminous propagandist use of this bit of misquotation—e. g., to denounce the efforts in our day to promote coöperation among nations—has been as uninformed historically as it has been unenlightened internationally. Both Washington and Jefferson favored constructive international relations.[1] The old accounts of the War of 1812 pictured the struggle as an unavoidable war growing out of British attacks upon American ships. The historian knows that the quarrel as to impressment was not most acute in 1812 but in 1807–08, when it was adjusted by diplomacy. It was Napoleon, not the British, who made the most serious attacks upon American ships. It was a few "war hawks" of the West and South, not the shipping interests of the East, that favored war, and it was not England that began the war.[2] The conflict is now regarded by competent scholars as a needless war due to a breakdown, or neglect, of diplomacy, and as one of the few dark and unfortunate chapters in American relations with Canada. Examples might be elaborately multiplied. The alleged "Mecklenburg Declaration of Independence" of May 20, 1775, is spurious.[3] The Caesar-and-Tarquin speech of Patrick Henry is no longer to be presented in the old grand manner.[4] Many other false ideas or fictional embellishments have had to be discarded.

One can trace the inception of legends in our own day. Stereotypes concerning matters of recent or present interest are thoughtlessly disseminated or deliberately propagandized. Made-up "stories," utterly fictional and outrageously false, have been transmitted by whispering campaigns, in which statements with no foundation whatever are irresponsibly repeated by thousands. It has been so in the past. When an event takes place or a leader emerges into prominence, a set of ideas becomes associated with the event or figure. These ideas are reiterated by speakers and editors; they pass into common parlance; they become almost automatic when particular topics are mentioned. Perhaps they find their way into textbooks. Superficial writers do not even check to determine in all cases what is the authentic historical finding. Many decades may pass before an old *cliché* or stock picture is reëxamined. Evidence is then studied, new evidence is brought to light, old presumptions are cast aside, past reality is recovered, and a truer account is presented. As the present writer has pointed out elsewhere, it is not adequate to refer to this as "revision."[5] It is historical restoration. The careful historian is not concerned with mere rewriting, certainly not with flippant destruction of popular ideas. He deletes only what is false. His work in the field of history is not unlike that of the art specialist who restores an Italian primitive or exposes a spurious Rembrandt. When the historian does his work faithfully he enhances the theme which he treats. It is the actual situation in Lincoln's day, not some modern pattern imposed upon the past, that we are to seek and present.

I

The appeal of the great pioneer West has been strong and virile in American writing, and with it has come the idea that Lincoln, whose pioneering and democracy were of the very essence in his development, was a kind of backwoods character. (One thinks thus of Jackson also, though he lived in the grand manner in one of the South's most stately mansions.) That Lincoln had a backwoods origin which powerfully influenced his character is significantly true. That he wielded the ax mightily is part of the record, but it was in 1860 that he was widely advertised as a "railsplitter" and by that time his life had long ago taken on other aspects.[1] Speaking of Lincoln at the time of his election to the presidency, thirty adult years—the whole of his mature life since coming of age in 1830—belonged to the post-railsplitting era. Those adult years meant much in terms of contact with intellectual movements in a vigorous period of America's rising culture. Lincoln was part of the frontier; but, as shown by his address before the Young Men's Lyceum at the age of twenty-nine, he was also a significant part of intellectual America.

As early as 1843—at the age of thirty-four—young Lincoln was characterized by opponents as "the candidate of pride, wealth, and aristocratic family distinction." The description, he said, would astonish his old friends of New Salem days.[2] Closeness to the great body of the people meant much to this prairie statesman, though he never paraded his humble origin as a politician's trademark. It was his genuine connection with common folk that he cared for. He was no "Bluejeans Williams" or "Sockless Simpson." He did not apologize for railsplitting; but his popular appeal, which he valued highly, was innocent of superficial and stupid claptrap. He did not descend to silly tricks to rake in the votes of the less thoughtful thousands.

To speak of "upper" and "lower" classes is one of the least inspiring types of human expression. It was a type of phrasing or thinking which Lincoln detested. As for the aristocratic reputation which opponents attempted to fasten upon him (without much success), it meant nothing as a characterization of Lincoln. It is nevertheless true that this unprofitable type of comment was not altogether without apparent basis. Lincoln had married into an aristocratic Kentucky family. His first law partner, John Todd Stuart, belonged to a related family of high social standing. He did not forget the humble occupations of his early days, but as a grown man and a rising statesman he was no stranger to the well-to-do and the politically favored. Had he remained all his life a poor man, that certainly would not have been against him. One needs to say this to avoid being misunderstood. The purpose is to state the fact as to Lincoln, not to generalize concerning wealth and poverty.

Some years ago there appeared a popular description of a man who suffered a love tragedy, tried this and that undertaking without success, underwent political defeat, and stood out as a pathetic example of failure at fifty.[3] After a string of such statements it was revealed that the man was Abraham Lincoln and that the next year he was elected President. This portrait does not fit Lincoln, however much it may have comforted the victim of depression and hard circumstance. Lincoln at fifty was a man of large success in his chosen pursuits. Having been for years the leading Whig of Illinois, he later became its leading Republican. He was a more than commonly successful lawyer, owned a substantial house and other property, had a sufficient income,[4] had served as his party's candidate for the United States Senate, and had become nationally known for his debates with Douglas and for other widely extended speechmaking. He had known disappointment and could sympathize with men less fortunate, but it was on a record of achievement, not failure, that he was nominated for the presidency at fifty-one.

It is said that Lincoln was a country lawyer. He did travel about from one county seat to another, mingling with people who regarded "court week" as a kind of show. Story telling and popular stump speaking accompanied the law practice of the eighth judicial circuit, which probably seems more picturesque in retrospect than it did at the time. The country lawyer, so affectionately treated in the pages of Bellamy Partridge, naturally and properly commands sympathy. To speak of Lincoln as a country lawyer, however, is to misapply the term. He handled important cases, practiced often before the Illinois supreme court [5] and the Federal courts, was admitted to practice before the Supreme Court of the United States, and served as attorney for corporations, as in the reaper case [6] and that of the Illinois Central Railroad. Lincoln's name as a lawyer carried prestige throughout the state. His was not a merely local reputation. He was an outstanding leader at the bar in the capital of one of the largest commonwealths of the Union. It was no minor legal business that claimed the energies of the Lincoln-Herndon office. Their methods may have been unsystematic, the manner of both partners informal, but the full record as found in the Herndon papers and in court reports adds up to an impressive total.

II

The sentimental tradition as to Lincoln and Ann Rutledge still persists, but informed readers are by this time well advised of the thinness of its historical basis.[1] This is especially true as to the notion that Lincoln's life after 1835 was continually and powerfully affected by the spirit or image of a loved and lost sweetheart. Contemporary evidence as to the romance is utterly lacking; supporting reminiscence is vague; other reminiscence discredits the story. Of course Ann was part of the New Salem community in which Lincoln was well acquainted, but if there is a fully authenticated statement by Lincoln himself, oral or written, in which Ann Rutledge is even mentioned, the present author is not aware of it. There is a statement attributed to Isaac Cogdal, transmitted indirectly through Herndon, in which Lincoln is said to have spoken as follows while President Elect: "I have loved the name of Rutledge to this day." It is represented in this Cogdal account that Lincoln "ran a little wild," that he "ran off the track," and so on.[2] There is insufficient support for this Cogdal record. Careful scholars do not accept it as a verified statement of anything that Lincoln said, nor do they accept an unidentified stone found at New Salem and bearing the inscription of a betrothal between Lincoln and Ann. It is known that the girl was engaged to John McNamar. That she was also, and simultaneously, engaged to Lincoln, which Herndon has claimed, is by no means proved.

In contrast to this vagueness as to Ann Rutledge, there is ample authentication for Lincoln's courtship of Mary Owens. Writing to Mrs. O. H. Browning on April 1, 1838, he referred, somewhat curiously, to an episode in which, as he said, "a married lady of my acquaintance, . . . a great friend of mine, . . . about to pay a visit to her father . . . in Kentucky, proposed . . . that on her return she would bring a sister of hers on condition that I would engage to become her brother-in-law with all convenient despatch." That was in 1836. Lincoln continued: ". . . I was most confoundedly well pleased with the project. I had seen the said sister some three years before [i. e., in 1833, two years before Ann's death], . . . and saw no good objection to plodding life through hand in hand with her [i. e., with Mary Owens]." In the days of his wedded life there is not the slightest evidence to support the idea that his heart belonged to Ann instead of to his wife.

It is seldom that the wedded life of any great leader has been so pitilessly treated as that of Lincoln. That is not to say that the treatment has been based upon any abundant analysis of evidence. It has been less a matter of informed investigation than of familiar repetition. In this connection we should stop and ask: What is biography anyway? Mark Twain said that biographies "are but the clothes and buttons of the man." [3] The man himself—his thought-life, his unexpressed feeling, his adjustment or lack of it, his meditations, the intricate interplay of character and incident—is not only "lost"; in Lincoln's case it was never made a matter of record. And without record, or some surviving evidence of reality, there can be no history. Daily happenings, seemingly trivial but constituting the very stuff of biography if they could have been preserved, have vanished with the years. Rather they disappeared with the very moment in which a word was said or a deed enacted, but found no Boswell. What do we really know of the sum-total of Lincoln's hourly experience? When we say that Lincoln's married life has been pitilessly treated, we mean that it has been mulled over. It has been "written up" (or down), largely by the repetition of Herndonian comments. Much of the writing has been unproductive.

It is upon Herndon's material, or the Herndon-Weik biography, that writers chiefly rely, but Herndon was never a Boswell as to Lincoln's home and he could hardly be regarded as the historian of that marriage. It was he who publicized the sentimental version of the Ann Rutledge romance. His recital of a wedding night with all the details of a bridal party, but with Lincoln, the groom, absent, is spurious. We know that Herndon had never got along well with Mrs. Lincoln and was not a welcome guest in the Lincoln household. It was the law-office personality of Lincoln that he saw, though even here he was not so much a Boswell as a transmitter of delayed reminiscence. He had observed the Lincoln of the court room, of politics, of the party canvass, of public appearance, of behind-the-scene conference. He did not always give the record with entire faithfulness even in these aspects, but this was the Lincoln he knew; these were the best parts of his contribution. It was very seldom that he saw Lincoln in his home; it is of course a truism to say that he never saw him in the full privacy of his home.[4] He did not get his material as to Lincoln's domestic life at first hand. His stories of the house on Eighth Street bear the earmarks of gossip. They were collected long after Lincoln's death and after Mrs. Lincoln's mind had begun to fail. It was upon indirect and fragmentary material that he built up a famous picture of a tempestuous, shrewish wife and a meek, indulgent, abused husband.

Among the strange theories on the Lincoln theme, one of the oddest is the Herndon notion that Mrs. Lincoln was in some way motivated by "revenge" in dealing with her husband. The theory was Herndon's own and he would not let it drop. In various connections one finds this interpretation bobbing up in his voluminous manuscript notes

and letters. At one point, writing to his friend Charles Hart and profes-
sing to be doing all he could to set Mrs. Lincoln right before the
world, Herndon referred to her domestic quarrels as due to a
"woman's revenge which she was not strong enough to resist." Then
he added: "Poor Woman! The world has no charity for her . . . ." [5]

In the Herndon-Weik biography the revenge idea appears more
as the pen swinging of an amateur psychologist than as a historical
contribution. We are not dealing here with a record based on evidence. Nothing as to revenge, for example, is actually affirmed in the
following statement: "Whether Mrs. Lincoln really was moved by
. . . revenge or not she acted along the lines of human conduct." [6]
At another point in the biography her "austere nature" is represented
as shrinking from the calm, imperturbable ways of her husband. Then
we have this: "Besides, who knows but she may have acted out in her
conduct toward her husband the laws of human revenge?" [7] This is
not a record of anything. It is not even an assertion, merely a query.
Yet the idea of a wife motivated by "revenge" toward her husband is
implanted in the reader's mind. On reading hundreds of Herndon-
Weik pages this is one of the few things that would be retained.

One should note what is meant by that retaining. The Herndon
passage is one thing: the manner in which the reader would remember
it is another. Many readers, if asked to reconstruct Herndon's theory
here, would answer that, to Herndon's mind, she *married him for
revenge.* We do not know that this was Herndon's meaning; if so he
was suggesting a thing which he by no means proved. The present
writer is not always able to follow Herndon's mental processes, and
he will not attempt to do so at this point, but one should notice how
in the context the revenge *motif* glides into a somewhat different connotation. Herndon was emphasizing that Lincoln was a difficult husband and expressing a kind of left-handed sympathy for the proud
wife of a man so absorbed in his own thought as to be absent-
mindedly neglectful in small matters of everyday life and partnerlike
duty. It was in this connection that he put in the revenge morsel. The
world, he said, did "not know what she bore, or how ill-adapted she
was to bear it." He meant to convey the idea that she was doing the

best she could, poor woman, but the situation, plus her own nature, got the better of her. She could not forget the picture of that (imaginary) desertion on her wedding night; to this was added her husband's bland indifference and "simple ways"; the result was too much; her better nature was kept in the background; during the married years the laws of revenge did their work. "In marrying Lincoln she did not look so far into the future as Mary Owens, who declined his proposal because 'he was deficient in those little links which make up the chain of woman's happiness.' " [8]

To deal correctly with this marriage would be to put in what Herndon missed. The total evidence is that of a normal American home, a devoted and united couple. When Lincoln and Mary were separated each felt the lack of the other's companionship. The best evidence on the whole subject is not second-hand gossip, nor Herndon's psychological clairvoyance reduced to a question, nor platitudes about human nature, but the actual letters which the pair exchanged, in which there was coquetry, teasing, humor, and playful affection. An example is a husbandly letter which Lincoln wrote from Washington to Lexington, Kentucky, showing concern for Mary's headaches, wanting to know how much she weighed, and adding: "I am afraid you will get so well, and fat, and young, as to be wanting to marry again." He confessed loneliness without her. She wrote: "I feel very sad away from you." At this time there were two Lincoln boys. "Don't let the blessed fellows forget father," he asked.[9]

In their mutual love of politics, their adored if unrestrained boys (whom Herndon regarded with something very different from Lincoln's clemency), and their everyday life (despite Herndon's theory), they were held together as surely as the typical American couple. There was imperfection, and there were defects on both sides, but imperfections are not incompatible with a satisfactory marriage.

In the presidential phase there is no denying that Mary had difficult qualities: jealousy, a tendency toward occasional embarrassing "scenes," a seeming obsession for extravagant expenditure, designing efforts to grasp and spend public money without Lincoln's knowledge. One can admit this, and without for a moment excusing it he can recognize those better qualities that have been drawn from life by such writers as W. O. Stoddard, Isaac N. Arnold, and Julia Taft Bayne. It is not without significance that children delighted in her, that colored people loved her,[10] and that soldiers felt her ministering hand as she carried food to the hospitals.

To say the last word as to Mary Lincoln, whether in Springfield or Washington, is not an easy task. One can summon up her deficiencies and put them down on paper, but the complexities of human nature are not reducible to a silhouette. Third-dimensional effects, primary and secondary lighting and shading, background and setting, interpretation, and depiction of personality, are attributes of a true portrait.

Lincoln is such a towering figure that his deficiencies and presidential frustrations are overlooked or sympathetically regarded; Mary's faults too often appear with emphasis and without relief. Herndon said a true thing when he remarked that the "world has no charity for her." In 1868 she wrote to a friend: "Since the birth of my youngest son [Tad was born in 1853] . . . I have been more or less a sufferer." In the same letter she had written: "My disease has been of a womanly nature . . ."; then with Victorian reticence she had crossed out these words, but physical distress was part of the reality, though it finds insufficient recognition in the record.[11] Part of the interpretation of Mrs. Lincoln should be medical.[12] In addition one should remember the unmerciful smearing (no other word is adequate) that she had to endure, her loneliness in those unfriendly presidential years, her pathetic wish to have Kentucky relatives to share the White House with her.

Even before April 1865 there were deep sorrows that hit the Lincoln family. The loss of Eddie at the age of three (almost four) in Springfield, and later of Willie after nights of heartbreaking vigil in the "Executive Mansion," were crushing bereavements. As for the shattering disaster of the assassination, no one can adequately portray its effect upon Mrs. Lincoln. In 1866, in a letter to the journalist Noah Brooks, she wrote: "I wish you were not so far removed from us—*true* friends, in these overwhelming days of affliction, I find to be very rare." She added: "In my . . . sorrow, how often I have prayed for death to end my great misery!" [13]

There are times when human nature breaks, when there is too much slander, too much abuse piled on devastating personal grief. There is a certain equity in remembering how cruelly one has suffered; there is need for a blending of tints in which the color is not all black; and there is appropriateness in applying Lincoln's own type of human understanding in dealing with the Lincoln marriage.

III

The subject of Lincoln and Douglas is almost invariably oversimplified. Though finality of appraisal may be unattainable, one of the essentials of a fair interpretation is to recognize the complexities of the subject. These can only be briefly suggested here.

Lincoln writers rarely go "all out" in their denunciation of his distinguished rival. Even more rarely do they do him justice. They make selections from the Little Giant's statements, but they seldom show his full meaning or quote him at his best. They may concede his strength, oratorical skill, debating strategy, prestige, popularity, and untiring energy. After these concessions they are apt to put in qualifying phrases disparaging his integrity, belittling his logic, and dismissing his reasoning as "sophistry." They go on to present the stanchness of Republican doctrine and the unswerving logic of Lincoln's arguments.

Full analysis of the debates, which are seldom read, requires uncommon historical restoration. Douglas had an impossible assignment if it was a matter of reconciling his view—that the people of a territory ought to settle the slavery question through their legislature—with the Supreme Court's decision in the Dred Scott case (1857), which declared it the duty of Congress to protect and maintain slavery in the territories. In truth these two things could not be reconciled, but in the troubled condition of the later fifties, with the lower South becoming increasingly militant, Douglas's solution was as favorable to freedom as any formula that was possible of en-

actment in the peaceable sense. It must be remembered that Douglas
was the main power in the Senate as to this type of legislation. He
was, perhaps, the foremost leader of the party then dominant. He had
to think, not merely of campaign oratory, but of responsible measures to be carried out—not by one section exclusively, but by national
action. He was not the author of the unfortunate Dred Scott decision.
It was a question of whether, because of the decision, he would give
up his "popular sovereignty" position, in which he sincerely believed
and to which he was in honor committed.

This he refused to do. In view of the turgidity of the Court's language, the ponderous technicalities involved, the legal doubt as to
what the judges had really "decided" (in what was judicially before
them), the *obiter dicta* nature of Taney's opinion, the obvious need of
further clarification, and the unwillingness of Douglas men to consent to the imposing of a slave code upon a territory against the
people's will—in view of these factors, one can hardly blame him.
Douglas did not come out and say that the Court had badly confused
the issue, but short of this he did the best he could to sustain the
position as to territorial popular rule which he deemed fundamentally
sound. This he did not by reaffirmation of the Court's doctrine, but
by his statement at Freeport that a territorial legislature would find a
way; they would "effectually prevent" the introduction of slavery
into their midst "no matter what the decision of the Supreme Court
may be on that abstract question." [1]

If there was sophistry here it was due to a dilemma which was not
of Douglas's choosing; if there was rough-and-ready self reliance,
that was characteristic of the West; if there was mental reservation as
to the pontifical finality of Taney and his Court, that was an attitude
which Lincoln shared. Furthermore, if it was a matter of a workable
national solution, Douglas was nearer to that in the peaceable sense
than the Republicans. Resentment toward this Freeport statement
came from the Southern pro-slavery element. Incidentally it should
be noted that Douglas's discomfiture in facing this pro-slavery element was due to his basic popular-sovereignty doctrine repeatedly
expressed. It is a mistake to suppose that his embarrassment was due

to being caught off guard or being pinned down by one of Lincoln's questions. He was not dodging the territorial issue, however much he wanted his party to remain national and to avoid offending Southerners. It was not that he was being forced into a corner and making an unguarded concession. Rather, he was explaining and applying his oft-stated policy. He did not suddenly reveal at Freeport that a territorial legislature could exclude slavery. He had contended for that all along, and now he said it could be done despite the "abstract" position of the Supreme Court. The Dred Scott opinion was "abstract" in the sense that the law then operating as to the territories— the Kansas-Nebraska act of 1854—was not specifically declared unconstitutional,[2] though the act permitted a territorial legislature to overthrow slavery if the people so desired, while the vague doctrine of the Court was that slavery in national territory was to be federally protected. The Douglas law and the Taney opinion did, of course, clash; yet in the absence of any specific Court statement that the existing law (that of 1854) was invalid, Douglas was entitled to his Freeport interpretation. It would have taken a Philadelphia lawyer to explain all the ramifications of the nine varying opinions of the justices, to comment on Taney's pronouncement in terms of the whole Court's intention (whatever that was), to apply the Court's reasoning to the existing Kansas-Nebraska act, and to show just where the vexed question stood after Taney's blast had been fired. Douglas's explanation was a useful and needful clarification directed to the practical situation at a time of misunderstanding and public confusion.

Here again one finds a need for blending and for authenticity in portraiture. It is not that Douglas was entirely free from the politician's tricks, or that Lincoln was for that matter. There is, however, a curious tendency to assail Douglas even at those points where he agreed with Lincoln—for instance, in his stout opposition to the imposition of a slave code upon Kansas. In the complex currents of that day this position cost Douglas dearly, bringing upon him the potent wrath of the Buchanan administration and of Southern leaders. In Lincoln's case the very same policy was a political asset.

One can perceive a difficulty in Douglas's position—that is not denied—but the main weakness was in the Taney pronouncement itself, which did not make sense except in terms of forcibly imposing a slave code upon the people of a territory. This was a solution that Douglas would not agree to. It would have been a negation of his party's position in 1856 and a betrayal of his own pledges. He was by no means laboring to impose slavery upon the territories. His principle, letting the people decide, would have produced freedom; much of the misconception is in ignoring that obvious factor. It does not assist an understanding of the subject to assert, contrary to fact, that Douglas was trimming his policy for the benefit of slaveholding interests. His fiercest opponents were extremists of the lower South. His unwillingness to yield to extreme pro-slavery claims and his firm support of the Union were impressively demonstrated in 1860–61.[8]

IV

No compromise should be ignoble; but there are times when a measure may be tolerable though lacking in ultimate perfection. Lincoln's party had agreed with that of Douglas in the matter of sectional compromise in 1850. In doing so they consented to the things for which Douglas continued to contend in the later fifties. Clay, whom Lincoln praised, had favored that compromise, being its reputed author. He had declared that in that mid-century adjustment the North got what was "worth a thousand Wilmot provisos." [1] Webster had also favored the compromise, for which he received undeserved castigation by Whittier, Parker, Phillips, Emerson, Garrison, and others. Douglas was applying to Kansas and Nebraska the formula which had already been supported by men with whom Lincoln agreed.

Lincoln denied that Douglas's Kansas principle was contained in the bipartisan Compromise of 1850, but that was a debatable point; it was a matter of stating in so many words what the compromise plainly implied as to giving up the earlier Missouri compromise. (That "giving up" did not mean a surrender of freedom. It meant substituting local self-determination for national prohibition.) Had Clay lived in 1854 it is likely that he would still have stood with Douglas, who claimed as great a part as the Kentuckian in the 1850 settlement. The difference between 1850 and 1854 was not so much a shift of principle. It was rather that in 1854 the great stretch of territory from the Minnesota-Iowa-Missouri tier of states to the Rocky Mountains, previously unoccupied, was now being opened up, so that specific territorial organization for that area was necessary. Such organization had to be provided by Congress at a time when national prohibition of slavery, admirable though it was in principle, was made impracticable by determined Southern opposition. Republicans might ignore or defy this Southern attitude; at least they might defy it until they got into power. Douglas, a prominent senator already in power, could not do so. Last-stand statesmanship ought to be reserved for occasions in which it is appropriate. Douglas was ready to stand at Armageddon when it came to defending the nation's integrity, but as for the unlikely chance that slavery would spread into the territories, he was content, as was Clay (Lincoln's former idol), to rely upon normal processes of democratic rule and American pioneer development.

Parties and statesmen of the North were wary of the slavery issue in its fundamental aspects. Here was the great social evil of human bondage, but the evil was not being tackled. To say that little was being done about it by responsible political leaders is not to ignore its seriousness. Serious as slavery was, those aspects of the institution that found their way into the agenda of prewar politics were of minor significance. Where struggle raged fundamentally against slavery itself it was not large controversy. It was rather the ardent agitation of small antislavery groups. Today those groups command respect, but it is only by a retrospective misreading of history that they can be associated with any large co-existing movement. In antebellum days they were negligible in politics and of no appreciable influence in the functioning of government.[2]

Political leaders of large influence were not trying to grapple with slavery in the basic sense. No party, not even that of Free Soil, advocated abolition of Southern slavery. What the Republicans did was to stress phases of the slavery problem that lacked substance—slavery in Kansas, for instance, not slavery in the South. In 1860 there were only two slaves in Kansas, in a day when the Kansas-Nebraska act permitted slavery if the people genuinely approved of it, and when by the Dred Scott doctrine of the Supreme Court the institution was to be both permitted and protected though the people disapproved. It may be hard now to understand how the brave question of stamping out Southern slavery by national action was avoided by all political parties, but in the contemporary scene such avoidance was axiomatic. To mention one of many factors, the Constitution then permitted no such national abolition. (The postwar anti-slavery amendment, in which North and South joined, belonged to a later period.)

The territorial agitation can be thought of as a kind of paradox: the issue of slavery in the territories was at the same time a factor of little practical concern and a matter of tragic importance. Slavery interests in the territories were hypothetical rather than actual. If Southerners had been less worked up about it they would have suffered not at all. The real "grievance" was thin, but emotions are stubborn facts. The tragic importance, or menace, was in the use of the issue as a fearful trouble-maker between the sections.

The negative facts of political avoidance and Southern sensitivity might make the problem seem hopeless, as if the nation were saddled with an institution it could not possibly shake off. It was characteristic of the nineteenth century, however, that one great humanitarian cause after another was moving toward fulfillment. Politicians were riding rather than steering. While Republicans in antebellum days were only nibbling at the slavery issue, conditions of the time were a controlling factor, being unfavorable to the spread of the institution. The economic and social fact was that slavery was so ill suited to the West and Southwest that it simply would not, and did not, take root. Elsewhere Republicans were not thinking of touching it, if one judges by their responsible spokesmen. Lincoln himself said: "I have said a hundred times . . . that I believe there is no right and ought to be no inclination in the people of the free States to enter into the slave States and interfere with the question of slavery at all. I have said that always . . . ." [3] In this declaration Lincoln was avoiding even the "inclination" to interfere with slavery in the area where practically the whole of it existed.

V

It has been often asserted that a comprehensive principle was bound up in the territorial issue. Prohibition of the institution in the territories where it would not go was said to be important as a way of checking slavery in the larger sense.

This concept had strength. It also had defects. In its support one could say that high-minded men thought of the Republican party as the elongation of the Free Soil party, and that many thousands of Northerners entered and promoted the party with the honest motive of checking what they considered the aggressive policy of Southern slaveholders. They thought the national government had long been over-weighted in favor of the Southern "slaveocracy." [1] By voting Republican they honestly meant to promote freedom in the nation's counsels. They were supporting a party that was but slightly anti-slavery in its platform, but perhaps they looked beyond platforms of the day. Their ballots would serve as a gauge of public sentiment. People could look at the size of the Republican vote and realize that slavery was on the way out.

For many earnest souls that would be a great gain. Opinion against slavery could be registered. Little might come of it in immediate measures, but there would be an entering wedge for freedom. From the vast literature one may select one or two statements by that upstanding New Englander, George F. Hoar of Massachusetts. He wrote on the subject with glowing fervor. As to the Free-Soil-Republican party (he considered these to be the same) his superlatives were unrestrained: "No political party in history [he wrote] was ever formed for objects so great and noble. And no political party in history was ever so great in its accomplishment for liberty, progress and law." [2] Of the agitation in Lincoln's day he said: ". . . there was something in that struggle with slavery which exalted the hearts of those who had a part in it, however humble, as no other political battle in history." [3] One cannot doubt in reading Hoar's pages that he meant this, that the thrill of righteousness which he felt was sincere, and that there were thousands like him.

That was part of the story. On the other hand, if one inquires how tendencies were actually working out, he may recognize that slavery was a sick institution without giving all the credit for the sickness to Wilmot-proviso advocates. Agitation for the proviso seemed actually to strengthen the proslavery element in its Southern influence. Politicians found it easy to represent such agitation as enmity toward the South and as Northern interference with its domestic affairs. Such a man as George F. Hoar might be militant in spirit and righteously fervid, but practical Republican managers were quite complacent as to slavery. Far-reaching statesmanship to eradicate the institution was not their main purpose. To them the Republican organization was not an elongation of Free Soil, but merely of the Whig party. That would go for Weed [4] and a great many others. These "practical" politicians wanted most of all to get into office and stay there. The concept that parties operate for the purpose of settling public questions is a way of viewing things in the upper air of pure political science. The purpose of politicians is often to dodge public questions, to make conflicting appeals to diverse groups, and to garner in all the votes they can get from men of differing, or diametrically opposite, views. It is the commonest thing in American politics to note that an election does not settle an issue in accordance with party pledges. The proliferation of such pledges in campaign time, to appeal to one group after another, is one of the most familiar factors in American politics. Republican managers of 1860 were using this or that issue with an eye to the main chance. Some of them were more concerned with the tariff, with the homestead question (as in Minnesota), or with "carrying Pennsylvania" than with the slavery problem, even in its limited form of party declaration. [5] The spread of slavery was being somewhat opposed, but it was far from an all-out opposition.

It is significant to remember that when Republicans in Congress came for the first time to pass territorial laws (for Dakota, Colorado, and Nevada in February-March 1861) they avoided applying the principle of slavery exclusion, though this was supposed to be the bedrock of Republican doctrine. They went not a step farther in stopping slavery in these new areas than Douglas had gone in providing for Kansas and Nebraska. They were dealing with the only territories coming up for organization by congressional legislation. If Lincoln's principle was to be applied at all, it should have been applied there; yet Daniel E. Sickles declared in the House of Representatives that "that principle is abandoned." [6] These laws were passed with Republican votes. Only ten Republicans in the House opposed the Colorado bill; the total of those supporting it was ninety, of whom eighty-six were Republicans.[7] It is fair, of course, to recall that Republicans were then motivated by a wish to avoid provocative legislation at a time of fearful crisis. There was also the reasonable argument that national abolition in the territories was unnecessary, but that had been precisely the contention of Douglas the Democrat and of Webster the Whig. J. G. Blaine remarked: "Every prominent Republican senator who agreed in 1861 to abandon the principle of the Wilmot Proviso . . . had, in 1850, heaped reproach upon Mr. Webster for not insisting upon the same principle for the same territory. . . . It was certainly a day of triumph for Mr. Douglas. . . . The political agitation and the sentimental feeling on this question were . . . exposed on both sides,—the North frankly confessing that they did not desire a Congressional restriction against slavery, and the South as frankly conceding that the demand they had so loudly made for admission to the Territories was really worth nothing to the institution of slavery. The whole controversy over the Territories, as remarked by a witty representative from the South, related to an imaginary negro in an impossible place." [8]

There was an easily won party advantage in having what appeared to be a big issue, not as a thing to settle, but as a thing to agitate. Earnest souls on the front of social reform wanted to grapple with slavery. That, of course, meant slavery in the South. Not so the politicians; they were content to skirt the subject. As Republicans approached the day of their power the moral zeal of their party managers seemed to diminish. A contemporary remarked that they would "drown the Giddings crew" and be "as harmless in office as most men are." [9] By the same token antislavery enthusiasts regarded practical Republican leaders as backsliders. Giddings wrote: "I am sorry to find so many cowards even among republicans." [10] Salmon P. Chase, sincere in antislavery principle, wrote of Republican attitudes in January 1861: "It is sad to think what is now yielded and by whom." [11]

It is in terms of such factors that a judgment should be rendered as to Douglas. If these and other complications of the time are not remembered, he cannot be rightly understood. Despite the cry raised against the Kansas-Nebraska act there were men of prominence in Lincoln's own party—Greeley, for instance—who thought of Douglas as a suitable Republican leader. This seems strange when one reads of it today, but Lincoln referred to the matter on several occasions. In his speech at Chicago on March 1, 1859, he spoke at some length on this point, admitting that the Republican party in other states could "make something" by electing men "who occupied a position similar to Judge Douglas" (this was quite an admission), but that they could not do so in Illinois; "let them . . . make him their candidate, and they do not absorb him—he absorbs them." Lincoln would not have devoted so much attention to this matter if the willingness of some Republicans to accept Douglas had not been an appreciable factor.

It is the part of statesmen to prevent an emotionally dangerous question from getting out of hand and to deal with problems on the level of adjustment. The "vexed question" (slavery in the territories) was tearing the nation apart. Lincoln and Douglas were alike in deploring any such result. In the debates Douglas was trying to clear up the subject so as to avoid the compulsory-slave-code interpretation. Perhaps the main difficulty was that the times were out of joint. Neither Lincoln nor Douglas ought to have been regarded as sectional trouble-makers, though both were so accused. Both men really wanted a peaceable solution: Lincoln by what the national government would do (though the Republicans did not do it in 1861), Douglas by what the people would do (and actually did) through a free vote in the territories.

Lincoln himself was not always free from stretching a point. His accusation that Taney, Buchanan, Pierce, and Douglas were in a conspiracy to impose slavery upon a free people was unjustified.[12] The main point as to Douglas and Buchanan was the feud between them. This may as well be admitted. It is an unrealistic kind of portraiture that would make the subject a plaster saint or a paragon of all the virtues with never a blemish. Lincoln, though usually logical, was descending to a non-sequitur in his prediction that the sequel of the Dred Scott case would be a future decision imposing slavery everywhere in the United States by the overruling of state laws for its abolition. At no point did the Court question the jurisdiction of the states to establish or abolish the institution within their borders. We have perhaps never had a Court so thoroughly minded toward state rights. Lincoln was seeking to associate Douglas with a hypothetical and imaginary future Federal decision by which Massachusetts, Illinois, and all the other free commonwealths would be changed into slave states against their will. When asked by Lincoln whether he would favor such a decision Douglas was "amazed" at the question. "It would," he said, "be an act of moral treason that no man on the bench could ever descend to."[13]

The seven forensic duels—the specific "joint debates"—were only part of the 1858 senatorial canvass in Illinois during which Lincoln traveled extensively and made over sixty speeches. The debates did not traverse the field of American politics or of national economy in any comprehensive discussion. Nor did they contribute to the solution of the question of slavery in the territories, certainly not in the anti-Douglas sense. It should be remembered that it was on the Douglas pattern of self-determination that slavery was actually abolished in Kansas. Republicans abandoned in 1861 the position that Lincoln took in 1858. When they voted, as above indicated, to organize three territories early in 1861, they did so not on Lincoln's Wilmot-proviso doctrine, but on Douglas's principle of allowing the free tendency in the territories to take its natural course.[14]

It is a misconception to suppose that Lincoln and Douglas were altogether opposites. Both were good Americans. The first presidential campaign in which the Wilmot proviso—to exclude slavery from territory acquired from Mexico—came up for discussion was that of 1848. In that year Lincoln supported, not Van Buren of the Free Soil party who upheld this policy of national exclusion, but the Louisianian, Zachary Taylor of the Whigs, a slaveholder who called the proviso a "mere bugbare" and a cause of needless excitement. It will hardly be contended that Douglas's candidate, Cass of Michigan, was more friendly to slavery than Taylor.

In 1850 the parties to which Lincoln and Douglas belonged—Whig and Democratic—acted together on slavery questions. Even after 1854, when the party situation was far more difficult, these political antagonists agreed much more largely than they differed. When in 1858 each tried to embarrass the other by a series of set questions, their answers showed agreement on important points.[15] They thought alike as to the social relation between the races, as to the fugitive slave law, as to the admitting of new states, and as to the iniquity of the Buchanan program by which slavery was to be imposed upon Kansas. (This, however, is hard to reconcile with the fact that politicians of Lincoln's party worked with the Buchananites in the 1858 canvass in Illinois.[16] As a matter of party strategy they coöperated with that element of the Democratic party that was definitely proslavery, the element that favored the Dred Scott decision and was bitterly seeking to destroy the Little Giant. To the politician's way of thinking consistency was less vital than maneuvering to defeat Douglas.)

If instead of exaggerating their differences Lincoln and Douglas had dissociated the slavery question from party politics, if then they had sat down at a table to arrive at solutions and recommend measures for nonpartisan adoption, they would have found much in common. When the country faced the tragedy of sectional hatred, disunion, and war Lincoln and Douglas stood together. They proved that it could be done. In the promotion of union and coöperation in the country's hour of danger they appear to better advantage than in the party maneuvers of 1858.

VI

The moral issue of slavery constituted indeed a great question, especially if one launches forth into an ambitious consideration of all its overtones, implications, and ultimate repercussions. The anti-slavery movement has sometimes been presented as a sweeping forward of epic forces or as evidence of a super-human or divine power mysteriously brooding over the nation and working out its great destiny through imperfect human instruments. If one deals with the subject on such a super-historical plane he should inquire whether these overruling and mysterious forces working through (or against) human instruments could not have operated to eliminate slavery by peaceable methods. Factory conditions in the North were as truly to be deplored as slave conditions in the South,[1] but they were peaceably ameliorated. Why must it be thought that divine power is necessarily catastrophic or violent? If slavery was a moral question, which of course it was, so was the avoidance of war. One should not too readily disparage the moral integrity of those who wished to deal with slavery, as with other social questions, on the plane of adjustment.

A historian should not be thought of as neglecting the ethical merits of the issue if he recognizes complex factors and seeks to show the manner in which the problem was actually presented to the nation. If one takes political parties (speaking of imperfect human instruments), he finds, for example, all sorts of conflicting interpretations as to what the Republicans meant to do. Southerners "made no distinction between abolition societies which sent armed bands to the territories to exclude forcibly the slave owner and his property, and a political party which purposed to exclude them by legislative enactment."[2] It was alleged by some that the Republicans would bring murder, poison, and arson to Southern homes, would sweep slavery away by violence, subverting Southern institutions, suppressing state rights, destroying "white civilization," setting up a consolidated government, and subjecting the whole country to the tyranny of numbers —i.e., allowing local customs to be upset by a distant, over-all majority. Others argued that the Republicans, when actually in power, would do next to nothing as to the basic situation, even with regard to slavery. A Republican editor before the election of 1860 declared that the party would "not interfere with any vested rights." [3] Other Republican editors said that their organization was "for non-intervention by Government with the subject [slavery]," that "natural forces" would "be sufficient to accomplish all that . . . [was] desirable in the restriction of slavery," [4] and that "many who voted for Lincoln" were "entirely indifferent to the subject of Slavery." While genuine abolitionists also voted the ticket, one of the editors stated that this was not true of "the more rabid ones, for these refused to vote at all, and denounced Lincoln more bitterly than did any other of his opponents." [5]

These are a few of the elements to be put together if one would "settle" the question of slavery in relation to social organization, economics, psychology, sectionalism, party hate, and fratricidal war. Though the problem is historical in the sense that conditions of the time must be brought into the picture, the main question is conjectural: it is a matter of what "would have" been done as to slavery if events as to strife had been different.

Charles W. Ramsdell, competent student of Southern institutions, wrote: "The ratio of slaves to whites was declining year by year in Virginia, Kentucky, and . . . Missouri. The industrial revolution was reaching into these three states, and promised within less than another generation to reduce the economic interest in . . . slaveholding . . . to very small proportions." Mr. Ramsdell added: ". . . it seems evident that slavery had about reached its zenith by 1860 and must shortly have begun to decline. . . . It could not go forward in any direction and it was losing ground along its northern border. . . . It had reached its limits in both profits and lands. . . . Even those who wished it destroyed had only to wait a little while— perhaps a generation, probably less." [6]

In like manner A. C. Cole has concluded that "in view of the increasingly unsound economics of slave labor, the doom of slavery in the Southern states was sealed more by the social and economic forces that had gained headway in nineteenth century America than by the immediate implications of the political revolution of 1860." [7]

VII

The intensely unfavorable caricature of such men as Garrison was as unfair as their own caricature of slaveholders. The present purpose is not to cast a slur upon them.[1] They were usually pure souls, such as Whittier, and they were ahead of their time. If one writes of them only he can have much to say, but if one attempts to deal with the history of the nation, the whole complex subject must be seen in contemporary setting. Their forte was in agitation, not in politics or government. They scorned politics, and one cannot well blame them for this in a day when the cards were stacked politically and party-wise against their type of crusade; but the other side of the truth is that these humanitarian enthusiasts had no guiding influence in parties or government in the days of Lincoln's rise to prominence.

It was their right, of course, to agitate against slavery as an unjustifiable social institution, and it would have been undemocratic to suppress them in exercising that right. When that was done their movement took on something of a crusade for freedom of speech and civil liberty. One can understand well enough why honest liberals today think highly of them. Their cause, however, depended not so much upon the immediate prospect for any practical measure they advocated as upon the hope that if there was sufficient agitation, some day perhaps there would be enough antislavery sentiment to relegate the institution to the past. While some felt this way, others could not wait; they approved of violence, which Lincoln did not; men of this opinion wanted war. Still other abolitionists did not want war or the Union either; they preferred to be dissociated from wicked slaveholders. There were men of fine caliber among the abolitionists, but their words were often reckless in the extreme, their speeches were abusive, they tended to approve criminality, and their self-righteous denunciation of Southerners, as well as thousands of Northerners, was hard to bear. In Northern conservative circles they were despised as vicious and highly subversive. In the South, where their movement was vastly exaggerated, they were assailed as human vipers and accused of that most dreaded of all crimes, the stirring up of slave insurrection against white masters.

That Lincoln did not want to be identified with them, which would have ruined his leadership and career without practically helping the antislavery cause, was obvious. Where they were more concerned with a crusade, Lincoln was mindful of governing realities. Where they disregarded, or transcended, legal and constitutional restrictions, Lincoln the lawyer and political leader had perforce to recognize such things. That he resented the abolitionist stigma being applied to himself, as Douglas sought to apply it, is too well known to require reiteration. One can deplore a system in which the humane purity of a Whittier or a George F. Hoar was denounced as conducive to social disorder, and one must condemn a Northern regime under which Garrison was mobbed and Lovejoy murdered; but for Americans who lived under the system the Lincolns of that day hoped that the door of escape would not be explosive, cataclysmal, and violent, but orderly and legal.

Lincoln believed in gradualism and in regard for established rights. This was no reactionary adherence to the status quo. It was rather that Lincoln, with his liberal fervor, believed in and expected human betterment. He did not oppose change; rather he had confidence that reasonable change would come. His liberalism embraced tolerance. This should not be understood as a tolerance of evil, but as a preference for peaceful correction of evil and as a recognition that virtue was not a sectional monopoly. Lincoln did not join in the abolitionist tendency to abuse all slaveholders. He did not blame the South for slavery more than he blamed the North. Resenting the misconstruction of his house-divided declaration, he thought there was a reasonable way of growing out of the institution and that is what he favored. There are writers who would have us believe, contrary to history, that the Civil War came because of a great, overwhelming Northern crusade to destroy slavery. We even have the war represented as a great Marxian wind, sweeping the nation into violent social upheaval.

Such writers, as well as others, object to the idea that the war was avoidable or that statesmanship could have prevented it. To understand Lincoln is to remember that he rejected the notion that violence and sectional abuse offered the solution to the nation's ills.[2]

VIII

As to wartime emancipation it is incorrect to suppose that Lincoln announced something far in advance of anything existing in national law. Before Lincoln's proclamation Congress had already done, on paper, more than the emancipation proclamation did, also on paper. In the peculiar legal reasoning of United States authorities all who resided in so-called "rebel" territory were rebels.[1] The second confiscation act (treason act) of July 17, 1862, which preceded Lincoln's proclamation, went farther than that edict, though one is considering here the provisions of a statute that was never effective. It declared all slaves of persons adhering to the "rebellion" to be forever free. The law was not qualified by the hundred-day warning or escape clause, or by the very considerable territorial exceptions of the President's decree. It was but one of several antislavery acts of Congress that antedated the proclamation.[2]

There is the stock picture of Lincoln the emancipator striking the shackles from millions of bondsmen by a stroke of the pen. What are the facts? Lincoln issued his proclamation and very little happened, so far as actually freeing particular slaves was concerned. The proclamation did not say that slavery was henceforth abolished in the United States. There were two proclamations. The first (September 22, 1862) said that one hundred days later (January 1, 1863) slaves would be free in regions then remaining in insurrection. If the Southern states would come back to the Union, the plain meaning was that slavery could be conserved in those states. Furthermore, when the definitive proclamation was issued on January 1, 1863, Lincoln was making declarations which, at the time at least, applied only where his arm could not reach. Tennessee and large parts of Virginia and Louisiana were excepted. The portions of the country to which the proclamation extended were regions in which the Confederacy was in control. It did not touch slavery in Kentucky or other border states.

In 1861 when the war began there were approximately four million slaves in the United States. How many of them were freed by the proclamation? As the Union armies advanced in the latter half of the war, Federal military control brought more and more slaves under the edict; but in February 1865 Secretary Seward stated with Lincoln's corroboration that "there were only about two hundred thousand slaves, who, up to that time, had come under the actual operation of the Proclamation, and who were then in the enjoyment of their freedom under it . . . ." [3] This was another way of saying that ninety-five percent of the slaves had not been liberated by the proclamation after two years.

The main significance of the proclamation is not to be found in its provisions, or in its immediate liberating effect. What we are dealing with here is a matter of psychology and opinion, of overtones and thought waves. Emancipation became a slogan. From the time of the proclamation the war came to be regarded in the popular mind as a struggle to overthrow slavery, and it is this popular concept that has given form to the whole tradition. Lincoln, in the September proclamation, had said that "hereafter, as heretofore" the war would be prosecuted "for the object of practically restoring the constitutional relation between the United States and each of the States . . . in which . . . that relation is or may be suspended or disturbed." He also declared his continued purpose to promote emancipation by voluntary state action, with Federal compensation and with colonization beyond national limits. He suggested that emancipation by states might be either immediate or gradual. Thus he showed the opposite of a change of war aim, assuming that the Southern states would peaceably and willingly return to the Union. (This was assuming a good deal, but one is speaking here of statements in Lincoln's September proclamation.)

What the edict was, however, or what it actually said, did not matter so much as its dramatization in the public mind. This slogan quality of the proclamation carried over into international relations. It was as a trumpet blast against slavery that the edict was heralded abroad so far as the general concept was concerned. In this sense it played its important part in the failure of "King Cotton" diplomacy in England and France.

It is a mistake to suppose that the famous proclamation was Lincoln's preferred solution of the slavery issue or that it embodied his whole policy of dealing with this heavy problem. Lincoln actually disparaged the importance of the proclamation, admitting doubts of its legal efficacy.[4] He wanted states by free acceptance to pass liberating laws. In return he wanted slaveholders to be compensated, the United States government assuming the burden of such compensation. Thus he envisaged that form of constructive state-and-Federal action which proceeds by way of the contribution of money by the national government in a project that is dependent upon state laws and state administrative coöperation.

Lincoln did not succeed in his plan of compensation, but the scheme throws a great deal of light on the workings of his mind as he pondered the toughest social problem of his time. In this program, more than in the edict of "military necessity," one may read his ethical concept that the North should share with the South the burden of liberation as it shared the blame of slavery, his innocence of self-righteousness, his recognition of consent of the governed, his caution as to legal matters, and his regard for property. Lincoln did not grow weary in his efforts to remunerate Southern slaveholders. As late as February 1865 he proposed, though unsuccessfully, to his cabinet that a recommendation be addressed to Congress providing that four hundred million dollars in Federal bonds be paid to the slave states in sums proportional to the number of slaves in each state, cessation of resistance to the Federal government being naturally required.[5] It is reliably reported that at the Hampton Roads Conference concerning peace terms (February 1865) he expressed willingness to be taxed to remunerate the Southern people for their slaves.[6]

IX

One could go on at length in this analysis of misconceptions and debatable points. It could be noted how the real Nancy Hanks is hard to reconstruct because of the vagueness of our far-away evidence concerning her, how alleged accounts of Lincoln's parentage are "too absurd to deserve serious consideration," [1] and how the more careful study of Thomas Lincoln has necessitated a revision of concepts as to his abject poverty and ne'er-do-well qualities.[2] The frequent outcropping of forgeries would make a book in itself. Another book could be written to show how anecdotes which are no more than stock stories have been "pinned on" Lincoln, and how made-up statements, the product of fictional invention, have been soberly put into his mouth.[3] Errors of misdating and of mistakenly locating Lincoln at certain times and places have had to give way under the honestly factual survey of the valuable day-by-day books.[4] The publication of his writings is an elaborate subject. In this connection one would have to observe how the "editorial tidying" [5] of Nicolay and Hay took flavor and force out of Lincoln originals; how the large twelve-volume edition bearing the name of these secretary-biographers, called the *Complete Works*, lacks completeness by hundreds of items; how fabricated material has crept into this edition; [6] and how the ten-volume Nicolay-Hay biography was marred by a more or less conscious and deliberate purpose to present a slanted and partisan interpretation which sometimes amounted to a distortion of history.[7]

For a prolific species of superficial popular writing one needs nothing better than the Horatio Alger success story or the romantic love tale that ends in exquisitely tragic grief. There are other sure-fire formulas for literature with a mass appeal and a huge sale: tales of detectives, mysteries, incredible plots, elaborate intrigue, psychological conflict, daring villainy, a sensational murder, a dramatically martyred leader. One has all these, tied together in a supreme bundle, in the Lincoln subject. There are serious reasons for writing of Lincoln and his era, but the more popular reasons have accounted for immense portions of the enormous and bewildering output. "Lincolniana" has become a rather loose term.

High flying psychoanalysis on the Lincoln theme must be taken with many grains of critical salt unless we are to give more attention to Freudian (or Herndonian) patterns than to historical reality. Lincoln's religion—free from cant, unresponsive to the antics of pioneer evangelists, distrustful of theology—was genuine, upstanding, and spiritual; yet on the one hand it has suffered from allegations of infidelism, while on the other hand it has been badly overwritten in terms of superficially pious stereotypes. So it is all the way through the Lincoln story. The vast and complicated Civil War, with its hectic and irrational prelude, is bound up with his election and administration. Lord Charnwood was not exaggerating when he wrote: "Hardly an action of his Presidency is exempt from controversy." [8] There are many matters that are merely undetermined; they are reducible to questions as yet unanswered. Why did Lincoln yield as to Cameron? We know he did not want him in the cabinet; we know the nature of the pressure put upon him as President Elect; do we know fully his feelings and reactions? What about Stanton? He had been contemptuously abusive of Lincoln; [9] his intrigues were hard to reconcile with loyalty; his arrogance and misdirection of military matters became a serious drag upon the Union cause; his fundamental policy was opposed to Lincoln's. Why was he ever appointed, and what did Lincoln think of him?

At the beginning of September 1862, when the government was shaken to its foundations by Pope's defeat, did Lincoln ponder the thought of his own resignation? [10] Did he do so at other times? What about that unsolved "Diary of a Public Man"? [11] Was it genuine? If so, who was the author? If it was not a genuine diary, one must consider the process of its fabrication, which showed remarkable skill and accurate knowledge of events and incidents unfamiliar to the wider public. Even if fabricated, then, how much of the substance of the "Diary" (as to movements, events, and episodes of the time) is historically sound? In the vice-presidential nomination of 1864, to what extent was the event shaped by Lincoln? What if the provocative

Benjamin F. Butler had been nominated in second place, becoming President on Lincoln's death? How near did that sensational possibility come to fulfillment? [12]

How shall we deal with long and detailed conversations with Lincoln, recorded after many years? When ten or more years have elapsed, how likely is it that a conversation can be adequately reconstructed from memory alone? Let any man try to recall specific conversations long past, for which no notes were taken. He will then understand the historian's caution in using this type of reminiscence. There is the pretty story of Lincoln, on his visit to Richmond after the Confederate evacuation, calling at the home of George Pickett, greeting the wife and kissing the baby of that general. Mrs. Pickett gives the story; can we accept it in the lack of supporting evidence?

Shall we credit the claim that the famous Bixby letter was composed by John Hay? [13] One can quote recollections as to what Hay is supposed to have said; but F. Lauriston Bullard, after elaborate study, finds himself unconvinced that authorship of this classic belonged to Lincoln's private secretary. The original of the letter appears to be irrevocably lost; it is a loss greatly to be regretted. One often sees alleged "facsimiles" said to be in Lincoln's handwriting. They are not to be accepted as genuine. Lincoln scholars do not believe that any maker of a facsimile had an actual handwritten letter of Lincoln (or a photographic reproduction) before him as he worked. Taking one of these facsimiles, of which several have appeared, and comparing it with genuine Lincoln letters of the time, one sees that the supposed facsimile lacks the easy vital flow of manuscripts penned by Lincoln's hand. It is studied and artificial, as if laboriously drawn, however clever the imitation. (Some say Hay did such an imitation. That would hardly do as explanation of a "facsimile" in the absence of the original letter which no one has located. Doubt or affirmation as to Hay covers both the problem of authorship and that of imitative handwriting.)

It is not that the Bixby letter itself was a fake, as some seem to have supposed. The letter was printed in Boston newspapers and in the *Army and Navy Journal* shortly after its receipt by Mrs. Bixby. The letter existed; it was authentic; it was lost; it is the facsimile that is a made-up affair. These questions, however, as to the facsimile and as to authorship are only a few of the problems to be studied concerning this one letter of Lincoln which Barton called a "beautiful blunder." [14]

How much "new" material will we have when the large masses of Lincoln papers, long held in the Library of Congress, are opened to investigators, as they soon will be? Reasonable conjectures can be made from what is now known. As to new writings by Lincoln, perhaps they will be few (though some important Lincoln originals are likely to be included). One can, however, expect that the collection will have considerable significance in its incoming papers, endorsements, first drafts, memoranda, and piles (as well as scraps) of material that will serve for significant reinterpretation.

What about the wave of emotion that swept over the North after Lincoln's assassination? Was there deliberate design in having the body slowly and circuitously moved and publicly displayed in many places as it lay in state? In this episode one should note the manner in which Lincoln himself was to a large extent overlooked. Instead of his spirit of tolerance and his well known desire for friendly reconciliation with the South (expressed with pathetic earnestness in his last speech), the post-assassination emphasis was upon hate, vengeance, and radical politics, associated with divine sanction and given out in homily, editorial, or memorial oration.[15] The irony is that while it was all done by way of honoring Lincoln's name, it served the purpose of men who had worked against him while living, who had wished him displaced, and who powerfully opposed the enactment and fulfillment of his policy.

One sometimes encounters the idea that Lincoln was a dictator. The fact of the election of 1864 was enough to refute the charge, if the word dictator is understood in anything like its modern meaning. Civil rights were partly suppressed under Lincoln, but only partly. The broad fact was that democracy still existed. Officials were chosen by the people; elections were not suspended (as in Europe) in war time; Stanton's secret police, bad as it was, could not be compared to

Himmler's gestapo; criticism of Lincoln was constant and vociferous. Criminal violence was not employed for a party purpose. Congress was not suppressed, mass terrorism did not become a regular policy of state, and, above all, the ideal of democracy was not contemptuously derided.[16]

X

A further consideration remains. One cannot deal with Lincoln by destructive emphasis. Let it not be supposed, however, that discrediting a legend has only negative value. To dispel false ideas is to give a clearer view. It is like washing the dust from a lens or window. Constructive values remain; indeed they stand out more distinctly. One gains in authentic reality by realizing that Washington never intended to guide distantly future generations in the direction of uncooperative isolationism, and that relations between the United States and Britain in 1812 could have been adjusted without a war which, in the result, settled none of the alleged "issues."

It takes nothing away from Lincoln to show that he was no crude product of the backwoods. The historian does not deny his homespun origin nor omit its picturesque flavor, but he is aware of cultural values as he studies the rising intellect of Lincoln even before the fuller period of his political career. None of Lincoln's greatness is lost when one points out that his uncouthness has been exaggerated. Association with families of social distinction did not make him any the less a democrat. Allowing a proper place to the stirrings of Lincoln's mind is part of that more mature and better informed appreciation which gives deserved value to the intellectual strivings of middle westerners in the day of "freedom's ferment." [1]

Lincoln's position in history does not suffer by the fact that he was an outstanding lawyer rather than an obscure one. If the betrothed of John McNamar has less, and Mrs. Lincoln more, of a place in his love and sentiment, that is not exactly a disparagement of his character. One's respect for him is not diminished by learning that he had a reasonably comfortable income and was no failure at fifty. That he had a worthy opponent in Douglas does not detract from his stature, nor should one feel regret to learn that his thought paralleled that of the Little Giant in certain essential respects. If they had differences they also had significant points of agreement. We know today that statements made in party campaigns must be heavily discounted; it does no harm to realize that the same was true in contests many decades ago. Such a realization is a wholesome factor. It tends toward normal, undistorted thinking. Patriotism and virtue are not the patented monopoly of one group. Life is not bounded on all sides by partisanship. It offers no inspiration to narrow the list of America's statesmanlike leaders or to suppose that only those leaders are genuine who have a particular party label.

In treating an unhappy era in American politics one does not make Lincoln a lesser man by recalling that he was no abolitionist. In common with other right-minded men he abhorred human slavery,[2] but his hope for eradication of the evil lay in the direction of peace and normal progress rather than in violence and catastrophe. John Brown's act was not so much a deed done for freedom as a prelude to civil war.

When one mentions how, as President, Lincoln hesitated, how careful he was not to offend Kentucky, and how little immediate effect the emancipation proclamation had as to particular slaves, the reason for such mention is simply that this is the record; but one can look ahead and realize also the part that Lincoln had in the ultimate triumph and the constitutional implementing of emancipation. It is no disparagement to bear in mind that his working toward ultimate liberation was not motivated by bitter anti-Southern prejudice. The moral uplift of his proclamation, despite its limitations, has already been pointed out. In all such matters we are in danger of losing Lincoln's solid significance if we fail to lift the discussion above the level of superficiality. It is a kind of integrity to face up to hard historical facts.

II. A BLUNDERING GENERATION

I

WHEN one visits a moving picture, or reads Hergesheimer's *Swords and Roses,* which is much the same thing, he may gather the impression that the Civil War, fought in the days before mechanized divisions, bombs, and tanks, was a kind of *chanson de geste* in real life. "The Civil War in America," writes Hergesheimer, "was the last of all wars fought in the grand manner. It was the last romantic war, when army corps fought as individuals and lines of assault . . . charged the visible enemy." "The war created a heroism . . . that clad fact in the splendor of battle flags." [1]

Hergesheimer feeds his readers chunks of sombre beauty, winterless climate, air stirred with faint cool music, fine houses, Spanish moss and cypress, trumpet vine and bay blossom, live oak and linden, bridal wreath, japonica, moonflower, and honeysuckle. In his foreword to "Dear Blanche" he writes: "Here is a book of swords . . . of old-fashioned dark roses . . . [of] the simpler loveliness of the past." His pages live up to the foreword. He gives dear Blanche "The Rose of Mississippi," "The Lonely Star," "Shadows on the Sea," and "Gold Spurs." Of "Jeb" Stuart he says:

Ladies in Maryland gave him the spurs and ladies wherever he chanced to be gave him the rosebuds. . . . Naturally he was in the cavalry. He was different . . . . [He] wore a brown felt hat . . . with . . . sweeping black plume; . . . his boots in action were heavy, . . . afterwards he changed them for immaculate boots of patent leather worked with gold thread; but he danced as well as fought in his spurs.[2]

Colorful touches fill in the picture: red-lined cape, French sabre, yellow sash and tassels, The Bugles Sang Truce, The Dew is on the

Blossom, orders given when asleep, animal vitality dancing in brilliant eyes.

Escapists may put what they will between the covers of a book; unfortunately the historian must be a realist. Whatever may be the thrill, or the emotional spree, of treating the Civil War romantically, it may be assumed that this has not been neglected. A different task, therefore, will be attempted in these pages—that of weighing a few Civil War realities, examining some of the irrational ideas of war "causation," and pondering some aspects of the Civil War mind.[3]

Without stressing the obvious fact that recent examples of heroism have matched any Civil War exploit, or that aviation is as smart as cavalry, it is sufficient to note a few comparisons. If World War I produced more deaths, the Civil War produced more American deaths. If weapons have become more brutal, at least medicine and sanitation have advanced. One seldom reads of the Civil War in terms of sick and wounded. Medical officers of the sixties repeated the experience of a British medical officer in the Burmese War who advised his commander how to avoid scurvy and was told: "Medical opinions are very good when called for." [4] A Union surgeon at Bull Run reported extreme difficulty in inducing field officers to listen to complaints of disease resulting from foul tents into which fresh air was "seldom if ever" admitted.[5] Because ambulances were on the wrong side of the road, this also at Bull Run, twelve thousand troops had to pass before some of the wounded could be taken to the emergency hospital.[6] Wounded men arriving from the field were thrust into freight cars where they lay on the bare floor without food for a day; numbers died on the road.[7] One of the officers refused hospital admittance to wounded soldiers not of his regiment.[8] Medical supplies were thrown away for want of transportation,[9] injured men were exposed to heavy rain,[10] gangrene resulted from minor wounds.[11]

Romance and glory suggest at least the memory of a name. This implies an identified grave, but after making calculations based upon the official medical history issued by the surgeon general, the student would have to inform dear Blanche, or perhaps Mr. Ripley, that if the surgeon general's figures are right the unknown dead for the

Civil War exceeded the number killed in battle! In round numbers there were about 110,000 Union deaths from battle, while the surgeon general reported that in November 1870 there were 315,555 soldier graves, of which only 172,109 had been identified by name,[12] leaving over 143,000 unidentified graves. The number of Union soldiers known in the adjutant general's records to have died during the war is much greater than the number identified as to burial or reburial. It must be remembered that the soldier regularly carried no means of identification, that graves of men buried by comrades were marked by hasty devices, that Confederates appropriated Union arms and clothing, that teamsters, refugees, camp followers, or even fugitive slaves might have been buried with soldiers, and that the number reported as killed in action, this being less than half the deaths, was inaccurate.[13] A full examination of these and other factors would throw further light on the matter; yet after making all such allowances, the vast number of the nameless leaves the inquiring mind unsatisfied. It is no more satisfactory to realize that about half the Union army became human waste in one form or another, as dead, disabled, deserting, or imprisoned.[14]

"Jeb" Stuart may have worn gold spurs, but the common soldier was more familiar with vermin. Sashes may have adorned generals, but privates were often in rags. It was reported that one of the army surgeons boarded for an entire winter on Sanitary Commission stores.[15] Camps were dirty, sanitation was faulty, cooking was shiftless. Reporting on one of the hospitals, an inspector referred to a leaky roof, broken glass, dirty stairs, insufficient sanitary facilities, and unclean disgusting beds.[16] The soldier who was brutally struck by a sentry of his own company or who contracted malaria would hardly think of his experience as a thing of romance. Without exposing all the euphemisms that obscure the truth of this subject, it may be noted that the great majority of Union deaths were from causes medically regarded as preventable, leaving aside the cynical assumption that war itself is not preventable.

Pneumonia, typhus, cholera, miasmic fever, and the like hardly find their way into the pages of war romance, but they wrought more havoc than bayonets and guns. Where there was danger of infection the rule-of-thumb principle of the Civil War surgeon was to amputate,[17] and from operating tables, such as they were, at Gettysburg, arms and legs were carried away in wagon loads. Discipline was slack, desertion was rampant, corruption was rife. Individual injustices of the war were shocking. Some generals got credit that was undeserved, others were broken by false report or slandered by an investigating committee of Congress. The men who languished in prison were several times more numerous than those killed by bullets. That there was heroism in the war is well known, but to thousands the war was as romantic as prison rats and as gallant as typhoid or syphilis.

II

One does not often speak or read of the war in reality, of its blood and filth, of mutilated flesh, and other revolting things.[1] This restraint is necessary, but it ought to be recognized that the war is not presented when one writes of debates in Congress, of flanking movements, of retreats and advances, of cavalry and infantry, of divisions doing this and brigades doing that. In the sense of full realism war cannot be discussed. The human mind will not stand for it. For the very word "war" the realist would have to substitute some such term as "organized murder" or "human slaughterhouse." In drama as distinguished from melodrama murder often occurs offstage. In most historical accounts, especially military narratives, the war is offstage in that its stench and hideousness do not appear.

In a subject so vast, yet often so imperfectly treated, it is difficult to achieve a full realization of how Lincoln's generation stumbled into a ghastly war, how it blundered during four years of indecisive slaughter, and how the triumph of the Union was spoiled by the manner in which the victory was used. In the hateful results of the war over long decades one finds partisanship at its worst. To see the period as it was is to witness uninspired spectacles of prejudice, error, intolerance, and selfish grasping. The Union army was inefficiently raised, poorly administered, and often badly commanded. In government there was deadlock, cross purpose, and extravagance. One can say that Lincoln was honest, but not that the country was free from corruption during the Lincoln administration. There was cotton plundering, army-contract graft, and speculative greed. Where Lincoln was at his best, where he was moderate, temperate, and far-seeing, he did not carry his party with him. Even those matters dissociated from the war, such as homesteading and railroad extension, came to be marred by exploitation and crooked finance. The period of the Civil War and the tawdry era of Jim Fisk and Jay Gould were one and the same generation.

If it was a "needless war," a "repressible conflict," then indeed was the generation misled in its unctuous fury. To suppose that the Union could not have been continued or slavery outmoded without the war and without the corrupt concomitants of the war, is hardly an enlightened assumption. If one questions the term "blundering generation," let him inquire how many measures of the time he would wish copied or repeated if the period were to be approached with a clean slate and to be lived again. Most of the measures are significant as things to be avoided. Of course it is not suggested that the generation of the sixties had any copyright on blundering.

It is not that democracy was at fault. After all, civil war has not become chronic on these shores, as it has in some nations where politics of force is the rule. One can at least say that the Civil War was exceptional; that may be the best thing that can be said about it. A fuller measure of applied democracy—e. g., a less precipitate casting of the die, a delay of secession till all the South could have taken part in a widely representative gathering, with the main issue reserved for popular vote—would probably have prevented the war. (In the secession movement of 1850 the more deliberate and coöperative method was used in the Nashville convention, and disunion was averted.) A better democratic expression—e. g., as to war department administration or exchange of prisoners—might have mitigated the war's abuses. To overlook many decades of peaceful development and take the Civil War as the exhibition of what American democracy does, would be to give an unfair appraisal. Nor does this probing of

blunders involve lack of respect for the human beings of that generation. As individuals we love and admire them, these men and women
who look at us from the tintypes and Brady photographs of the sixties,
though we may have "malice toward some." The distortions and
errors of the time were rather a matter of mass thinking, of unrea-
soning obsessions, of social solidification, and of politics.

III

In the present vogue of psychiatry, individual mental processes
and behavior have been elaborately studied. Psychiatry for a nation,
however, is still in embryo, though it is much the fashion to have
discussions of mass behaviorism, public opinion, pressure groups,
thought patterns, and propaganda. Writers in the field of history tend
more and more to speak in terms of culture; this often is represented
as a matter of cultural conflict, as of German against Slav, of Japanese
against Chinese, and the like.[1] Scholars are doing their age a disservice if these factors of culture are carried over, as they often are,
whether by historians or others, into justifications or "explanations"
of war. The note of caution here should be a note of honest inquiry.
If one talks of social forces they should be adequately understood. In
the Nazi case, for example, it may be seriously doubted whether war
arose from valid fundamental motives of culture or economics so
much as from the lack of cultural restraint or economic inhibition
upon militaristic megalomania. Modern wars have not relieved population pressures. In the days when Germany and Italy had African
colonies the number of genuine, voluntary German and Italian set-
tlers in those colonies was so small as to be practically negligible. Nor
was Japan's population pressure appreciably relieved by the acquisi-
tion of Manchuria.

The idea that aggressive or imperialistic war is required in order to
obtain raw materials is a colossal fallacy. A nation does not need to
own or govern distant rubber producing or oil producing areas in
order to have oil or rubber. As to "have not" nations, it is fallacious
to apply that term to such a country as Germany in the Hitler days.

Contemplating the tremendous munitions plants and factories of Germany and the manner in which raw materials were flowing in to support those plants, one could hardly say that Germany was a "have not" nation. Nothing is more fallaciously artificial than to suppose that a nation must make war and seize the areas from which its raw materials are to come. For how many countries would such a development be practically feasible? Of the more than sixty nations in the world of today, hardly more than one or two could actually seize and govern the raw material areas requisite for a whole nation's economy on the complex industrial pattern of present times. Hitler did not make war because Germany was actually being denied access to raw materials. War makers do not open up economic benefit so much as they stifle it. Their relation to culture is no better than their relation to economy.

There is the word *astrology* for bogus astronomy and *alchemy* for false chemistry. Ought there not to be some such word for the economic alchemists of this world? Perhaps it exists in the word *autarchy*. Is it not in the category of bogus economics, or *ersatz* economics, that one should put those who present war as a matter of trade, supply, resources, needs, and production?

As for the Civil War the stretch and span of conscious economic motive was much smaller than the areas or classes of war involvement. Economic diversity offered as much motive for union, in order to have a well rounded nation, as for the kind of economic conflict suggested by secession. One fault of writers who associate war-making with economic advantage is false or defective economics; another is the historical fault. It is surprising how seldom the economic explanation of war has made its case historically—i. e., in terms of adequate historical evidence bearing upon those points and those minds where actually the plunge into war, or the drive toward war, occurred. Cultural and racial consciousness are as strong in Scandinavia or the Netherlands or Switzerland as in militarist-ridden countries. To make conquest a matter of culture is poor history. It may be the vanquished whose culture survives. Culture is not easily transplanted if force be the method. When war comes by the violence of a few in control and by the stifling of economic and cultural processes, it ill becomes the scholar to add his piping to the cacophonous blare of militaristic propaganda.

War causation tends to be "explained" in terms of great forces. Something elemental is supposed to be at work, be it nationalism, race conflict, or quest for economic advantage. With these forces predicated, the move toward war is alleged to be understandable, to be "explained," and therefore to be in some sense reasonable. Thought runs in biological channels and nations are conceived as organisms. Such thought is not confined to philosophers; it is the commonest of mental patterns. A cartoonist habitually draws a nation as a person. In this manner of thinking Germany does so and so; John Bull takes this or that course, and so on. When thought takes so homely a form it is hardly called a philosophical concept; on the level of solemn learning the very same thing would appear under a Greek derivative or Freudian label. However labeled, it may be questioned whether the concept is any better than a poor figure of speech, a defective metaphor which is misleading because it has a degree of truth.

Ruritania—to be no more specific—does so and so in the sense that it has a government, the government is presumed to act for the nation, and for political purposes there is no other way in which the country can act. The doubtful part is to infer that there is one directing mind for Ruritania which is the distillation of all the millions of minds. Where government has a bogus quality such an inference is more doubtful than if government is well grounded or soundly established. Given certain conditions of forced leadership and suppressed thought, the oneness of executive action in a nation may in fact represent nothing at all in terms of consolidated will and intent distilled from the whole mass. What passes for mass thought these days is not so much distilled as it is translated from golden plates handed down on some ideological Hill of Cumorah and read through the magic of authoritarian Urim and Thummim. The terrifying fact is that such bogus thought can be manufactured; it can be produced wholesale and distributed at top speed; it can control a nation; it is the shabby mental *ersatz* of an abnormal period.

War-making is too much dignified if it is told in terms of broad national urges, of great German motives, or of compelling Italian ambitions. When nations stumble into war, or when peoples rub their eyes and find they have been dragged into war, there is at some point a psychopathic case. Omit the element of abnormality, of bogus leadership, or inordinate ambition for conquest, and diagnosis fails. In the modern scene it fails also if one omits manipulation, dummies, bogeys, false fronts, provocative agents, fifth columns, made-up incidents, frustration of elemental impulses, negation of culture, propaganda that is false in intent, criminal usurpation, and terrorist violence.

IV

There is no intention here to draw a comparison of the American Civil War with recent wars. The point is that sweeping generalizations as to "war causation" are often faulty and distorted, and that when such distortion is assisted by taking the Civil War as an alleged example, a word by the historian is appropriate. Unsound historical analogies may have present-day effects. The "explaining" of war is one of the most tricky of subjects. If the explanation is made to rest on the cultural or economic basis, it is not unlikely that the American war in the eighteen-sixties will be offered as a supposedly convincing example. The writer, however, doubts seriously whether a consensus of scholars who have competently studied that war would accept either the cultural or the economic motive as the effective cause.

If one were to explain, or record, the relation of this or that group or individual to the Civil War, he would have to recognize influences, situations, forces, or perhaps mere tricks of fate, that existed to a large extent outside the rational life of the particular group or individual. In such an inquiry he could rely on no one formula. He would have to make up a series of situations of which the following are only a few that might be mentioned: the despairing plunge, the unmotivated drift, the intruding dilemma, the blasted hope, the self-fulfilling prediction, the push-over, the twisted argument, the frustrated leader, the advocate of rule or ruin, and the reform-your-neighbor prophet.

Robert Toombs said he would resist Stephen A. Douglas though he could see "nothing but . . . defeat in the future"; [1] there is your despairing plunge. Young Henry Watterson, then a Tennessee antislavery Unionist who fought for the Confederacy, is an example of the unmotivated drift. To many an individual the problem was not to fight with the side whose policies he approved of, but to be associated with the right set. Such an individual motive could not by a process of multiplication become in any reasonable sense a large-group motive. Yet it would be understandable for the individual. Usually in war time individuals have no effective choice of side, though in the American Civil War they sometimes did, especially on the border. Even where such choice was possible, the going to war by the individual in the sixties was due less to any broad "cause" or motive than to the fact that war existed, so that fighting was the thing to do. War participation is one thing; genuine and reasoned choice between war and peace, while that choice is open, is quite another.

The intruding dilemma was found in the broad border and the great upper South. The true interests and wishes of those regions did not determine the pattern that was set up before April of 1861. It was rather that, in a situation created by outside forces and thrust upon them, the people of Virginia, Kentucky, and neighboring areas were faced with two alternatives, both of which were utterly distasteful: either to fight against sister states of the lower South, or to join with those states in breaking the Union. The self-fulfilling prediction is recognized in the case of those who, having said that war must come, worked powerfully to make it come. The blasted hope—i. e., the wish for adjustment instead of butchery—was the experience of most of the people, especially in the border and upper South. The frustrated leader is seen in the Unionist who came to support secession, or in such Northerners as Thurlow Weed and William H. Seward who sought compromise and then supported war. The plea that "better terms" could be had out of the Union, implying a short, temporary secession gesture though uttered by determined secessionists, was the crafty argument used in enlisting Unionists for the cause of disunion. This might be dubbed the twisted argument. The push-over is seen in the whole strategy of secession leaders by which anti-secession states and Union-loving men were to be dragged in by the accelerated march of events.

These are things which belong as much to the "explanation" of the Civil War as any broad economic or cultural or elemental factor. It should be remembered how few of the active promoters of secession became leaders of the Confederacy; their place in the drama was in the first act, in the starting of trouble. The Rhetts and Yanceys were not the ones who steered the South through the bitter four-year crisis produced by secession. Nor should sectional preference cause one to forget how large a contribution to Union disaster, and how little to success, was given by Northern radicals during the war.

Clear thinking would require a distinction between causing the war and getting into it. Discussion which overlooks this becomes foggy indeed. It was small minorities that caused the war; then the regions and sections were drawn in. No one seems to have thought of letting the minorities or the original trouble makers fight it out. Yet writers who descant upon the "causation" of the war write grandly of vast sections, as if the fact of a section being dragged into the slaughter was the same as the interests of that section being consciously opera-tive in its causation. Here lies one of the chief fallacies of them all.

Virginia would be an example to illustrate this point. Suppose one inquires into the "causes" of the Civil War. Suppose, then, he asks: Why did Virginians fight? Already he has shifted the discussion, per-haps without noticing it. In the period before Sumter Virginia avoided secession, having no important motive for leaving the Union. In fact, Virginia made a notable effort, through the Peace Convention, to preserve the Union, to keep things as they were, and to prevent war. The prevailing element in Virginia was not making a drive for secession and for a Southern Confederacy. The proceedings of the Richmond convention of 1861 proved that. Then events got out of hand. War broke out *for reasons outside Virginia.* The Old Do-minion was *drawn into a war,* but as of early April 1861 it could not have been said that someone would have to begin a war in order for

Virginian homes to be safe.

There was no prewar grievance, or Northern threat, or brutal aggression, that made the Union culturally, economically, or politically unendurable, or continued peace intolerable, to Virginia.[2] There was no controlling belief that an outside power was oppressing Virginia, and that war was required to throw it off. As for helping sister states, Virginia was willing to help them stay in the Union. Yet, war having been launched, men and women of Virginia verily believed that their homes and their true interests were at stake, though some of them, who had been strong Unionists, supported the Confederacy because in their view they could not loyally do otherwise once their state government had acted. While Virginia is presented as an example, the principle could be much more broadly applied. If the question before us is that of causing a war, one should speak to the point of causation. He merely clouds the issue if he confuses causation with those motives, sentiments, loyalties, unwelcome dilemmas, and necessities as to governmental adherence which exist in a given region after war has been launched, when the clock has passed the hour of causation or prevention, and when the practical question is that of participation.

V

In writing of human nature in politics Graham Wallas has shown the potent effect of irrational attitudes.[1] He might have found many a Civil War example. Traditional "explanations" of the war fail to make sense when fully analyzed. The war has been "explained" by the choice of a Republican president, by grievances, by sectional economics, by the cultural wish for Southern independence, by slavery, or by events at Sumter. But these explanations crack when carefully examined. The election of Lincoln fell so far short of swinging Southern sentiment against the Union that secessionists were still unwilling to trust their case to an all-Southern convention or to coöperation among Southern states. In every election from 1840 to 1852 Lincoln voted for the same candidate for whom many thousands of Southerners voted. Lincoln deplored the demise of the Whig party and would have been only too glad to have voted in 1856 for another Harrison, for another Taylor, or for Fillmore in the old Whig sense. Alexander H. Stephens stated that secessionists did not desire redress of grievances and would obstruct such redress. Prophets of sectional economics left many a Southerner unconvinced; it is doubtful how far their arguments extended beyond the sizzling pages of *DeBow's Review* and the agenda of Southern commercial congresses. The tariff was a potential future annoyance rather than an acute grievance in 1860. What existed then was largely a Southern tariff law. Practically all tariffs are one-sided. Sectional tariffs in other periods have existed without producing war. Such a thing as a Southern drive for independence on cultural lines is probably more of a modern thesis than a contemporary motive of sufficient force to have carried the South out of the Union on any broadly representative or all-Southern basis.

It must be remembered that the secession movement of 1860–61 proceeded, not by coöperative action of various states joining to deliberate and choose, as a group, between secession and union. It proceeded by separate state action, which was much easier for secession leaders to manage. Not even by separate state action was the upper South drawn in until after the formation of the Confederacy and the beginning of war. Robert Barnwell Rhett, father of secession, was distrustful of coöperative action, or of anything like an all-Southern gathering to ponder the merits of secession. If modern writers have discovered a dominant movement over a wide region strong enough to have broken the Union for cultural reasons, they have found something which the promoters of secession did not know was there. Cultural factors are important; they should be studied for what they were, not cramped into a twisted or artificial formula or thesis.

It was hard for Southerners to accept the victory of a sectional party in 1860, but it was no part of the Republican program to smash slavery in the South, nor did the territorial aspect of slavery mean much politically beyond agitation. Southerners cared little about taking slaves into the territories; Republicans cared so little in the

A BLUNDERING GENERATION 49

opposite sense that they avoided prohibiting slavery in territorial
laws passed in February and March of 1861.[2]

Things said of "the South" often failed to apply to Southerners, or
of "the North" to Northerners. "The North" in the militant prewar
sense was largely an abstraction. To mention "Southern rights" as a
generalization was easier than to analyze what the term meant. The
Sumter affair was not a cause, but an incident resulting from pre-
existing governmental deadlock. Sumter requires explanation, and
that explanation carries one back into all the other alleged factors.
In contemporary Southern comments on Lincoln's course at Sumter one finds not harmony but a jangling of discordant voices. Virginia resented Lincoln's action at Sumter for a reason opposite to
that of South Carolina. Virginia wanted to preserve the Union; her
resentment was in the anti-secessionist sense. By no means did all
"the North" agree with Lincoln's course as to Sumter. Had Lincoln
evacuated Sumter without an expedition, he would have been supported by five and a half of seven cabinet members, Chase taking a
halfway stand and Blair alone taking a positive stand for an expedition.[3] What Lincoln refused as to Sumter was what the United States
government had permitted in general as to forts and arsenals in the
South. Stronger action than at Sumter was taken by Lincoln at
Pickens without Southern fireworks. Search as one will, he simply cannot find an aggressive North bound up in the Sumter episode. Lincoln hoped the men in authority would realize that. There is no general North-versus-South pattern that covers the subject of the forts.
Nor can the war itself be adequately explained by the glib repetition
of North-versus-South terms. These terms are usually excessive in
what they purport to signify. Instead of denoting proved reality,
phrases of this nature—"the North" wanted this; "the South" demanded that, etc.—should be regarded as a kind of stereotyped vo-
cabulary.

Let one take all the factors traditionally presented—the Sumter
maneuver, the election of Lincoln, abolitionism, slavery in Kansas,
prewar objections to the Union, cultural and economic differences,
etc.—and it will be seen that only by a kind of false display could

any of these issues, or all of them together, be said to have caused the war if one omits the elements of emotional unreason and over-bold leadership. If one word or phrase were selected to account for the war, that word would not be slavery, or economic grievance, or state rights, or diverse civilizations. It would have to be such a word as fanaticism (on both sides), misunderstanding, misrepresentation, or perhaps politics. To Graham Wallas misrepresentation and the coarser type of politics are the same thing.

The fundamental or the elemental is often no better than a philosophical will o' the wisp. Why do adventitious things, or glaringly abnormal things, have to be elementally or cosmically accounted for? If, without proving his point, the scholar makes war a thing of "inevitable" economic conflict, or cultural expression, or *Lebensraum*,[4] his generalizations are caught up by others, for it would seem that those authors who do the most generalizing, if they combine effective writing with it, are the ones most often quoted. Sometimes an author's pronouncements are taken as statements of laws whether he means them so or not; he is quoted by sociologists, psychologists, behaviorists, misbehaviorists, propagandists, and what not. When history is distorted it becomes a contributor to those "dynamic" masses of ideas, or ideologies, which are among the sorriest plagues of the present age.

VI

As to wars, the ones that have not happened are perhaps best to study. Much could be said about such wars. There has been as much "cause" for wars that did not happen as for wars that did. Cultural and economic difficulties *in wars that have not occurred* are highly significant. The notion that you must have war when you have cultural variation, or economic competition, or sectional difference is an unhistorical misconception which it is stupid to promote. Yet some of the misinterpretations of the Civil War have tended to promote it.

This subject—war scares, or vociferous prowar drives which happily fizzled out—is a theme for a book in itself. There was the slogan "Fifty-four Forty or Fight" in 1844. If it meant anything, it meant

10203040

5060708090100

that, in the international territorial difficulty as to the far Northwest, the United States should demand all the area in dispute with England, should refuse diplomatic adjustment, and should fight England if the full demand was not met. The United States did not get Fifty-four Forty—i. e., an enormous area of Canada—but it did not fight. The matter was easily adjusted by treaty in 1846. In retrospect, the settlement made the earlier slogan, and war drive, seem no better than sheer jingoism.

That was in the roaring forties. In the sixties the arguments with England, despite war cries, were adjusted by diplomacy; after the war they became the subject of successful arbitration. In the nineties the Venezuelan trouble with England caused a good deal of talk of coming war, while at the same time there was patriotic advocacy of peaceful adjustment. In the result, the Monroe Doctrine was peaceably vindicated. If that war over Venezuela had happened, one cannot doubt that writers would impressively have shown, by history, economics, etc., that it was "inevitable." Previous troubles with England would have been reviewed with exaggerated emphasis on a hostile background and with neglect of friendly factors.

There were those who said the United States would have to fight Mexico in post-Wilson days. Some talked as if they knew, from inside information, that it would occur in 1927. Let one take the elaborate discussions concerning security in relation to international agreement for naval limitation in the 1920's—what will he find? It seems incredible now, but in a certain type of newspaper, and in statements of some of the leaders, it was considered axiomatic that we had to deal with such matters as if we feared England, or contemplated war with England. It was in that false mental climate that we conducted much of our discussion of the Washington conference of 1921, the Geneva conference of 1927, and similar matters. To talk of possible future war is to suppose a future enemy—i. e., to put a particular nation in that hypothetical role. In those days it was England that was so regarded by not a few Americans.

It would be instructive to examine such episodes and to show how easily the country accepted peaceful adjustment, or how life simply went on with continued peace; then, after the frenzy of war agitation had passed, reasonable men everywhere either forgot the agitation altogether or recognized how artificially and how mistakenly the "issues" had been misrepresented by those who gave out the impression of "inevitable" war. All the familiar arguments, replete with social and economic explanations, could be mustered up for "wars" that were avoided or prospectively imagined. The whole subject of war "causation" needs far more searching inquiry than it has received.

<h1 style="text-align:center">VII</h1>

What was the mind of America in Lincoln's day? It was human, which means that it was partly simian! It was occidental. It was New World. It was American, though it would take a Benét or a Sandburg to suggest the vast and varied content of that word.[1] One could speak of its different "levels," but what would that mean? There were small intellects among scholars, great minds among men who worked with their hands. The "learned blacksmith," Elihu Burritt, would work ten hours at the forge and in the same day peruse works of science while also finding time for long passages in Hebrew, French, and Syriac. Naturally one does not try to "cover" such a subject. One can, however, recognize the existence of a continent he is not exploring. He can stand in awe of it, as Lincoln did in some of his best speeches,[2] and if one takes but a few steps in such contemplation his effort is as worth while as to devote hundreds of pages to the sterilities of politics or the elaborate details of military campaigns.

The mind of America in that day was Victorian. It had inhibitions which today appear as droll as its unrepressed whiskers. It was of the horse-and-buggy age. It was the mind of the McGuffey reader, by which a world of ready-made ideas is suggested. It was soul searching. It was Christian and it was chiefly Protestant; yet the Catholics were numerous, especially in the North. Religiously it was fundamentalist. It was not profoundly philosophical. Its mental climate was not suitable for the reception of Darwinism. As in other generations there was the sorry tendency to misinterpret science as if it were in conflict with religion. Though polyglot the generation was far from cosmopolitan. The soapbox flavor or backwoods tang was characteristic of its humorists.

If one remembers that it was Southern, Yankee, mid-western, or otherwise sectional, how far does that modify the fact that it was American? It was partly conditioned by racial backgrounds, such as the Dutch, German, Irish, Anglo-Saxon, or Scandinavian. It differed in the degrees of its Americanization. There was a staggering at variant distances from immigrant ancestors. Often the recent immigrant, such as the German or Scandinavian, took American democracy with more simple faith than the seasoned American. When disillusion came to such, it came hard.

The mind of the time was many things socially. Diners and dancers in New York's "high society" had their being on a different plane from the farmers whose rusticity was no more deserving of ridicule than their own clannishness. Those whom we describe as the Brahmins of Boston, highly vocal and expressive, were aware of little in common with the so-called "laboring class," which was less vocal and should not have been called a "class" at all. If one were to search for class consciousness in the Civil War age, it would be found less among underprivileged masses than among the aristocrats, the planters, the capitalists; it was they who were indeed class-conscious. Such a matter as the Southern gentleman's conventionalized code of honor, including the *code duello,* was a bulwark of exclusiveness and a deliberate social barrier.[3]

As to its war attitude, the mind of Lincoln's day was in part a mind during war, in part prowar, in part antiwar, in part merely at war. It was not predominantly militaristic. Where it was German it was usually not Prussian, being spiritually closer to Weimar or Frankfort-on-Main. What we envisage here are minds that were more or less genuine; this would rule out the unenlightened politician whose mind was usually a synthetic affair made up for the vote-getting occasion.

The mind of the time was often the product of intra-American migration. Thus it was Virginia or Kentucky in Illinois, Tennessee in Missouri, Massachusetts or upstate New York in Ohio. Rural areas had contributed more to these migrations than cities; not much relief of urban congestion had come by way of the westward movement. Perhaps predominantly the mind of America was rural. Yet hardly at all was it a peasant mind, much less proletarian. Never would its educated people have called themselves the *intelligentsia*. To refer to its middle class as *bourgeois* would be to use a non-American concept. The middle class did not function as a set social type or bloc.

It would be of interest to examine this mind in segments, but they would have to be complex segments. There would be the American-Victorian-New York-élite mind, the midwest-German-farmer mind, the Irish-Tammany-Eastside mind, the immigrant-labor mind, the old American frontier mind, and so on. Quite generally it was three things: Victorian, restless, and habituated to politician-like thinking. The puritanical Victorianism of the age combined with financial imperatives when one of Jay Cooke's cashiers committed the astounding indiscretion of driving a four-in-hand in Central Park on a Sunday afternoon. Cooke warned him that if that were known "amongst financial People" it would bring "great discredit to the Bank." "Credit," he admonished, "is a tender plant." Its delicate growth would be affected by "such a stupid display as a four-in-hand." [4] Business men who did not walk the straight and narrow were "under suspicion." Wall Street was an uplifting factor. Sabbath observance had its Bradstreet rating.[5] Yet it may have been the appearance of evil that was detrimental, for corruption was rampant and social disapproval by no means always attached to methods of questionable financial dealing. Graft and special privilege were respectable. Many a fortune of Civil War origin belonged to the ill-gotten class. Defrauding the government did not make one a social pariah.

In spite of much nobility of sentiment on its higher levels the Civil War mind seems, at least in large part, a sorry *mélange* of party bile, crisis melodrama, inflated eloquence, unreason, religious fury, self-righteousness, unctuous self-deception, and hate. Bad party feeling was evident when Seward, after a prolonged visit to Europe, appeared in the Senate on January 9, 1860, "& not a man from the democracy save Douglas . . . came to greet him." "D—n their impudence,"

was the comment of William P. Fessenden.[6] Yet this was more than a
year before the war opened.

It was, among startled, thoughtful souls, a time of stirring crisis.
Men felt they were living in great days. The generation had its self-
consciousness of mission and destiny. Even the private soldier filled
his letters with exalted talk. At the beginning of the war a Massachusetts soldier, telling of a rail journey from Boston to New York,
wrote: "Refreshments were lavished upon us . . . cannon sent their
boom over hill and dale and bells peeled [sic] their tocsin of warning
. . . that our train was approaching bearing a Regiment of brave
hearts to the defence of our country's capitol [sic]." Passing the Constitution he wrote: "May they [the colors] ever float over that notable
ship . . . as she rides proudly upon the waters of the Union." This
proudly riding epistle was but a soldier's letter to his brother.[7]
Similar attitudes were characteristic of the South. Mrs. Chesnut referred to "the high-flown style which of late seems to have gotten into
the very air." [8]

What the war did to the mind of Ralph Waldo Emerson deserves
careful study, though here it can be only hinted. To the Emerson of
the sixties New England was the custodian of sense and elegance,
Boston superiority was axiomatic, the South was boorish as well as
wicked, and John Brown, well-known in Concord, was a martyr. There
are "crises which demand nations," he thought, and a generation
might well perish to insure a better life for generations that follow.[9]
"What a healthy tone exists!" he wrote in May 1861.[10] To Emerson
not merely *the war* but *war* was an elemental, purifying force. Ridi-
culing the sentimentalist, demanding that the North must conquer
as a matter of culture, he wrote grandly of a strong wind, of "one
energetic mind" where there had been "incapacity to move," of
war as a searcher of character. War to Emerson was a "dynamometer,"
taking the "fop in the street, the beau at the ball," and lifting them up
by something "in the air." [11] "A civil war," he naïvely wrote, "sweeps
away all the false issues . . . ." [12] "This revolution," he said, "is the
work of no man, but the effervescence of Nature." [13] Reaching almost
Nietzschean ecstasy, he exclaimed: "War is a realist, shatters every-

thing flimsy and shifty, sets aside all false issues . . . breaks through all that is not real . . . ." "On with the war" might have been his slogan. "Let it search," he said, "let it grind, let it overturn, and . . . when it finds no more fuel, it burns out." [14]

To illustrate the benefit of war he looked for a simile and found it in the cholera! On this theme he wrote: "We watch its course [that of the war] as we did the cholera, which . . . took only the susceptible, set its seal on every putrid spot . . . followed the limestone, and left the granite." [15] What to David Starr Jordan was an annihilator of the finest and of potential descendants of those best fit to reproduce,[16] was to Emerson a beneficial cosmic force finding its origin in the motion of the planets. The "great illusion," as we now see it in the searching analysis of Norman Angell, found impressive and distinguished spokesmen. They did not, however, include Lincoln. The nation's affliction set his mind to wondering as to the ways of Providence and the mystery of men in deadly combat praying to the same God, but it did not find him extolling the grandeur of war.

VIII

When philosophers turned war apologists it was not to be expected that pacifists would have a hearing. The broad cause of peace was one of the casualties of war. In its antebellum background the peace crusade in America was a small affair of humanitarian groups with variant attitudes. It embraced men of intelligent idealism, but its efforts never bore fruit as did other crusades such as that of Dorothea Dix for the neglected insane or of Horace Mann for public elementary education. The Peace Society, launched with the impetus of Christian evangelism by William Ladd in 1828, and promoted by Elihu Burritt and other choice spirits, was thirty-three years old when the guns spoke at Sumter. In those years the society had not been idle. It had made use of the familiar techniques of agitation: lectures, local agents, local chapters, tracts, prize essays, magazines, books, national congresses, and petitions to the seat of government. International understanding was fostered, "popular handshaking" across the ocean sincerely encouraged. A vigorous literature was produced, world peace congresses were held, arguments against war were marshaled, arbitration among nations urged, disarmament advocated. Diverse elements were enlisted, such as Quakers, insurance men, free-traders, and merchants.[1]

Pacifism of the early nineteenth century differed from that of the twentieth chiefly in this, that it was economically and socially conservative. Peace agitation was a matter of Christian evangelism and social stability. It did not march with socialism. Christian and conservative though it was, it often met opposition or at least noncooperation from ordained ministers. Taking a stand against war was difficult and complex. Questions arose touching the duty of fighting a defensive war or concerning the right of revolution. To favor peace in the sense of having governments avoid the outbreak of war was very different from avoiding individual participation once war had broken out. Organized peace men were chiefly Northerners, rather Northeasterners, and the movement was interlocked with collateral movements, especially antislavery. Peace advocacy might or might not mean non-resistance. Not all peace men could accept Garrison's formula of doing nothing to preserve the Union against armed secession.

When war came and as the struggle dragged on, demands for peace were regarded as a kind of defeatism, of surrender to forces which Northern idealists considered destructive and evil. Peace became a matter of politics, of anti-Lincoln agitation, of what was called Copperhead disloyalty. Forces of institutional Christianity denounced it the loudest. Though praising Seward's peace efforts before Sumter, the Peace Society formulated its wartime position after Sumter as follows: *"Peace is always loyal. . . . We cannot . . . tolerate rebellion. . . . The cause of Peace was never meant to meet such a crisis as is now upon us."* [2]

The society was a negligible thing. One could read many tomes of American history without seeing it mentioned. It did not associate itself with opposition to the war powers, with anti-Lincoln demands for civil rights, with Vallandigham partisanship, or with obstruction of the draft. It never made enough of a stir to become notorious. Many of its members preferred war to the continuance of slavery; others preferred war to disunion; still others deemed human slaughter not too high a price for ascendancy of a favorite party.

Denunciation of war easily became denunciation of rebellion; this readily passed over into a demand to put down rebellion. The cause of peace as a peacetime crusade found a new orientation when war actually existed; non-resistance could not stop the torrent. It was the dilemma of the pacifist. When peace men face an existing war begun by what they consider an aggressor, their attachment to peace becomes outraged indignation against those who, in their opinion, have broken the peace. Such a feeling is consistent with the motive of stopping the war maker.

It is only the cynic who would laugh at the discomfiture of the pacifist when once war exists and when the choice of peace is no longer open. The contradiction belongs to those who would put the label of "war monger" or "interventionist" upon peacetime efforts to implement international coöperation and to buttress war prevention. The inconsistency is in misapplying the term "peace bloc" to those isolationist groups which have worked to frustrate international security and to break down peaceful organization among nations.

For the Civil War generation the problem of the advocate of peace was only in a limited sense the problem of the conscientious objector. Objectors in the Lincoln period were chiefly associated with well established antiwar creeds of religious groups. General objectors on other than religious grounds were not much in evidence. In this the Civil War presented a contrast to the World War of Wilson's day, wherein refusal to fight was associated not only with specific religious groups—Quakers and others—but with broad philosophical and social attitudes. In both wars the mass effect of organized religion was the opposite of pacifist. In each war administrative authorities of the United States respected the idealism of the objector and gave him the alternative of noncombatant service. In the Wilson period more objectors were relieved than imprisoned, though the imprisoned received the most attention. Imprisonment of objectors as such was not a Civil War practice.

If the pacifist had a dilemma, so did the government. The sincere and serene Christianity of the Quakers could not but command respect, and those who stood their ground were, as a rule, honorably excused from fighting. That Lincoln understood the Quaker's war problem was shown by his sympathetic letter to Eliza P. Gurney, September 4, 1864, in which he promised to do the best he could (under his "oath to the law") for those who appealed to him "on conscientious grounds." In keeping with this spirit a lenient policy was adopted which was at first an administrative adjustment in a situation where the objector might have expected severe treatment; late in the war it was a matter of statutory amendment to the conscription act. As originally passed the conscription act of 1863 did not even exempt ministers. On February 24, 1864, however, along with other modifications of the law, it was provided that members of religious denominations whose articles of faith opposed the bearing of arms were to be considered "non-combatants" when "drafted into the military service." In this capacity they were to be assigned to duty in hospitals or in the care of freedmen, or they were to pay $300 for the benefit of sick and wounded soldiers.[3]

For the objector to stand his ground in early Civil War days meant something like defiance of the government; the government was demanding a service which the objector refused; leniency was an afterthought. Non-resistance was a Quaker tenet, but here the Quakers, or rather the strictest of them, would have to resist, as did Cyrus Pringle of Vermont, unless their government would make a concession which in such cases it did make. No government can be completely unbending. Government is, after all, an art, perhaps a compromise. If the objector remained obdurate, either the government had to withdraw somewhat from the principle of compulsory military service or the uncompromising objector whose creed forbade war would regard himself as being punished for being a Christian. The government took an attitude toward Quakers which it could not take toward all, where conscription was its principle. The Quaker came through the dilemma with less compromise than the government.[4]

IX

It is not of record that Lincoln's cabinet contained a "minister of national enlightenment and propaganda"; yet propaganda itself was not lacking.[1] In the public "enlightenment" of that time there was boasting, there was rumor, there were atrocity tales, and there was falsehood. Atrocity stories were found not only in newspapers but in congressional reports. There were circumstantial accounts of Confederates bayoneting wounded captives, kicking heads about like footballs, insulting women, and engaging in gruesome tortures. William B. Hesseltine has shown that anti-southern horror tales were not without governmental inspiration in the North and that the secretary of war, the surgeon general, and the committee on the conduct of the war took pains to spread tales of the sufferings of Northern prisoners in the South.[2] Motives were various: tales might be spread to carry forward the abolitionist's denunciation of Southern cruelty, to satisfy the war mind by besmirching the foe, or to discourage surrender into Southern hands. When the backfire came and these atrocity stories led to questions as to why prisoners were not exchanged, it became necessary to invent the tale that exchange had been stopped by a vicious South intent upon destroying the lives of prisoners. Even the humanitarian motive promoted atrocity tales, and the report of the Sanitary Commission on this subject in no way fell short of governmental accounts.

Lincoln's attitude on such matters was expressed in a speech delivered at a Sanitary Fair in Baltimore in 1864. Referring to the rumored massacre of colored prisoners at Fort Pillow, the President carefully avoided pointing up the reputed atrocity, declared that the event was not known to have occurred, and promised an investigation. He also promised retribution if needed; but, as in the case of similar threats by the Confederacy, his motive here was humanitarian. The threat of retaliation was intended to make actual retaliation unnecessary, as well as to satisfy, and thus partly restrain, that type of vindictiveness at the North which was strangely bound up with humanitarianism. On this point Lincoln reached the height of caution when he said: "It will be [a] matter of grave consideration in what exact course to apply the retribution . . . ." [3] What seemed to worry Lincoln was not a vicious South, but the need to satisfy his own Northern public, including the humanitarianly vindictive public. For the latter he gave a threat of retribution which in fact he never carried out, and probably never intended to.

In spite of its lack of modern carriers, such as radio and the movies, Civil War propaganda found many devices. There were drawings in *Harper's Weekly, Leslie's,* and *Vanity Fair,* though not daily cartoons. There were popular songs such as "Father Abraham" which gave the chief a nickname and personified the cause in a benevolent President. There was recruiting propaganda by poster and otherwise, and there was a mixture of partisan and patriotic propaganda in appeals for soldier votes. Generals of the political variety made impressive speeches. The Loyal Publication Society sent out its material by the bushel, including stereotypes to local editors, tracts, broadsides, pamphlets, and in one case a forged speech attributed to Alexander H. Stephens, whose alleged language was startlingly similar to that of Helper's *Impending Crisis*.[4]

The word "propaganda" is an inexact expression which eludes definition. Every public appeal to support a cause could be loosely called propaganda. An advertisement might be propaganda in this broad sense, so also an editorial, a parade, a novel, a Sanitary Fair, a request for funds, a Thanksgiving proclamation, an anecdote, an envelope, a letterhead, a postage stamp, a dollar bill, a legislative preamble, a sermon, a petition, a sewing circle, or a school primer. One might use propaganda in christening a baby, naming a street, or addressing the Almighty.

Motives in reaching the public were mixed. Propaganda in Lincoln's day was more often complex than simple, hybrid oftener than thoroughbred; it had one purpose grafted upon another. Publicity for the national cause was universal, but this broad appeal was often linked with an ulterior purpose which was in fact the main interest of the promoting agency. Thus a party rally would masquerade as a Union mass meeting, a volunteer fire brigade would be a unit of Tammany Hall, and the anniversary at Baltimore in 1862 of the anti-Union riot of April 1861 was a boost for the newly elected mayor and council. When Jay Cooke urged people to buy bonds he did not hesitate to blend self-interest with patriotism as he stressed the advantages of tax-free seven percents. Even the name "Union" applied to the Republican party in Civil War days was an example of this tendency. Among themselves Republican leaders understood each other perfectly and continued to refer to their party as Republican, while for public consumption it was called "Union." [5]

Much could be said concerning party propaganda, but this was not peculiar to war time; party agitation is always with us. That the national cause was appropriated for a party purpose was seen in the Union League. It is unnecessary to comment on the League at large, with its expensive club buildings, its social impressiveness, its exploitation of the American propensity for joining, its masses of war literature, and its showy efforts toward recruiting and soldier relief; but there is need for further study of its campaign activities, especially the procedures of its local chapters. The minute-book of a local league in the nineteenth ward of New York City belongs to the type of sources that are seldom dug up.[6] The minutes here recorded are generally quite sterile as they creep along with routine matters till the approach of election time. Indeed it was not until September 19, 1864, that the nineteenth-ward leaguers "heartily approved" the early June nomination of Abraham Lincoln and Andrew Johnson at Baltimore. It was in October and the first days of November 1864 that this local league suddenly came alive, sending loyal newspapers to soldiers, passing sizzling anti-Democratic resolutions, publishing campaign documents, and appointing poll-watchers to swing into action at sunrise on the eighth of November. Just after the election the minutes report "no quorum," and from that time this patriotic organization sank back into utter inactivity. Repeatedly there was the "no quorum" record; in February 1865 it was voted to adopt measures to increase interest in the meetings. On April 3, 1865, the minutes flicker out altogether. Similar accounts with different terms, including the names of Tammany and the Knights of the Golden Circle, would illuminate the history of certain elements in the Democratic party.

Official propaganda took many forms, including governmentally inspired foreign missions of prominent Americans. Thurlow Weed promoted the Union cause in the British press, Archbishop John Hughes sought contact with Catholics in Europe, Bishop McIlvaine of the Episcopal Church made his appeal to the British clergy. In addition, the irrepressible Robert J. Walker appealed to British financial groups in opposition to Southern bond sales, while John M. Forbes and William H. Aspinwall labored to halt naval building for the Confederacy in Britain.

President Lincoln, who once owned a newspaper, by no means neglected publicity. Naturally he addressed the people in occasional speeches, in his two inaugurals, his proclamations, and his messages to Congress. Beyond this there was the use of patronage for newspapers (an obscure subject yet to be explored), and there was the case of John W. Forney whose Philadelphia *Press* and Washington *Chronicle* were known as Lincoln organs. In March 1862 the President asked Henry J. Raymond for an article in the *Times*.[7] So much of the writing on Lincoln has been of the sentimentally stereotyped variety that people have overlooked his trenchant comments on his own times— on profits,[8] on corruption, and on the manner in which every "foul bird" and "every dirty reptile" came forth in war time.[9] It is safe to say that Lincoln saw the war more clearly and faced it more squarely than Emerson. He faced it with an amazing lack of hatred and rancor.

The Civil War generation—not alone military and political events, but life and *mores,* social conditions and thought-patterns that accompanied the war as well as non-war aspects of the age—need further attention by inquisitive historians. In Arthur C. Cole's pages in the Fox-Schlesinger series one finds products of mature study and cues for further investigation.[10] Beyond the boundaries of even the newer books lie disappearing and forgotten stories. Where the stories are recoverable the present age of historiography, as shown in Cole's book, is more capable of accomplishing the recovery than previous ages. As history has its vogues and movements, so the retelling of the Civil War is a matter of changed and changing viewpoints. In the present confused and troubled age it is of more than academic interest to reëxamine the human beings of that war generation with less thought of the "splendor of battle flags" and with more of the sophisticated and unsentimental searchlight of reality.[11]

III. THE UNPOPULAR MR. LINCOLN

ALL the world is familiar with Lincoln the emancipator, the author of the Gettysburg address, the timeless spokesman of democracy. Few of us are acquainted with Lincoln the baboon, the imbecile, the wet rag, the Kentucky mule. Yet these are typical examples of the names heaped upon him in those cruel days when high office brought him less of glory than of insult and abuse within the ranks of the nation he was struggling to save from dissolution. Some of these utterances, voluminously given in contemporary correspondence long since forgotten, are presented here not for their own sake, but as evidence of the extent to which a leader may be reviled in his own time and yet go down in memory as a national hero. One does not take the full measure of the man's character unless he remembers that while Lincoln was battling a formidable enemy in arms and studying to avert international disaster, foes within his own political household were like choking fingers at his throat.

In the thinking of the nation Lincoln is remembered by what his friends have said of him, for the most part after his death. This is fortunate. If, like Wilson, he were remembered by what enemies have said, the picture would be amazingly different. For in the eyes of contemporaries Lincoln was a President who offended moderates without satisfying extremists, who issued a tardy and incomplete emancipation proclamation after showing a willingness to conserve slavery, who suppressed civil rights, headed a government marred by corruption, bungled the war, and then lost the peace, his postwar policy being blocked by congressional leaders in his lifetime before being wrecked in the reconstruction period. These denunciations are preserved only in fading manuscripts and yellowing newspapers, while

Lincoln's fame is a living thing, as if Fate had been struck with re-
morse and had made a belated effort to even the scales.

I

It was with incredibly low prestige that Lincoln in March of 1861
took the helm of a badly shaken ship. That form of studiously favorable publicity that modern journalists turn on or off was denied him.
A "good press" was lacking. Showmanship failed to make capital of
his rugged origin, and there faced the bewildered country a strange
man from Illinois who was dubbed a "Simple Susan," a "baboon,"
and a "gorilla." In Washington chatter and in news sheets he was
labeled an "ape," a "demon," an "Illinois beast." His tariff speech
at Pittsburgh in February, 1861, was described by a Washington correspondent as "crude, ignorant twaddle, without point or meaning." [1]

Publicity was unfortunately given to his kissing a little girl while
en route as President Elect, the same girl who claimed credit for suggesting the ill-designed whiskers that disfigured his fine chin. To
Charles Francis Adams the younger it seemed that while Sumner
"talked like a crazy man" and Seward labored "under a total misconception," the "absolutely unknown" Lincoln was "perambulating
the country, kissing little girls and growing whiskers!" [2] An imper-
tinent journalist linked the whiskers theme with the choice of a New
York hotel: "Mr. Lincoln, having . . . brought his brilliant intellectual powers to bear upon the cultivation of luxuriant whiskers . . . , has now . . . concentrated his mental energies upon
the question—what hotel he shall stop at in New York." [3] Men of the
East thought him unaccustomed to polite ways and lacking in *savoir
faire;* from this it was an easy step to consider him deficient in statesmanship. Breaking his published schedule and entering Washington
by a secret night trip in order to avoid threatened assassination in
Baltimore—a thing forced upon him by friends and detectives against
his preference and judgment—he became the butt of sarcastic comment and insulting cartoon just before taking the oath of the highest
office in the land. [4]

Inadequacy, weakness, vacillation, even "imbecility" (a favorite word) were attributed to the new leader. It is well that Lincoln had a sense of humor, for along with some of the sorriest "politics" this country has ever seen he had to endure the venomed barbs of the cruelest abuse. The smart thing to do was to ridicule Lincoln; thereby a writer would show his sophistication. The President is "about played out," was one of the belittling comments.[5] Others were in like vein. "You can not . . . fill his . . . empty skull with brains." [6] We "are sold out at Washington." [7] Lincoln "has done for the Republican party what John Tyler did for the Whig party." [8] The President was "unfit," a "political coward," a "dictator," "timid and ignorant," "pitiable," "too slow," a man of "no education," "shattered, dazed, utterly foolish." [9]

There was the impression that Lincoln could not cope with his problems. "It seems . . . our whole government is about the meanest & most inefficient in the world." [10] "Our people feel disheartened, discouraged & disgraced and are ready to curse the administration and all that belongs to it . . . ." [11] "Every one is . . . disappointed at the Presidents course . . .—the first man I met . . . this morning [this was in December 1861 after Lincoln had just sent an annual message to Congress] in a rage declared that if a speedy change . . . did not soon occur, he hoped some Brutus would arise and love his country more than he did the President." [12] "I . . . fear that the President is rapidly alienating his friends and will soon find himself without a party, if not without a country." [13] The North *"fights without a General, without a Statesman."* [14] "Lincoln is doing twice as much today [June 1862] to break this Union as Davis is. We are paying . . . [the] penalty for having a *timid & ignorant* President, all the more injurious because honest." [15] These bits of private correspondence, however devastating they may seem, are authentic and representative samples of opinion.

To say that people were dissatisfied with the conduct of the war and the performance of the administration under Lincoln would be the blandest understatement. Less than a year after Lincoln took office a disappointed citizen wrote to his senator that the Republican party in Illinois was "nearly paralyzed by the imbecility of President Lincoln in the management of the war." He added: "No Republican in Illinois doubts the honesty . . . of Abe Lincoln, yet his . . . opposition to striking rebellion where a blow is . . . effectual, has utterly destroyed all confidence in his statesmanship . . . . Nothing is more common than to hear men who did all in their power for the election of Abe Lincoln . . . say that Lincoln has done more to aid Secessia, than Jefferson Davis has done. Were the trial made to-day, [February 4, 1862] Mr. Lincoln would not receive one in ten of the votes given him in Illinois at the late presidential election." [16] A confidant of Governor Andrew of Massachusetts talked with a cabinet minister in Washington and then wrote: "There is no Cabinet. No Council. No union upon a policy nor a principle . . . . This cabinet minister asked me how Hamlin [the Vice-President] would do in place of Lincoln. I said first rate, . . . he would . . . make mince meat of . . . the cabinet . . . ." [17]

Within that very cabinet Salmon P. Chase, secretary of the treasury, was writing: "The President's great mistake has been . . . that he has made excuses for blunders . . . instead of dismissing the officers who made them . . . ." "If I were President," added the secretary, "it should be done." "We are in a deplorable condition," said Chase, "—armies inactive—councils uncertain—credit drooping." [18] A Connecticut friend of Chase was "unable to discover any serious, earnest, . . . overmastering purposes on the part of the administration . . . ." "What . . . does it mean," he asked, "that at such a time of darkness . . . there comes not from Washington a stirring word or courageous utterance . . . ?" [19] Another friend of Chase wrote: "Many of our best citizens say the President should resign . . . ." [20] Back in Illinois Billy Herndon, Lincoln's partner, wondered whether Lincoln supposed he could "crush . . . this huge rebellion by pop guns filled with rose water," [21] while Governor Yates was lamenting the President's "habitual disregard" of all his requests. [22]

II

In a naïve and simplified view the public—some of them at least —may tend to think of a President as having the controlling voice in the government, but the truth is that Lincoln found it increasingly difficult to get along with the powerful group of radicals whom John Hay dubbed "Jacobins," though they might better have been termed reactionaries or Bourbons. They had, and they exercised, the power to obstruct what Lincoln wanted and to enact what he distrusted. If some of our men in office have been "cheap politicians," these men might be considered costly politicians if one remembers the unenlightened policies they promoted.

In a careful study of the radicals one is impressed with the contrast between the pious unction of their public profession and the unscrupulousness of their methods and motives. They worked their intrigues behind the banner of a fine ideal, a people's indignation at the wrongness and injustice of slavery. With the driving power of self-importance and ambition they pushed forward their program by unethical politics, party "discipline" (i. e., the destruction of those who did not conform), intimidation, patronage (which traditionally has been largely influenced by congressmen), propaganda, and trickery. (The fully buttressed pages of *Lincoln and the Radicals* by T. Harry Williams give abundant evidence of the tricks they used and of their obstructive attitude toward policies which Lincoln favored.) As a contemporary observer remarked, their efforts gave "another turn to the screws under which the President was writhing." [1]

These anti-Lincoln vindictives, with apology for the anachronism, would have furnished models for a "modern" art class that likes its paintings strong. Thaddeus Stevens sat for an early portrait which shows a handsome type of hopeful young manhood, but now hate, sourness, and the disillusion of rejected idealism had etched their heavy and repelling lines upon his visage. Though "never . . . sparing of his insinuations against the [Lincoln] administration" [2] (these were the words of a Boston journalist) he was actually the leader of the Republicans in the lower house of Congress. Nature had afflicted him with a limping clubfoot; his sneering lower lip was his own.

Charles Sumner is less easy to characterize. Pompously elegant and rhetorically impressive, he was at times insufferable in the eyes of his colleagues. In speaking of Southerners he tended to become offensively insulting. Yet he had a scholarly background, mastery of foreign tongues, and legal learning. He also had the courage to champion unpopular causes. He opposed the "lords of the loom" as well as the "lords of the lash" and he favored the outlawing of war by way of "a Congress of Nations, with a High Court of Judicature." Peace and emancipation were the great movements for which he worked. In the *Trent* affair he served his country grandly, as did Bright in England. In the main result the Massachusetts senator was less of a headache to the President than other radicals. Lincoln and Sumner were unlike. The senator could never bend to the President's humor; yet Lincoln could and did keep on good terms with him as friend and co-laborer. The senator probably flattered himself that he was the author of some of Lincoln's measures. Lincoln was not the man to upset such an illusion.

Portraiture for those two westerners—"Bluff Ben Wade" of Ohio and Zach Chandler of Michigan—would have to be strong in the sense of bold, forceful in the sense of over-bearing. Little could be seen in their faces except petulance, insolence, unscrupulousness, and vulgarity. Wade's dislike of Lincoln was well known; Ohio politics as well as national polity became more difficult because of the intrigues of such a man. Joshua Giddings, stanch and forthright in his antislavery position, was utterly disgusted with Wade, whose hostility to Lincoln he attributed to bad feeling because of the Ohioan's failure to win the presidential nomination in 1860. The following was a typical example of Giddings's opinion: Wade, he said, "denounced the President as a *failure* from the moment of his election and began to lay his plans for his own advancement. . . . Wade proclaimed that no party could succeed on *moral principle.* That if we intended ever to elect a President we must cease to avow immutable truth as the basis of our party . . . . He was a candidate for nomination at Chicago [1860], and his friends were anxious to strike from our [Republican] platform all allusion to principle." [3] Giddings wrote indignantly to George W. Julian: "he [Wade] has demoralized the party which you and I had spent our political lives in building." [4] Sneering at Lincoln as a person descended from "poor white trash," Wade declared, when the President overruled Frémont in 1861: "I shall expect to find in his annual message, a recommendation to Congress, to give each rebel . . . a hundred and sixty acres of land." [5]

Of like caliber with Wade was Zachariah Chandler. A colleague dubbed him "that Xantippe in pants"; [6] Gideon Welles described him as "steeped . . . in whisky . . . coarse, vulgar and reckless." [7] There were, of course, other names on the roster of radicals: Ashley and Bingham of Ohio, Roscoe Conkling of New York, James H. Lane of Kansas, S. C. Pomeroy of Kansas, and so on. Such were the men who shaped the measures and cast the congressional votes in what was nominally the President's party.

In the congressional "committee on the conduct of the war" the Jacobins found their chosen instrument. It is not merely that in this committee as elsewhere one finds non-coöperation with the President. The committee has been aptly called by T. Harry Williams "the spearhead of the radical drive against the administration." [8] Partisan in all its activities, dominated throughout by radicals, this organ of congressional investigation was a continual embarrassment to the President, while its inquisitorial proceedings against able generals and its bandying of unproved charges of treason created dissension within the sadly disrupted Union lines. Perhaps it is a sufficient characterization of this radical agent to say that Wade and Chandler, crudely bitter in their opposition to Lincoln, were its leading spirits.

III

In the distorted vision of the Jacobins, Lincoln as President was hopeless. They distrusted him at every point. They disliked his slow-ness, his tolerant patience, his regard for border-state sentiment, his willingness to keep such men as Blair and Seward in the cabinet, and his reluctance to approve proscriptive measures against Southerners as persons. They were outraged at his veto message expressing disapproval of the act of July 17, 1862, to confiscate the private property of "rebels." In the final result Lincoln signed this distasteful bill, but in spite of this he sent to Congress the veto message he had prepared; his dislike of the bill was widely advertised.

These radicals did not understand Lincoln's policy. They saw none of the complications that Lincoln saw. They detested the generous things that the President ardently desired. It is impossible to understand the period unless one takes into account the political contradictions and distortions of that day, especially the manner in which vindictive leaders with well calculated motives took the popular votes of well meaning and righteous men and twisted these votes to partisan uses. Thus good men would vote and verily believe they were performing God's will, but politicians would shape the result.

By demanding the death of slavery the Jacobins were able to rally the support of many thousands of the nation's best citizens. To the eyes of many of these citizens, here was a President of their own choosing who actually tried, early in the war, to preserve slavery. "A more ridiculous farce was never played," wrote one of them, than permitting slaveholders to keep their human property on taking oath of loyalty. Let the administration continue thus and the Republican party would be forever broken and Lincoln "the most unpopular man in the nation." [1] To Salmon Chase's mind it was folly to think of winning the war while permitting slavery. "The government," he thought, could not succeed "in the attempt to put down this rebellion with the left hand while supporting slavery with the right hand." [2] To an Ohioan writing to Chase it seemed that if the President saved slavery in the struggle, not only would he fail after all to save the Union, but he would "be ruined & forever disgraced." [3]

One must remember that in the first eighteen months of his administration Lincoln withheld antislavery measures, overruled those who took liberating steps without authorization, showed a willingness to save the Union with slavery if that were possible, and in any case did not intend to impose abolition upon loyal men. It is true that he adopted emancipation in September 1862 (to become effective in January 1863), but this measure was considered halfway since it did not decree abolition in the Union slave states nor even in those portions of the seceded South where Union armies stood, such portions being specifically exempted. The emancipation proclamation was a kind of slogan for the ultimate freeing of Negroes, but as issued it was and remains a slightly understood measure whose actual immediate effect in the liberating of particular slaves was almost negligible. The fiercest attacks of the radicals against Lincoln came after his famous edict of liberation.

Lest readers be misled by a matter of terminology here, it should be added that the group known as "radicals" in Lincoln's day ought more properly to be designated vindictives. It is true that they opposed slavery, but they did a disservice to this good cause by the partisanship and exploitation that accompanied their opposition. They preferred military repression to the free play of public opinion. In 1866, for example, they were furious in their denunciation of the Supreme Court for its upholding of civil rights as against martial law in the Milligan decision. Looking back at that period, liberals of today would more readily agree with Lincoln than with Thaddeus Stevens, Ben Wade, or Zach Chandler.

Having observed the quality and motives of these Jacobins, one may note some of their comments selected at random. "Be sure that Lincoln is at heart with Slavery." [4] "No man . . . ever threw away so completely, an opportunity . . . to make himself revered, and loved by millions, and to secure to himself a place and a name in history . . . ." [5] " 'Old Abe' . . . is as stubborn as a mule." [6] Instead of "inspiring the people, he represses their ardor." [7] "Public sentiment is . . . deep and bitter . . . against Mr. Lincoln because he is looked upon as an obstacle in the way of closing up this war. Men are losing all respect for him and . . . for the office he holds and in these days of revolution God only knows what may come forth if the people get grounded in the belief that the inertia . . . of the President is . . . sapping the life of the Government." [8]

It is a surprise and a shock to observe how far morale had dropped in the days of Lincoln's ordeal.[9] Though expressions of wartime despair could be vastly multiplied, a few must suffice. We "must have a victory soon or we are . . . lost. Unless Richmond is occupied before winter by the federal Army [this was written in August 1862, two and a half years before Richmond was taken] Mr. Lincoln cannot complete his term of office." [10] "The President has given respectful audience to every mad agitator, whose presumption has been increased by the patience of the administration." [11] "Universal distrust begins to prevail. Even while sending troops the people distrust the Pres. Cabinet & . . . Generals . . . ." [12] The country "seems trembling on the brink of the precipice." [13] Trembling on the brink so continuously, and, in the inspired words of the politicians, quadrennially threatened with destruction, doom, and utter ruin, it is a marvel that the nation yet exists.

IV

It must not be supposed that in disappointing the radicals Lincoln satisfied the conservatives. Far from it. The radicals were in some respects conservatives, even reactionaries, the term being a misnomer. They were quite ready to allow plundering groups to use the war for exploitive purposes. On the other hand the moderates or true conservatives were offended by Lincoln's alleged dictatorship (this again being a misnomer), his denial of the habeas corpus privilege, and his partial suppression of civil rights. The moderates did not want Union victory to be envisaged as hateful subjugation. They stood at the opposite pole from the vindictives, to whom suffering on the part of slaveholders was relished as divine vengeance and to whom continuing domination over the Southern people offered the indispensable weapon of power politics. Conservatives were ready to treat the South fairly once the Union was restored. Such men were Browning of Illinois, Cowan of Pennsylvania, Henderson of Missouri, and that "Jeffersonian Republican," Doolittle of Wisconsin.[1] Being of a cultured temper, they had less boldness, forwardness, and dominant influence than the Jacobins. Success of the extremists was a matter of drive, tactics, organization. Moderates made speeches; sometimes they warmed up, but they did not go to bat.

The matter was further complicated by an unnatural party situation. Instead of a true alignment, Lincoln's party came increasingly to be dominated by radicals who were essentially anti-Lincoln, while the few efforts that were made to consolidate the moderates, including antislavery men of constructive rather than punitive intent, were abortive. The party that won success under Lincoln and Johnson in 1864 turned promptly to harsh, anti-Lincolnian policies in postwar days. Some who worked for that success did so with ulterior motives of which Lincoln would have thoroughly disapproved. He did, of course, hold the radicals partly in check, which is one reason they disliked him. In the larger picture war conditions, always difficult for a democratic-minded leader, plus the inadequacy of parties for the focusing of issues, made it hard for Lincoln's essentially liberal views to be fully implemented.

Few men in Washington could have been found who were at the same time friends of the administration and satisfied with existing political trends. Lincoln's old-time colleague of the law circuit, Judge David Davis of Illinois, wrote that Lincoln did not see his Illinois friends. They did not offer advice unsolicited, and could not afford trips to Washington. He added: "I do not believe that Judge Trumbull & the men he represents wish well to the administration. The true well wishers to the administration & to Mr. Lincoln's fame . . . are I am afraid, not often seen about Washington. . . . The tribune of Chicago (which I take to be Judge Trumbulls organ) is in my opinion doing infinite harm." [2] In the summer of 1862 Joseph Medill of the *Tribune* expressed disgust with the moderates of the time, referred sarcastically to "constitutional platitudes," and revealed his expectation that there would be but "a feeble response" to Lincoln's call for 300,000 troops.[3] Of Wendell Phillips it can be said that few men spewed out more offensive abuse of the nation's chief, whose renomination he opposed in 1864.[4] Frémont, Republican candidate in 1856, made a determined effort for Lincoln's defeat in 1864, heading (for a time) a presidential ticket of the President's opponents. There were whispered slanders against Lincoln's wife, preposterous allegations of her disloyalty, industriously circulated rumors that this or that man was about to leave the cabinet, and the like.[5] A collector of anti-Lincolniana would not have to go into the ranks of Democrats to find the President referred to as "a Damed [sic] old traitor"[6] and "as near lunacy as any one not a pronounced Bedlamite."[7] This last touching comment was offered by William Lloyd Garrison on September 9, 1862.

V

A major factor in producing dissatisfaction with Lincoln was the unfavorable military outlook, to which, incidentally, Lincoln's radical opponents made their contribution. Only slowly did the American people manage the transition from a little war, a mere sequel of the Sumter incident, to a long, serious, gigantic struggle. The first major battle, coming at Bull Run in July 1861, when militia terms were expiring, was a stinging Union defeat, after which months dragged while McClellan trained a real army. In 1862 came the Peninsular campaign and the Seven Days before Richmond. The campaign was a draw, though it need not have terminated so, for McClellan stood firm at Malvern Hill as the Seven Days ended. At this critical point new commanders were brought in—Pope and Halleck—and there occurred the ruinous removal of McClellan from the Peninsula, where Washington was in reality defended at the same time that the enemy's capital was threatened. In the meantime the Washington authorities had denied McClellan the troops he needed, those under McDowell and Blenker, and had kept considerable forces in the Valley of Virginia without accomplishing anything with them.

McClellan's demotion and removal led promptly to the startling defeat of Pope almost at the gates of Washington. Then at a dark moment McClellan took hold again, stopping Lee at Antietam, and saving the Union cause at a time when international complications as well as Lincoln's evolving emancipation policy made a show of military strength indispensable. Weeks passed and McClellan was finally ousted. Burnside followed him, then Hooker followed Burnside, and with these men came additional Union disasters, though with a fine army, at Fredericksburg and Chancellorsville.

War dragged on, casualties mounted, a drastic conscription law was passed (1863); yet the poignant hope of victory was deferred. A brighter prospect came with Gettysburg, Vicksburg, and Chattanooga; yet it was not in these brighter days that Lincoln came up for reëlection, and by the time of the next presidential campaign in 1864 the North was again in the depths of gloom, war-weariness, and defeatism.

In the days of deep military discouragement late in '62 there came an ill-timed congressional election which has been referred to as a repudiation of Lincoln. In this election five important states (New York, Pennsylvania, Ohio, Indiana, and Illinois) which had given their electoral votes to Lincoln in 1860 now chose Democratic delegations to Congress, while in a number of other states Republican congressional majorities were cut down. Though a Republican majority in Congress was not in fact a Lincoln majority, the whittling down of Republican strength naturally constituted a blow to the President's prestige. In the Springfield district in Illinois Lincoln's first law partner, John Todd Stuart, Democratic candidate, opposed Leonard Swett, Republican, who supported Lincoln's policies. Swett's decisive defeat, whether justly or not, was regarded as a verdict of thumbs down in Lincoln's own home.[1]

After the congressional election, the removal of McClellan, and the smashing defeat at Fredericksburg, there came a full-sized effort of Republican leaders to take matters out of Lincoln's hands. In December of 1862 Republican senators held a caucus in which biting remarks were directed against the administration. They then called at the White House and demanded changes in the cabinet, such men as Blair and Seward being unpalatable to the radicals. It was a time of intrigues, mutterings, and rumors, the bewildered country meanwhile being unable to understand what was afoot. Lincoln managed to ride the storm, coming out without a clipping of authority and with the same cabinet as before, but behind his skillful tact and calm bearing the President felt, though he hardly revealed, a feeling of deep personal hurt. "What do these men want?" he asked his friend Browning. "They wish to get rid of me, and I am sometimes half disposed to gratify them. . . . Since I heard . . . of the . . . [Republican] caucus I have been more distressed than by any event of my life." [2]

VI

When in 1864 the time came for Lincoln to face up to the test of reëlection, there were among other factors, three developments which showed the low state of the President's prestige: (1) the attempt of Republican radicals to prevent his nomination; (2) the utter despair of his own managers and supporters in that dark summer; (3) the movement within his party to force his withdrawal even after his nomination, and to substitute another man at the eleventh hour.

(1) When in December 1863 Lincoln clearly stated his peace aims in non-radical terms (promising pardon and generous reconstruction to Southerners in return for renewed loyalty) he brought upon his head a torrent of vindictive opposition that never spent its power until it ultimately swept away his plan of restoration under his like-minded successor. Part of this opposition expressed itself in the "Chase boom" as seen in the private circular sent out in February 1864 by Senator S. C. Pomeroy of Kansas. This document, which expressed the Jacobinical view, objected strenuously to "party machinery . . . being used to secure the perpetuation of the present administration." In briefest form, the gist of the circular was that "even were the reëlection of Mr. Lincoln desirable, it is practically impossible" and that Salmon P. Chase had "more of the qualities needed in a President . . . than . . . any other available candidate." It is true that the Chase boom was abortive, made so in part by Lincoln's quiet shrewdness; none the less it was an authentic expression of the thought and purpose of precisely that element which was so soon to take the saddle in American affairs.

Despite the radicals, Lincoln's nomination was smoothly and regularly achieved in early June 1864 at Baltimore. Directly after that,

however, Ben Wade and Henry Winter Davis, determined to kill his
plan of restoration, launched a caustic "manifesto" against the President for his courageous conduct in scotching by pocket veto their
"Wade-Davis bill" for a vindictive treatment of Southerners. This
manifesto was an emphatic public attack by Republicans upon the
man whom their party had just renominated.

(2) In the midst of the presidential campaign of 1864—when it
seemed that Grant, in spite of frightful casualties, as at Cold Harbor,
was getting no farther against Lee than Pope or Burnside—the apathy
or antipathy toward Lincoln became so serious that Henry J. Raymond, Republican national chairman, wrote: "We must have a
radical change in the *spirit* prevailing at Washington or we don't stand
the ghost of a chance in November." [1] In addition to all his other
troubles, Lincoln at this time was confronted with a peace drive
based on the erroneous assumption that the war could be satisfactorily
ended by negotiation, and was subjected to the unfair accusation of
refusing the boon of peace to a war-weary people, while at the same
time accomplishing nothing in prosecuting the war. Under these
circumstances Raymond wrote privately: "I find everywhere a conviction that we need a change,—that the war languishes under Mr.
Lincoln and that he *cannot* or *will* not give us peace." He then referred to a letter by Lincoln concerning peace maneuvers sponsored
by Horace Greeley, and added: "It was a most unfortunate document
. . . and is contributing . . . not a little towards the manifest
unpopularity of Mr. Lincoln." [2]

Raymond's gloom showed a depth of despondency among Lincoln's
managers which seems almost incredible when read today. In August
1864 an Illinois colonel, having visited the Republican chairman,
quoted Raymond as telling him "that the game was up—that there
was no chance whatever for Mr. Lincoln." The officer suggested that
while there was life there was hope. "By God, sir," said Raymond,
"there is no life. Mr. Lincoln will do nothing. He refuses to change
his cabinet or do anything else to promote his election . . . ." [3]
The young Republican, Whitelaw Reid, then Washington correspondent for the Cincinnati *Gazette*, wrote late in this campaign to the

girl orator Anna E. Dickinson: "I know one young person, who . . .
will vote for Mr. Lincoln, if at all, very much as he has swallowed
pills." [4]

(3) Many other examples could be presented to show Republican
lethargy during this political campaign, but perhaps the most startling
was the backstage effort of leading Republicans in the late summer of
1864 to oust Lincoln *after he had been regularly nominated*—that is,
to force him to withdraw and allow another candidate to be chosen.
In this development one finds the very nadir of party morale. The
movement was unique. It is the sort of thing that "is not done." Even
yet it is forgotten history. If the documents were not before us (for
those who search) the fact would seem impossible of belief. Secret
meetings were held, letters were circulated, and a new nominating
convention was all but called, with the purpose of getting another
head for the Republican ticket. At this time a New York Unionist
wrote: ". . . there are *no* Lincoln men . . . . We know not which
way to turn—none of us have any confidence in the re-election of
Mr. Lincoln . . . ." To this man there seemed "one possible chance
of saving the Nation, and only one;—. . . the voluntary withdrawal
of Mr Lincoln and the substitution of another candidate." [5]

An observer in New York, writing of "the radical portion of the Republican party," remarked that they were "entirely *out* with Mr. Lincoln." [6] George W. Julian of Indiana wrote as to the contest in his
state: "Old Abe is rather a burden than a help to our cause," [7] while
a friend of Sumner wrote: "Our boys all agreed in desiring another
candidate than Mr. Lincoln . . . ." [8]

Active in this movement to displace Lincoln as Republican nom-
inee late in the campaign were David Dudley Field, John Austin
Stevens, Parke Godwin, and Henry Winter Davis, conventions being
tentatively planned to make the substitution, with Buffalo and Cincinnati as the places suggested. [9] In this connection a despairing questionnaire was sent by three Republican editors in New York (Horace
Greeley of the *Tribune,* Parke Godwin of the *Post,* and Theodore
Tilton of the *Independent*) to Republican state governors, asking
whether another man ought to be named as standard bearer of the

party. Though doubting the feasibility of such a substitution, the governors sent replies which uniformly showed their lack of confidence in Lincoln, whom Andrew of Massachusetts described as "essentially lacking in the quality of leadership." [10]

About two months before the election of 1864 a curious letter was written by Lincoln's old friend and former supporter, Orville H. Browning of Illinois, to Senator Edgar Cowan of Pennsylvania. In a quandary as to which candidate to support, Browning mentioned the enthusiasm with which McClellan's nomination was received, and was "inclined to think there are many republicans . . . [who] will secretly support him." Then he wrote: "You know, strange as it may seem to you . . . I am personally attached to the President, and have . . . tried to . . . make him respectable; tho' I never have been able to persuade myself that he was big enough for his position. Still, I thought he might get through, as many a boy has got through college, without disgrace, and without knowledge; but I fear he is a failure." [11]

Such was the dark picture in the summer of 1864. By mid-September, however, the situation had notably changed and Lincoln's prospects had brightened. Several factors produced this result. The Democrats played into their opponents' hands by a plank in their platform, put there by the Vallandigham group, which demanded a cessation of hostilities on the ground that the war for the Union was a failure. Despite its decisive rejection by the Democratic candidate McClellan, this plank did enormous mischief to the party that adopted it, being interpreted as a "Copperhead" gesture to favor the enemy. Other factors were Sherman's capture of Atlanta, Blair's retirement from the cabinet, Frémont's withdrawal from the presidential race,[12] and Republican victories at the polls in Maine and Vermont.

Shortly before this favorable turn Lincoln himself recognized his difficulties in a memorandum of August 23, 1864, in which he wrote: "This morning, as for some days past, it seems exceedingly probable that this administration will not be re-elected." [13] If the election had been timed in August, when men of Lincoln's own party were wishing that he could be dropped, or if the August situation had persisted into November, the prospects, by Lincoln's own appraisal, were for his defeat. As it turned out, the President won the election by a wide electoral margin, "carrying" all the Union states except three; yet McClellan showed considerable popular strength, as in New York City.

The President's victory caused previous mutterings and doubtings to be forgotten. In the sequel, however, it was the anti-Lincoln vindictives within the party who profited by the election, and it was the anti-Lincoln ideology that was dominant in the postwar result, despite the nation's majorities for Lincoln and Johnson, and despite the fact that the vindictive candidate, Frémont, had withdrawn from the race before election day.

VII

In the statements here selected from slightly known sources, chiefly contemporary manuscripts, the half has not been told. Such passages could be continued indefinitely, with citations from the writer's files as to date, place, and author. Most of them have been photographically reproduced for the writer's use. It is from Lincoln's own party that the unflattering opinions given above, and many of like tenor, emanated. For views disparaging to Lincoln it has not been necessary to go into the opposite political party, whose leader, Douglas, gave the President notable support, nor does it seem worth while to repeat the vilification that came from enemy lips.

Some of the most crushing sarcasm against the President came from the successful and influential New York *Herald*, whose notorious proprietor-editor, James Gordon Bennett, claimed to "care nothing for any election or any candidate, from President down to constable." [1] The following passage, taken from the *Herald* of February 19, 1864, is a sample of the daily editorial pabulum that was fed to thousands of readers:

President Lincoln is a joke incarnated. His election was a very sorry joke. The idea that such a man as he should be the President of such a country as this is a very ridiculous joke. The manner in which he first entered Washington—after having fled from Harrisburg in a Scotch cap, a long military cloak and a special night train—was a practical joke. His debut in Washington society was a joke; for he introduced himself and Mrs. Lincoln as "the long and short of the Presidency." His inaugural address was a joke, since it was full of promises which he has never performed. His Cabinet is and always has been a standing joke. All his State papers are jokes. His letters to our generals, beginning with those to General McClellan, are very cruel jokes. His plan for abolishing slavery in 1900 was a broad joke. His emancipation proclamation was a solemn joke. His recent proclamation of abolition and amnesty is another joke. His conversation is full of jokes . . . . His title of "Honest" is a satirical joke. The style in which he winks at frauds in the War Department, frauds in the Navy Department . . . and frauds in every department, is a costly joke. His intrigues to secure a renomination and the hopes he appears to entertain of a re-election are, however, the most laughable jokes of all.

VIII

Within the citadel of his character Lincoln did not lose poise; in the administrative sense he rode the storm. He won the tricks in the senatorial attack of December 1862. The "Chase boom" was beaten before it was launched; Lincoln, for the time, kept his troublesome secretary in the cabinet where he could do the least harm. Reëlection came despite party gloom and without the President seeming to raise a finger. When presented with the question of Frémont's revolt in 1864, Lincoln made use of the Biblical allusion later employed by John Bright: "And everyone that was in distress, . . . and every one that was discontented, gathered themselves unto him; . . . and there were with him about four hundred men." [1] With a story, a humorous quip, or a gesture of adroit diplomacy, he turned opposition to his own advantage.

So handsomely did Lincoln survive that there will be those who say "What of it?" What if Lincoln was abused? His memory and his fame came through triumphantly. All great leaders have had opponents. It all came out right in the end. Unfortunately, to one who considers something other than superficial impressions of history, no such easy dismissal of the subject is possible. In at least two respects the thrusts and stratagems of Lincoln's opponents did incalculable harm: (1) they probably prolonged the war; (2) carrying over into the days and years after Lincoln, the devices of opponents within his own party produced a period of postwar abuse and confusion which is one of the crying tragedies of American history.

(1) As to the first point, looking beyond voluminous generalizations to the sources and the evidence, one cannot help noting that the unfair and successful drive against McClellan was with the intent of ruining him at the time when he commanded the main Union army. In McClellan's place the intent was to substitute such a military incompetent as Frémont, Pope, or Butler. What happened when Pope took command is a matter of history. Nor can one forget that this drive was promoted by the same radicals who assailed Lincoln. If coöperation had been offered in place of such weighty interference, there is reason to suppose that the war could have been shortened.

McClellan created an efficient army out of an unmilitary aggregation. The army that fought at Gettysburg was largely of his building. He operated against the Confederacy at its military peak; only an amateur would suppose that he was unwise in demanding full preparation when taking the offensive against Richmond. His requests for troops and supplies, so sarcastically denounced, were a matter of appraising what was needed to overwhelm Confederate defense under able Southern commanders. (This problem is not so much a matter of judging McClellan's information service, which is not to be taken very seriously, but of considering realistically what was required, not merely to face the Confederates in battle, but to put an end to their military power at the strongest point of their competent defense.) Never did the Union army under McClellan suffer a major defeat. The worst that Lee accomplished against him was to administer a temporary setback at Gaines's Mill. The campaign against Richmond was in mid-progress when the incredible order came from Washington to drop it all and leave the Peninsula.

That withdrawal allowed Lee to move north, overwhelm Pope, and create panic at the Union capital. At this hour of peril McClellan saved Washington and the Union cause at Antietam. In 1862 he had planned to operate against Richmond from the south as Grant did in 1864; there is reason to believe that he would have succeeded as well as Grant did, and far sooner. One could make out a case to show that Grant was as slow as McClellan. It is simply that history is not usually written in those terms. Among surviving veterans no tradition was stronger than admiration for "Little Mac" and confidence in his leadership. No one can measure the effect of the attack behind the lines which destroyed him, and nearly destroyed the Union cause. There were times when it seemed that radicals actually dreaded Union victory if it should come too soon and under McClellan.

(2) It cannot be said that Lincoln's cause was in fact uninjured. Reconstruction came in harsh, non-Lincolnian terms, and with it an exploitive era of corruption, scandal, and low-grade politics. Ungenerous and vindictive subjugation of the South after Appomattox left a more cruel sting and a more lasting resentment than military defeat, which Lincoln and the army leaders would have followed with a reasonable settlement and a true restoration. Looking back to the day when Lincoln's policy might have been chosen, it can be said that the Union side, at a moment big with possibilities, missed an opportunity. Here was a chance for a magnanimous peace, the terms of which Lincoln had repeatedly stated, particularly in the last speech of his life, three days before the assassination. The chance was lost, and in its place was substituted an unworkable partisan program of radical abuse misnamed "reconstruction," which had to be abandoned by its own promoters. This development was not without its relation to the abuse of Lincoln. Much of that abuse, or distrustful obstruction, came from the radicals. The time was to come when these radical leaders would use the martyred Lincoln's prestige to promote non-Lincolnian reconstruction, but that merely showed that misleading lip service was part of their attitude.

In a democracy the right to criticize is essential. It is a fallacy, however, to proceed from this to the assumption that all criticism is justified. If there is the democratic right to tear down a leader, there is also the right to uphold and support him. It sometimes seems that the ablest of our leaders have been targets of the most abusive attacks, while one can point to mediocre men who have enjoyed favorable publicity. Assaults upon a leader, if dictated by factional motives and carried to excess, can have disastrous results.

IX

After the passage of eight decades, turbulent and noisy voices in the record are forgotten. The thing that solidly remains is the bearing of Lincoln facing colossal tasks when his own hearth was saddened by the death of a loved son during the war, when co-workers met him with gestures of scorn, when newspapers made it their business to besmirch him and magazines to present him in distorted caricature. His last pictures show heavy lines etched about the patient mouth and eyes. One can read the story of the war in the contrast between these final portraits and the sculptural vigor of the pre-presidential face. Men of the time all had war faces—Halleck's showing a pop-eyed uncertainty, Sherman's a powerful resoluteness of battle strength, Stevens's or Wade's an unholy scowl. Lincoln's countenance never wore the frown of hatred even when the war had done its worst. In the final days his aspect had taken on an added quality; despite the wear and tear, he had kept his ideals.

No one knew better than he the values at hazard. If the United States broke into pieces, it was a question whether any nation based upon popular rule could succeed. The issue was democracy at large. If America failed in its experiment of free government, if it fell apart from some inherent defect, the loss would be world wide. Looking abroad, one noted that those in England who believed in democracy and broader human rights, such as John Bright, supported Lincoln's cause, while aristocratic and reactionary elements that hated democracy wanted the Washington government to fail.

If the picture given in these pages is disheartening it may not be without value to recall that in past days our nation has lived through cumulative months of darkest military discouragement, has struggled to think straight in the midst of clamoring politicians and flying propaganda, has accomplished tremendous tasks, and withal has kept ideals that have come down from the settling of the wilderness, through the Revolution, and on through the furnace of civil war. If democracies exhibit tragic episodes due to partisan excess, they also present a perennial power of renewal if only statesmen can grasp their opportunity.

It was in this context of democracy and high ideals, without which a leader is not worth his salt, that Carl Sandburg wrote: "The man Lincoln . . . had come to be the pivotal issue . . . . Some would vote for him with no particular faith, . ; . preferring him to the only other candidate. Others would vote for him in a loyalty that had seldom or never swerved since he became President; they had arrived at an abiding faith in him . . . . In the chaos of the times he was to these folk a beacon light that shone, that wavered, that in moments almost flickered out into a black despair, yet returned to shine without wavering." [1]

IV. LINCOLN'S SUMTER DILEMMA

THE Sumter dilemma, with all its exigent factors, presented the hardest and most far-reaching decision that Lincoln ever had to make. Normal instincts cried out against war when Lincoln assumed office, but the forces making for peace were deeply-lying and inarticulate, while the alarms and agitations tending toward war were precisely of the superficial sort which in a time of emotional excitement may disturb the balance of rational life and precipitate a conflict that calmness and statesmanship would avoid. There are writers who would have us believe that fundamental motives produce war (as noted above), but a study of modern warmaking reveals that such an idea is a fallacy. In contrast to the normal and basically valid demand for peace, the desire for war, or the whipping up of hostile feeling by those who begin a war, is artificial, unnatural, and abnormal.

I

What were the conditions in 1860–61 which tended to plunge the nation into war? There was a background of irrational antagonism between what was called, not altogether correctly, North and South. Cultural differences between the Yankee world and the South are facts that the historian recognizes; that these differences at any time constituted valid reasons for war is by no means so evident. Similar differences—e. g., between Chicago and downstate Illinois—have often existed in a nation or a commonwealth without producing war. Southerners of Lincoln's day who found the peacetime Union culturally intolerable and who desired an independent Southern nation for that reason were, according to available evidence, a minority; secession *per se* would hardly have carried the South. In the absence of genuine antagonism there had been years of hectic propaganda which had dramatized "the North" or the "Black Republicans" as the enemy, or the potential future enemy, of "the South," while a small minority of extremists at the North had harped on the idea that Northern liberty was threatened by a wicked slaveocracy.

In this atmosphere there had occurred a series of provocative incidents which had inflamed passion. Among these were the mid-century crisis resulting from the Mexican War, the Kansas-Nebraska act, vigilante war in Kansas, the Sumner-Brooks affair in the Senate (a most unfortunate Southern assault in retaliation for a Northern insult), the Dred Scott decision, the Lincoln-Douglas debates, the excitement over escaping slaves, resentment (which now seems excessive) over *Uncle Tom's Cabin*[1] and Helper's *Impending Crisis,* the promulgation of propagandist economics in terms of "King Cotton," the fanatical and meaningless John Brown raid, the split in the Democratic party, and the challenging election of Abraham Lincoln by a sectional party.

Basic facts seemed not to matter. The true situation was that the Republican party was pursuing a policy of moderation and expediency and that Lincoln in the debates with Douglas had disclaimed any radical purpose. What mattered was that people were told on each side that they had an enemy on the other side. This prewar enmity agitation was of the sensationally patriotic type that serves quickly to manufacture public opinion. As of 1860 this factor constituted merely a potential danger; events would show whether it would become dominant, or whether, like other war scares, it would blow over. Ominously it seemed that the minority trouble makers might be those who would control events.

In the period of intensified excitement that must be retrospectively called the prewar months, leaders of the bolder type had taken "a stand." Uncompromising positions had been assumed not so much by the people of either section as by groups and individuals. It was a matter of finding "quarrel in a straw" when "honour's at the stake."

Stands having been taken, that abused factor called "honor" or "prestige" or "face saving" demanded that a holocaust of violence be precipitated upon an unwilling nation rather than that "demands" be examined and adjusted. In such matters it is easy to forget that adjustment and conciliation are as honorable as strife and bloodshed. There was the usual superficial talk that war had to come, that it was "inevitable," that it was only a question when and where it would break. There was less of this than is often supposed, but dangerously enough such talk came to the lips of those extremists who posed conspicuously as patriots. If agitators, however rashly, declare often enough that war is inevitable, they may *ipso facto* make it a reality. Then, having produced war by predicting it, they may strengthen their case by saying "I told you so." Thus they pose as the hard-headed patriots who saw what was coming and did not listen to prattle concerning peace.

In the secession crisis itself, along with the tendency of a few states to involve other states, there had been the inconsistent and troublous factor of unilateral action. Demands and assumptions had been too readily accepted as accomplishments. Where various parties to a controversy were inseparably involved, one party had taken action, had produced *de facto* changes, had assumed at once that full warrant existed for those changes, and had proceeded from there as if the main question in dispute was already closed. Realities had not been fully faced; too much had been taken for granted. At a time when most of the slave states were considering conciliation, South Carolina and other cotton states had so acted that one of two alternatives had to be accepted: war for a goal not desired by the upper South, or surrender at some point by one side or another. Emphasis was too soon shifted from the weighing of objectives to the humiliation of surrender and the hurt prestige of abandoning a governmental position. At a time when it was easy to do so, leaders had told their people that things must be done "at all hazards." They had prematurely closed doors for adjustment and discarded instruments by which demands and objectives could be weighed against hazards. Statesmen had been overbold in the advance stands taken.

Nor was this all. There was at Fort Sumter a particular locale where these advance stands and these facile assumptions of hazards seemed to be all concentrated and distilled. Here was an emotionally unstable danger spot where a mere incident might be suddenly transformed into a war. This meant that war could come not so much by any deliberate process as by a kind of explosion. The cart would be before the horse. An act of war might happen; then the declaring of war, or perhaps the making of war without a declaration, would follow. People would suddenly rub their eyes and find that war existed. From that point, however adventitiously reached, the overwhelming wish still to pursue methods of peace would have suddenly become hopeless.

II

Against these tensions there were, of course, basic factors tending toward peace. Peace existed. It was a thing that the nation already had if it could only value it. There was widespread Northern sympathy for the South, matched by true Unionism among Southerners. There were high-minded leaders who counseled moderation—such men as Crittenden, Douglas, Bell, Everett, Seward, Lincoln, Stephens, Benjamin Hill, Herschel Johnson, and Alexander H. H. Stuart. Lincoln's Cooper Union speech at New York in February 1860 was a plea for peaceable adjustment and for a program of live and let live. Among the potential influences for adjustment was the upper South, the region of Virginia, North Carolina, Tennessee, and Arkansas, where Union sentiment combined strongly with peaceable impulses. Of equal significance was the vast border region of Maryland, Kentucky, and Missouri, where Southernism in the cultural sense coexisted with vigorous Unionism. In sympathy with this region were the broad areas of southern Ohio, Indiana, and Illinois, in which the people were Southern by origin and thought. Such people would have no stomach for an anti-Southern war. If they should fight because pushed too hard, they would do so with revulsion and indignation at the failure of statesmen.

Throughout the great Yankee world there was the wish of the

masses of the people to go on living their lives, the desire of millions that leaders find a way to peace. If there were exhortations for a policy that would mean breaking with the South there were also petitions rolling in upon Congress urging adjustment. Over twenty-two thousand signatures were placed on one such petition from Massachusetts alone.[1] Some who had voted for Lincoln regretted the fact when they saw the sorry consequence in terms of Southern agitation. Southern editors in this period were not all hotspurs; some of them bespoke a calm mind and a second thought as they urged that Lincoln's legally valid election in no sense justified secession. Some went further and hotly denounced the agitators in their midst who, as they said, were driving the South to destruction while blocking all programs by which states of the South would act together in deciding the main issue. Not all leaders of one "side" denounced the other side. Many a Northern leader asked for moderation in those things that aroused Southern anger, such as "personal liberty" laws which hindered the recovery of fugitive slaves. Thoughts of Southern moderates likewise turned to questions of adjustment. The actual stuff or substance of controversy was thin. The "issues" were forced and unnatural.

President and Congress were aware of this popular demand for peace. The outgoing executive was a man devoted to the use of law against force, a leader in sympathy with the South, yet zealous for the Union and resolutely determined to resist warmaking activity. At the turn of the year his cabinet was reconstructed on vigorous Union lines, but both the earlier and later Buchanan cabinets favored peace measures. Buchanan was working for peace at a time when that was the overwhelming wish of his countrymen; yet he was severely denounced by Southern extremists for not yielding everything to them. He has been equally denounced by men of the other side who believed that he was giving away the Union case. Historically, he has had perhaps the worst "press" of any Chief Executive. The almost universal condemnation of the man has largely been in terms of the repetition of stereotypes; few writers have honestly and thoroughly restudied his policy step by step with his bitter problem.

As for Congress, adjustment was its main preoccupation as it pondered Buchanan's plea for the quieting of angry agitation and the avoidance of war. Not content with dependence upon Congress, however, certain groups labored to effect conciliation in terms of a national convention, or a border-state convention planned for Frankfort, Kentucky. There actually met at Washington a Peace Congress summoned by Virginia for the purpose of repeating in 1861 what had been done in 1850 and thus producing compromise where secession loomed. The whole situation could perhaps be summed up as follows: peace forces were real and deep; war tendencies, though largely false distortions, were ominous and menacing. It was the premature crystallization of governmental attitudes, together with the trigger-like character of the situation, that portended trouble.

III

In the months that intervened between election and inauguration Lincoln himself was hardly the central and dominant force.[1] South Carolina rushed ahead with its secession, envisaged as a Southern movement but maneuvered and managed as a separate-state movement. The easy device of a state convention with full constituent powers gave strong constitutional sanction to this development, while on the other hand the Unionists failed to use a broad national convention of the sort favored by some of Buchanan's advisers. Nor in the South was there any all-Southern convention to determine whether secession should be tried. Secession grew state by state till it quickly engulfed the lower South. Well before Lincoln's inauguration seven states had gone out of the Union and had set up their own confederacy. As Federal forts, arsenals, navy yards, and custom houses in one Southern state after another fell into secessionist hands, Lincoln said little; what he did say in moderation and in honest disclaimer of any aggressive purpose was too often said confidentially. On the territorial question, magnified far beyond its significance, he took an unyielding position and tended to take the Republican platform seriously at a time when Republicans in Congress withheld application of their platform and avoided prohibition of slavery in territorial acts for Colorado, Nevada, and Dakota.

Congress adjourned without having arranged either compromise or military preparedness. Amid threats and rumors of assassination plots the homely new President traveled to Washington. One wonders how in the pre-inauguration period he had time to think as he dodged office seekers, greeted multitudes, struggled with heavy correspondence, conferred with leaders, selected a cabinet and prepared a difficult inaugural speech. As best he could he avoided commitment, at the same time seeking to avoid offense. At Washington Lincoln was even more moderate than at Springfield. Thus in the preparation of his inaugural address in consultation with national leaders the whole tendency (as shown in many significant deletions and insertions in the process of final revision) was toward conciliation and nonaggression.

Peaceable adjustment was the main burden of the inaugural; "dissatisfied fellow-countrymen" of the lower South were promised peace and noninterference if there should be no attack. At the same time the holding of Federal "property and places" (though in as unprovocative a manner as possible) was clearly announced. The inaugural was unfavorably received in the South, where it was even termed a "war message," [2] though Jubal A. Early of Virginia, speaking in the Virginia convention, referred to Lincoln's intent to execute the laws as "a guarantee that he would perform his duty." [3]

IV

As to Sumter, Lincoln faced a dilemma. Fate had given this fort an undue emphasis. The near exhaustion of food for the garrison meant that some kind of executive decision would have to be made; Charlestonian threats made decision doubly difficult. Any conceivable choice of conduct, whether evacuation or reprovisioning, would, in the distorted circumstances of the time, have been bitterly distasteful. Buchanan had faced the same dilemma as to unhappy alternatives, but under Lincoln a change of some sort impended, whereas Buchanan could continue for his few remaining months to worry along with a situation which he would bequeath to his successor. Any steps taken by Lincoln would be watched as an indication of the policy of an incoming administration.

Of all the forts in the seceded areas of the South the only important ones still in Union occupation when Lincoln became President were Fort Sumter at Charleston (other Federal forts in Charleston harbor having been yielded) and Fort Pickens at Pensacola. Two others on the Florida coast, Forts Taylor and Jefferson, were of minor significance. Trouble had been caused, though avoidance of conflict had been the intent, by the removal of Major Anderson's Federal garrison from Fort Moultrie to Sumter at the end of December 1860, and a serious incident had occurred soon after, when South Carolinian guns had fired upon a United States supply ship, the *Star of the West*. The governor of South Carolina had taken the position that Sumter must be evacuated and had shown a tendency to deal with the fort as a Carolinian, rather than a Confederate, affair. It was not that he expected a Federal attack from Sumter under either Buchanan or Lincoln. He said definitely that he did not expect this; yet he asserted that South Carolina, as a matter of sovereignty and status, would be under the necessity of reducing the fort.[1] He said this knowing that it would probably mean war. When the Confederacy was organized the authorities at Montgomery recognized the same "necessity" while at the same time respecting Anderson's honor as an officer and hoping that somehow trouble could be averted.

Neither side actually wanted war; yet hopeless deadlock and complete antagonism of governmental position existed. To the Confederacy and to South Carolina secession and entire independence of the seceded area were finalities; to Lincoln the breaking of the Union was unthinkable. How far either "side" considered war too high a price when separation or Union should be put to the ultimate test it is not so easy to say. It is partly a question of how many you are counting when you speak of a "side." Readiness to accept war if disunion should be resisted was almost axiomatic at Charleston and Montgomery, as shown by active military preparations in the South; this, of course,

did not mean that peace (with disunion) would not have been preferred by secessionists. In the North a similar belligerency was shown
by such a radical Republican as Zachariah Chandler, who, in opposing
the Peace Congress, declared that without "blood-letting" the Union
would not "be worth a rush." [2]

On the other hand the atmosphere in government circles in Washington under Lincoln as well as under Buchanan was far from belligerent toward the South; indeed a number of Northerners seemed
to think that the erring states should go in peace. This attitude is
usually associated with Greeley, or rather Greeley in one of his moods,
but it was by no means confined to him. Chase, for example (though
this is not widely known), held this view for a time. Some who thought
thus considered that secession would be temporary; others were ready
to accept final separation as preferable to war. It must be remembered
that at this stage only a minority within the South had acted for
secession; the upper South and the slave states of the border were
still in the Union. In border and upper South the emphasis was upon
Union with conciliation.

In contrast to Sumter, though in status the two forts were analogous,
the case of Fort Pickens was psychologically less provocative. The
keeping of Pickens on the Florida coast would probably not bring
war; whether an effort to hold Sumter against South Carolinian and
Confederate opposition could be so managed as to avoid hostility was
a far more serious question. The Sumter matter had been the subject
of negotiation between Confederate commissioners and Secretary of
State Seward. Intermediaries had provided a kind of backstairs communication with officials whom the government of the United States
would not recognize, and in this unsatisfactory way Seward's word
had actually been given that the fort would be evacuated. When the
alternative of evacuating the fort or provisioning the garrison was
put to Lincoln's cabinet (March 15) the answer was in the Seward
sense. Five members advised withdrawal; one (Chase) gave an ambiguous answer; Blair alone unequivocally counseled holding the
fort. (When cabinet opinions were again taken two weeks later only
Chase, Welles, and Blair definitely favored a Sumter expedition.

Seward and Smith opposed it, Bates gave an uncertain answer, and Cameron gave no written opinion.) [3] Military authorities, including General Scott, head of the army, advocated evacuation and pointed to the impossibility of defending the position against Southern attack. The army could not avoid measuring its resources against the task it was asked to perform. In the previous two months the forces and armament of the United States at Charleston had notably decreased in proportion to those of South Carolina and the Confederacy.

In all this prewar excitement and tension there were three things that Lincoln did not do. (1) He did not order what would now be called mobilization. For the Lincoln case the term is, of course, a misnomer; any plan for warlike operations in the South would have required a vast increase of existing forces. The militia of the United States was a shadowy thing, trained reserves did not exist, and the regular army numbered no more than sixteen thousand at a time when the holding of the Federal position at Charleston alone in case of Southern attack was supposed by some to require twenty thousand. (2) Lincoln did not issue or inspire any public statements designed to inflame passion or intensify Northern hostility against the South. (3) Lincoln did not attempt to retake any of the already occupied forts in the lower South. Logic based on Union premises would have required this as much as secession logic required reduction or Federal abandonment of Sumter.

Lincoln did not think of his government as merely that of the North. It was for him the Federal government for the whole nation. That nation, in logic, could not be broken by unilateral action; to him secession was a nullity. Yet logic is not always wisdom, and Lincoln took care to avoid any demand that captured positions be reclaimed by force. To give up the few that remained was a different matter. That would have looked like a deliberate choice of Federal surrender. Yet as he pondered the dilemma, exploring all its phases, the President studied the policy of evacuating Sumter for what it was worth. He conferred with John B. Baldwin, a Unionist member of the Virginia convention which was considering secession. The holding of this conference presented to some minds the possibility of some kind of bargain whereby Lincoln would perhaps renounce Sumter while Virginia would renounce secession. The conference occurred very late in the Sumter imbroglio (later than Lincoln hoped) and in fact it came to nothing; none the less it appears that the thought of possible evacuation had for some time been in the President's mind.[4] To the historian the incident serves not only to underline Lincoln's willingness to explore peaceable methods; it also brings into view, as Southern writers have shown, the uneasy conviction of Virginians that a military outbreak would help secessionists. While serving no upper-Southern objective, such an outbreak would unite upper and lower South in common opposition to "coercion." By the same token the more extreme secessionists seemed to desire the outbreak.

The manner in which the Sumter question occupied Lincoln's mind is shown by his efforts to get information on the spot. Two close friends of Southern origin, Ward Lamon and Stephen Hurlbut, were sent to Charleston as the President's informal emissaries to report on the situation there. The irrepressible Lamon, profanely anti-abolitionist in sentiment and full of Washington gossip, managed to convey to South Carolinian authorities the impression that the fort would be evacuated, as indeed seemed likely in view of Seward's commitments. A third exploratory visit was that of Gustavus V. Fox of the United States navy. In Fox's mind the purpose of this visit was that of preparing a plan for a Sumter expedition. In the President's mind there was the realization that as long as the Sumter problem remained open the military and naval possibilities would have to be studied.[5]

V

After painful deliberation and amid conflicting advice and cruel pressure, Lincoln made his decision. One can find his own explanation of this decision in the message to Congress on July 4, 1861. If this message be considered special pleading, one can study the orders and events of March and April of 1861. Both the message and the contemporary orders serve to underscore one very important factor: the distinction between Sumter and Pickens. For the Florida fort Lincoln would do one thing; for Sumter another. It is an instructive exercise to note how clear-cut this distinction was between the two forts and how far it extended.[1] Lincoln intended to keep and reënforce Pickens, being well assured it could be done peacefully. For the Florida position he was preparing *and sending* an expedition; for the South Carolinian case he was making preparation but withholding sailing orders. The Pickens plan was launched more than two weeks earlier than that for Sumter. The expedition for Pickens was to proceed without delay and to act for the reënforcement of the fort. Ships meant for Sumter were given no such orders to reënforce or even to sail, but were directed to be "in readiness for sea service." The Sumter expedition, though made ready (and of course the preparation of an expedition, though tentative, required time), was, in Lincoln's own words, to be "used, or not, according to circumstances." [2] The Pickens expedition, destined for a point where trouble was not anticipated, would serve, however partially, to underscore Lincoln's announced plan to hold Federal property. Before starvation actually descended upon the Sumter garrison, Pickens could be reached, so Lincoln hoped, and reënforced without an outbreak. No Federal attack from Pickens was intended, merely reënforcement.[3] This, Lincoln said in his July message, would be a "clear indication of policy, and would better enable the country to accept the evacuation of Fort Sumter as a military necessity." [4]

How far does this statement constitute evidence of Lincoln's actual willingness to evacuate? The implication of the July message is that under a given set of circumstances—i. e., the prior reënforcement of Pickens—Lincoln would have renounced the Sumter expedition entirely, though his secretary-biographers, Nicolay and Hay, are very reluctant to admit any such possibility. On the other hand those who doubt the message might assert that, once the expeditions had been planned, he meant for them both to sail. One deals in conjecture when he attempts to say what "would have" occurred "if things had been different"; yet the case of a statesman actually canvassing alternatives may be a matter of history, and the historian can point to Lincoln's statement that the Sumter enterprise was tentatively planned for a "conjuncture" or a "contingency" and that the unexpected Pickens failure supplied the contingency that caused it to be sent.[5] It can be established that April 6, the day the disappointing news as to Pickens reached Washington, was also the time of various facts concerning the expedition for Sumter. It was the date of readiness for possible sailing as indicated in Lincoln's order of March 29 when tentative Sumter preparations began.[6] It was the date when an important instruction to Anderson, informing him that an expedition would go forward, was sent by Lincoln though it was dated April 4.[7] It was also the date of Lincoln's instructions to Chew to notify Governor Pickens that a supply fleet would be sent.[8] Finally, it was considered to be the date beyond which hesitation as to sending the expedition would hardly be possible because of the low condition of Anderson's supplies.

Up to April 6, then, the expedition, though prepared, could have been held back. In fact the actual sailings occurred mostly on April 8 and 9. To one who seeks to understand Lincoln's thought on this painful Sumter problem the tentative planning, the eager hope for a strengthening of Southern unionism, and the long waiting as to sending ships, are significant factors. The expedition was not sent until, after arduous consideration, the President felt (1) that he could not surrender the fort, and (2) that he could delay supplies no longer.

It has been noted that April 6 was the date when news came to Lincoln that his Pickens arrangements—the order to Captain Vogdes on March 12 which he regarded as essential to his Pickens-Sumter plans —had not been carried out. The reason for this failure was a kind of quasi-armistice or understanding concerning the Florida fort made under Buchanan but not considered binding by his successor. Lincoln was reluctant to give up Sumter unless authority could somehow be upheld in terms of his inaugural promise, which he thought might have been done peaceably by holding Pickens. Now the news of April 6 made this plan impossible. Further Pickens orders would have to be sent, and before the Florida fort could be reënforced the deadline at Sumter—i. e., the exhaustion of supplies—would be at hand.

Gustavus Fox later stated that on April 4 the President said he had

decided to let the Sumter expedition go. It appears however, that Fox
was not in possession of all the facts nor conversant with the President's full intentions. A few days before this, March 30, Fox had been
directed to go to New York, the point of departure, "with verbal instructions to prepare for the voyage, but to make no binding engagements." Lincoln knew that even after April 4 there would be a short
interval of a few days before the Sumter expedition would actually
sail, during which time it could be held up by telegraph. It was at this
critical stage, the Sumter expedition having not yet sailed, that Lincoln learned of the Pickens muddle. Under pressure from firm Unionists and sternly admonished by old Frank Blair that evacuation would
be treason, the President faced the bitter necessity of exhibiting firmness at some point; Pickens was the innocuous point he had chosen.
None of the Sumter orders were ever as firm as the Pickens orders.
The news of April 6, however, made it impossible to strengthen
Pickens in time to offset the Sumter situation. "In precaution against
such a conjuncture," wrote Lincoln, "the government had . . .
commenced preparing an expedition . . . adapted . . . to relieve
Fort Sumter, which expedition was intended to be ultimately used,
or not, according to circumstances. The strongest anticipated case for
using it was now presented, and it was resolved to send it forward." [9]

At Pickens as well as Sumter United States efforts were nonaggressive. Colonel Harvey Brown, U. S. A., informed General Braxton
Bragg, C. S. A., that he would hold himself on the defensive. Contemporary records show "how earnest the wish of Colonel Brown
[under orders from Washington] was that no act of hostility should be
committed which might provoke retaliation or serve as an excuse
. . . for an attack on the fort . . . ." [10] By April 17 the Florida fort
was quietly reënforced with no firing and no bloodshed. It showed that
such a thing could be peaceably done.

Attention now turns to one of the most important aspects of the
whole crisis—i. e., the purpose of the Sumter enterprise. When finally
and tardily released for sailing, the expedition still had no perempt-
tory orders to reënforce. The full object was to supply the men with
food. Only in case of attack by the other side were additional troops

to be placed in the garrison, or the attempt made to do so. There was a further thing: to show that hostile surprise was not intended, Lincoln sent a messenger, R. S. Chew, to notify Governor Pickens of South Carolina of his nonaggressive purpose to land provisions.[11] Provisioning was to be attempted only if Major Anderson's flag was still flying over the fort; there was to be no attack in terms of an attempted retaking. The major, according to war department instructions written by Lincoln, was expected to hold out if possible till the arrival of the expedition, but after acting on the defensive to the point of satisfying military pride, he was authorized to capitulate if that should be necessary. One aspect of these orders to Anderson is that they were the kind that would have to be given unless a large and really formidable force were to be sent to Charleston. They underline the mildness of Lincoln's Sumter undertaking.

The Sumter expedition sailed without the warship *Powhatan,* owing to a bungling of orders. This was a matter of opposite maneuvers on the part of Welles and Seward, each in his way seeking to use Lincoln's authority. Contrary to Lincoln's intent the secretary of state managed to keep the *Powhatan* for the Pickens fleet, which, as the diary of Montgomery C. Meigs shows, was a kind of Seward pet.[12] In this he showed something very much like defiance, or disregard, of the President. This extraordinary conduct of Seward was of a piece with his previous negotiations and unauthorized commitments concerning Sumter. The incident illustrates the looseness of administrative methods in the Lincoln cabinet. It also shows Seward's eagerness to justify his sobriquet of "premier" by assuming what amounted to presidential duties, as well as secretarial functions outside his proper department.[13] As for Lincoln, while giving the closest attention to the Chew instructions which were drafted in his own hand, and while keeping his finger on the methods by which South Carolina would be notified of non-hostile intent, he had paid little heed to the ships of the expedition itself, even signing orders without reading them. In orders as to the use of the ships he had emphasized caution and avoidance of attack.

It must be remembered that, after all, the main question of the day was the challenge of a new-formed Southern nation and the complete deadlock caused by the non-recognition of that nation at Washington. Lincoln was talking and thinking in familiar terms, while secessionists were speaking a novel language of changed allegiance, consummated dissolution of the Union, and displaced Federal authority in the lower South. States other than the seceded ones were regarded as foreign nations. On February 16, 1861, Toombs reported in the Confederate Congress a resolution in which certain action was to be taken ". . . against all foreign countries except the State of Texas." [14] That Lincoln should avoid such unfamiliar terminology and speak in established Federal terms was the thing expected of the President of the United States. Swift moving leaders of Southern independence spoke of a dissolved union before the country had time to rub its eyes.

To Charleston and Montgomery, where dissolution of the Union was a *fait accompli,* the mere sending of the expedition, or the mere non-withdrawal from Sumter, was regarded as "invasion." The expedition having been sent, Confederate officers visited the fort; orders were examined; Anderson predicted evacuation unless relieved; he also promised that he would not fire upon Confederate forces unless attacked. Despite Anderson's nonaggressive attitude Confederate authorities, to whom the retention of Sumter spelled "coercion," saw no choice but to reduce the fort. The responsibility of Confederate aides (who consulted Major Anderson in person, received an answer which went as far as the major could go to meet Southern conditions, and gave the order to fire without referring the matter either to Beauregard or Jefferson Davis) has perhaps been overstated. The historian Rhodes believes that Anderson was earnestly endeavoring to meet Beauregard half way and that the action of the aides was due to impetuosity rather than sound judgment.[15] The other side of the question is that Confederate authorities at Charleston were under orders from Montgomery to reduce Fort Sumter unless it should be evacuated.[16]

Firing began at 4:30 on the morning of April 12; over thirty hours of bombardment occurred without loss of life but with heavy damage to the fort; on April 13 Anderson agreed to evacuate; on April 14 he surrendered with colors flying, bringing away company property and saluting his flag. Military courtesy and regard for Anderson's feelings had been carefully observed by Southern officers. Thus it turned out that Sumter was not held. The few vessels of the relieving fleet that arrived remained at a distance and did nothing in the Sumter battle. The force sent to Sumter had been much smaller than that sent to Pickens; this force was not intended to be landed at all if attack had not occurred. The Sumter menace (to the South, or to South Carolina) had been overstated.

VI

Many post-mortems on the Charleston tragedy, some anti-Lincoln, some otherwise, have been conducted. Until the Sumter outbreak, peace, though not union, existed. Until then Virginia and the other commonwealths of the upper South remained firmly within the United States. Voluntary evacuation at Charleston would probably have tended to hold them there. What would have been the history of the Union from that point is not so clear. The Sumter clash, plus Lincoln's call for militia which immediately followed, put the upper South in such a dilemma as between secession and coercion of sister states that withdrawal soon followed. The tragedy of the Sumter imbroglio was that in the immediate sequel it was followed by war. Furthermore, Lincoln was considered by Southerners to have broken a pledge. Seward had given a promise of evacuation and such a promise from the secretary of state was considered meaningless unless it controlled Lincoln. It seems incredible, but it was characteristic of Seward that he made these commitments without Lincoln's permission. The charge that Lincoln knew of Seward's promises has never been proved. The evidence points the other way. One of the difficulties was that the Lincoln administration was not a coördinated unit.

Anger toward Lincoln was now almost universal in the South. In Southern eyes he had done the thing which made it impossible for Virginia unionists to hold their state. So also North Carolina, Tennessee, and Arkansas. Each side declared that the other began the war. Southerners argued that Lincoln's provisioning expedition amounted to invasion; Lincoln and his supporters held that he meant no aggression in merely holding a Federal fort. Logic on each side was faultless; it was only the premises that differed!

Explanation of Lincoln's action in terms of deliberate provocation —making the whole affair a matter of strategy to "begin the war" but to put the Confederacy in the position of firing the first shot—is not of recent origin. That theory is virtually as old as the event itself. In the Tilden manuscripts at the New York Public Library one finds a letter of August 1, 1861, from John L. O'Sullivan, spirited Democratic journalist and champion of lost causes, to Samuel J. Tilden, written at Lisbon, Portugal, in which O'Sullivan argued that Lincoln's acts were but an "adroit manouvre" to draw Beauregard's fire and "precipitate the attack upon Sumpter [sic] . . . for . . . its . . . effect upon the public feeling of the North." This theory reappears in an independent and scholarly article by Charles W. Ramsdell, published in 1937,[1] and the same interpretation has been advanced by other writers.[2] Professor Ramsdell's interpretation is in terms of a query which, he says "must have" arisen in Lincoln's mind: "Could the Southerners be induced to attack Sumter, to assume the aggressive and thus put themselves in the wrong in the eyes of the North and of the world?" Professor Ramsdell adds in a footnote: "The general idea of such an outcome was in the air; the contribution of Lincoln himself was the maneuver by which this desirable solution was brought about." [3]

In the elaboration of this thesis various factors that might have influenced Lincoln are presented, this presentation being combined with interpretations, queries, and conjectures as to the purpose and the meaning of the factors mentioned. Admitting his inability to read Lincoln's thoughts, Professor Ramsdell seems almost to show a sympathy for the harassed President in his difficult dilemma. The impatience and disgust of aggressive Republicans is mentioned, also the President's need to find some method of satisfying moderates. Lincoln is represented as having "rejected all overtures" [4] toward compromise. This is incorrect: Lincoln agreed to various concessions. He favored repeal of the "personal liberty laws" (laws of the states to obstruct recovery of fugitive slaves). As President Elect he had no thought of recommending abolition in the District of Columbia, though as congressman in 1849 he had favored such abolition in very conservative terms. On that and other questions he adopted a "hands off" policy. He did not insist on abolition of the slave trade among the states, nor was he much concerned as to possible extension of slavery in New Mexico. He took no stand against the admission of new slave states. He did not propose to use the patronage against Southerners, and he even consented to the curious constitutional amendment which would have prohibited Federal abolition of slavery in the states and would have made such a constitutional guarantee unamendable in the future. (This was a considerable concession.) As to his view that slavery should be prohibited in the territories he said he would not yield, and that is what writers probably mean when they say he refused compromise; but it has already been seen that Republicans avoided enactment of the Wilmot proviso early in 1861. Going over Lincoln's attitude in the crisis of 1860–61 one can see that he was willing to yield a great deal.[5] It is true that he was advertised as refusing compromise, but that was an overstatement.

Other points are included in the Ramsdell analysis. He mentions the inability to restore the Union by compromise, the necessity to "do something," the advantage to Lincoln of having the Confederates take the initiative, hence the motive to "induce" them to do so. The Lamon mission is mentioned with a suggestion that its purpose may have been "camouflaged." A "mysterious conference" of state governors with Lincoln in early April is treated with no proof of its purpose but with various queries, and with intimations of "rumors" that they "had gone to demand of the President that he send relief to the garrison at Fort Sumter." Lincoln's conference with Virginians is mentioned without settling the dispute as to what was offered and what was refused. The President's July message is analyzed in terms of an alleged discrepancy with April orders. The message through Chew to Governor Pickens is interpreted as a threat and a direct challenge,

while the timing of the message to arrive April 8, when excitement
raged high as to newspaper guesses concerning the destination of an
expedition known to be preparing, is treated as giving Confederates
time to act before the fleet should arrive. In addition, rationalizations
by Nicolay and Hay as to Lincoln putting the South "in the wrong"
are mentioned. Then comes the capstone with a now famous statement by O. H. Browning, incoming senator from Illinois. On July 3,
1861, having talked with Lincoln, Browning wrote in his diary that
Lincoln spoke as follows: "The plan [sending supplies] succeeded.
They attacked Sumter—it fell, and thus, did more service than it
otherwise could." [6]

The present writer has an affectionate memory for the late Professor Ramsdell, together with high regard for his scholarly methods
and his competence in the field. If there is disagreement, as there was
during Professor Ramsdell's lifetime, it is an entirely friendly argument. In this type of historical inquiry one should distinguish between findings and interpretations, between actual evidence and conjecture as to motives. It will be impossible to reconstruct all that
went on in Lincoln's mind. It is a matter of evaluating the elements
of the problem, noting that a given incident would look differently to
secessionists and to unionists, and recognizing that finality is hardly
attainable when the same evidence is susceptible of opposite explanations. Much of the material presented by Professor Ramsdell per-
tains not so much to something shown to have been in Lincoln's mind
as to the sending of the expedition and the circumstances under which
it was sent. Passages bearing upon Lincoln's motive in what he is
known to have done are largely a matter of interpretation. Professor
Ramsdell is on solid ground in concluding that mere non-evacuation
was thought of as aggression or provocation from the secessionist standpoint. At least that was true at Sumter; it was not so as to Pickens.
That it was conceived as provocation in Lincoln's mind in April 1861
is not so easy to say.

To show how interpretations differ, the same evidence that
Professor Ramsdell uses, with the possible exception of the Browning remark, could be given a non-provocative interpretation. Thus if

Lincoln needed to "do something" at Sumter without forcing civil war, doing something did not necessarily imply that war had to happen because of any Lincoln act. Firmness is not the same as violence, and firmness itself is a matter of degree. If Lincoln was to assert Union authority, that was not incompatible with a wish to avoid an explosion. The pressure of peace men upon Lincoln in April 1861 was at least as strong as that of aggressive Republicans. Those who were steering the none-too-steady Republican craft considered that "aggressive" (or radical) brothers within the party were rocking the boat. It is as reasonable to consider the Lamon mission a genuine attempt to study the situation at Charleston as to call it a camouflage to conceal an ulterior purpose. As for Lamon's predicting evacuation, that could be explained not as a Lincolnian ruse (there is no evidence that it was that) but as Lamon's overstepping of authority. The Virginia consultations are treated with emphasis upon the disputed question whether or not Lincoln offered evacuation if Virginia would avoid secession. It might be equally important to emphasize Lincoln's wish that the consultations had come sooner and his distress at Virginia's inability to put its unionism on a stronger basis than a Sumter evacuation when non-evacuation to Lincoln was a peaceful affair. Lincoln's July suggestion that the Sumter expedition might not have been sent except for the failure of the earlier Pickens plan is treated as unsound because Lincoln's Sumter orders were on April 4 while news of the Pickens failure came on April 6. This argument gives a mistaken impression by presenting only a part of the truth. It is true that by an order dated April 4 Captain Fox was put in charge of an expedition to take supplies to Anderson's garrison, and that certain other orders for the expedition were issued on that date. It is also true, however, that none of the sailings occurred (or were planned to occur) prior to the sixth; most of the ships sailed some days later.[7] Thus on the sixth, as Lincoln well knew, the expedition could have been checked before sailing. There are abundant evidences of the President's delay as to Sumter plans and of Anderson's continued uncertainty concerning the government's intentions. These considerations point up Lincoln's many difficulties in handling the problem, including the planning of an expedition which might possibly have been withheld.

The inducing-to-attack argument does not proceed far before it involves a subtle change of approach, so that the very decision to send the expedition is treated as the aggressive or provocative thing, whereas the point at issue—the Q. E. D. of argument—is whether the sending of supplies to feed the garrison was not in Lincoln's mind compatible with continued peace efforts. The "mysterious" conference with governors bears not upon provocative or warmaking intent in provisioning the garrison, but rather upon the alleged urging by the governors that the fort be not evacuated. It is, of course, well known that from some Northern quarters Lincoln was urged to avoid evacuation. It is not shown that the governors caused Lincoln to adopt an intentionally provocative maneuver, nor that he or they thought in terms of inducing war by a first shot on the other side.

The mild and cautious message of April 6 to Governor Pickens is treated as a threat. It does not read like a threat and could as readily be considered a reassurance and a non-hostile pledge. What Lincoln said in this message to the South Carolina governor was that an attempt would be made to supply Sumter with "provisions only," and that if there should be no attack there would be no reënforcement without further notice. (In the instructions and orders it was indicated from Washington that if the Charleston authorities should permit the fort to be supplied, there would be no further service required of the expedition; if forcible effort was made to prevent the landing of supplies, reënforcement was to be attempted.) [8]

It is suggested that a man of Lincoln's perspicacity would know that different interpretations would be put upon his words in the North and in the South, but it is difficult to believe that his message to Pickens was deliberately phrased as a thing of guile and double meaning. In dealing with an affair of state it was not in Lincoln's nature to mean one thing and say another. Secessionists were placing their own interpretations upon Lincoln's actions (was that perspicacity?), but it is a different matter to suppose that the President was purposely dealing out words of trickery and deception.

Misunderstanding between the Washington government and the lower South was, of course, a basic factor in the problem, and misunderstandings may lead to war. Lincoln, strong in Unionism, is known to have had Southern sympathies. In his efforts to sound out Southern feeling he may have optimistically overestimated Southern unionism as a hopeful or practical force, but it does no violence to known facts to believe that in his message to Governor Pickens he meant what he said, that he hoped his words would be understood in his own sense, and that he phrased his statements in strongly reassuring terms for that very reason. Instead of ignoring Southern suspicion, he tried, though unsuccessfully, to overcome it and to give the Confederacy the cue for avoiding attack from their side as Lincoln was from his. If it be answered that such forbearance by Southern authorities was impossible, the rejoinder is that precisely such an avoidance of assault on either side did occur at Fort Pickens.

The historical problem bears upon the question how much is proved (or convincingly indicated), and it may be doubted whether proof has been given that Lincoln actually hoped that the South would put the worst construction upon his motives. If suggestions of a Sumter maneuver were "in the air," urgings toward peace were equally so, being strongly supported in the cabinet. One can take any prewar situation—or any period in which threatened bloodshed is averted—and find talk of possible war "in the air," as well as talk of preventing war. Talk of all sorts was floating about. Lincoln's sending of the fleet was not the only factor. His manner of doing so was significant. His emphasis on "provisions only," together with other circumstances, could well have been understood as taking from his expedition the appearance of a hostile maneuver, unless the status quo of non-surrender was the hostile thing, which he did not admit.

As to the indication that Lincoln sought to stir up moderates to "flame out against the secessionists and in support of the government," [9] it may be noted that Lincoln's administration was the target, not the haven, of radicals, and that deliberate inflaming of sentiment against the South was precisely the kind of thing that the President was avoiding. Lincoln's conduct and words in March and April give no evidence of such an inflaming; there are many opposite evidences He was hoping for more moderation, not less. His language was that of restraint, caution, and cooling off. His manner was as different as possible from that of the famous Prussian leader in 1870, and one may question the analogy that has been drawn between the Sumter policy of the American President and the Ems dispatch of which the aged Bismarck boasted (as a war-provoking factor) when writing his memoirs.

VII

There remains the July remark which Browning attributed to Lincoln. "The plan succeeded. They attacked Sumter—it fell, and thus, did more good than it otherwise could." This diary record is a strongly emphasized link in Professor Ramsdell's chain. No one who holds the provocation thesis can be criticized for attaching weight to this remark; rejection of the thesis would probably have to be in spite of it.

Of course it could be shown that the Lincoln-Browning conversation occurred on July 3, that the very subject of the conversation was Lincoln's July 4 message, that the famous remark is reported to have followed Lincoln's reading of the message to Browning, and yet that the remark and message would seem at first sight to contradict each other. In the message Lincoln said that Southerners knew the government desired to keep the garrison in the fort, not to assail them, but merely to maintain visible possession, trusting to the ballot-box for final adjustment. This is precisely the opposite of deliberately maneuvering a war. The message comes to us direct in Lincoln's words, while the Browning statement is an indirect quotation. One is a formal public document; the other is a fragmentary bit of reported conversation. They seem to say opposite things. Which offers the more significant guide to the truth?

Was Lincoln revealing himself in the reputed remark to Browning, while using a kind of window-dressing in the July message? If he did so reveal himself, did the remark not sound a bit queer immediately after a reading of the message to his friend? Does the remark give a basis for doubting the message, or is it the other way round?

Was Lincoln merely rationalizing when he presented the subject to
Congress, or was he rationalizing when in July he proceeded, after
eighty days of actual war, to recall to Browning what was done in
April, and why?

The question, however, goes still further. Are we sure that we have
the full meaning Lincoln meant to convey to Browning? The now
famous remark was reported as part of an extended conversation.
Lincoln had just read his July 4 message to the new Illinois senator.
At this point we have the following diary record:

> . . . He told me that the very first thing placed in his hands after his
> inauguration was a letter from Majr Anderson announcing the impossi-
> bility of defending or relieving Sumter. That he called the Cabinet to-
> gether, and consulted Genl. Scott—that Scott concurred with Anderson,
> and the cabinet, with the exception of himself and P M Genl. Blair were
> for evacuating the Fort, and that all the troubles and anxieties of his life
> had not equalled those which intervened between this time and the fall
> of Sumter He himself conceived the idea, and proposed sending supplies,
> without an attempt to reinforce giving notice of the fact to Gov Pickins
> [sic] of S.C. The plan succeeded. They attacked Sumter—it fell, and thus,
> did more service than it otherwise could [1]

It is not a very illuminating account. Browning was wont to fill his
journal with details as to the weather, his flowers, his boarding arrangements, or the number of hours he traveled on a train. His entries
on public questions are often disappointing. On June 16, 1858, he
had been in attendance when Lincoln gave his house-divided speech
but did not even mention it. When Lincoln gave one of his most
famous orations (at Bloomington, May 29, 1856) Browning's record
was as follows: "I was called out and made two speeches in the afternoon Convention also addressed by Lovejoy, Lincoln, Cook &
others . . . ." The polished diarist had no very high opinion of the
President, though he had the friendship of both Mr. and Mrs. Lincoln. In the record as he gives it Lincoln's mind went back to his inaugural. (In that speech the President had declared his intent to hold
remaining forts but to avoid all irritation and seek a friendly solution.
If he had carried out the purpose of his inaugural address, that would
have been to hold Sumter, but he had said there was no need of

"bloodshed or violence.") Anderson and Scott advised that the fort could not be defended. The cabinet, except Blair, counseled evacuation. Lincoln was studying whether evacuation could be avoided. Never in his life had he suffered greater trouble and anxiety. If he was to keep Sumter in the face of all the conditions, how should he do it? "He himself" thought of a plan: "sending supplies, without an attempt to reinforce giving notice of the fact to Gov Pickins . . . ."

Does the context show that this was a plan for beginning a war? Does it not rather show that in what he "himself conceived" Lincoln was as unbelligerent as he could well have been without evacuting the fort? It is after this reference to an unwarlike act that we have the quotation: "The plan succeeded. They attacked Sumter—it fell, and thus, did more service . . . [etc.]." There is a hiatus in the Browning record. The plan did not "succeed" in any sense consistent with Lincoln's known statements on other occasions. It did not accomplish the purpose indicated in the inaugural address or the July message. It did not lead to the holding of Sumter. If it meant a deep-laid plot to induce a war, the record of what Lincoln was saying and thinking is, to say the least, incomplete. It stands as a detached statement with no elucidation or explanatory comment. Assuming that Lincoln used the words quoted, we do not know what other words he used along with them, and we do not know from Browning what he meant. It would be going rather far to take this uncorroborated and unexplained remark as a thing of greater weight than masses of known facts and statements in the Lincoln evidence.

In actual fact the manner of the April expedition in its execution was as appropriate for inducing ballot-box settlement (by continuing the status quo and not giving up the whole case) as for war settlement. The challenge of the provisioning expedition was certainly no greater than the secessionists' challenge to the Union. In spite of that challenge Lincoln did avoid attack. If conjecture as to Lincoln's possible intent and ruminations can be reduced to a hypothetical question, it might be worded thus: After reluctantly deciding to release the fleet tentatively prepared for Sumter, could Lincoln have determined to manage the expedition in such a way as to avoid hostile provocation? In the writer's opinion, an affirmative answer to this question is entirely consistent with the established facts as seen in the contemporary record.

VIII

Since the message and the remark, simultaneously spoken, seem to suggest different July meanings, and since the remark has a considerable margin of vagueness, we are thrown back upon the March-April evidence, which in any case is in the main field for historical inquiry. When two expeditions were preparing, the one ultimately directed to the fort where popular feeling was keenest and where trouble might be feared was the one in which the least provocative conduct was chosen. It is not as if the Sumter provisioning was a made-up incident; it was, on the contrary, a necessary and obvious thing for Lincoln to do in the line of duty unless he should give up the fort. Essentially it was a decision not to evacuate a Federal position. The expedition was merely to maintain the status quo, so far as that was possible, by giving food to the garrison. Only in case of Southern attack was there to be forcible effort to land troops. As it turned out, this attempted forcible landing of troops, or even supplies, by the fleet never occurred. Except for the fact that Lincoln was not surrendering the fort as demanded by Charleston and Montgomery, it is hard to see how orders and actual measures were provocative. He can be convicted of refusal to surrender if that is the point, but if in that refusal he was provoking to war, then perhaps we need to search for some impartial plane of judgment, some objective criterion for determining what the word "provocative" means. The fleet was sent with publicity and with prior notification to Governor Pickens. Instead of a secretly prepared Sumter expedition, with a calculated leakage of information and a hint of hostility, there was advance official notification with emphasis upon non-hostile intent and with a pledge not to reënforce unless attacked.

It was not from Lincoln that truculent actions and utterances came. His avoidance of any effort to recapture Southern forts was of a piece with his whole policy. He was far from demanding everything which strict Union logic required. People often forget how far his concessions went. Affirmation of principle was to be combined with moderation in practice. To see the laws of the Union "faithfully executed" he declared to be his "simple duty"; he would perform it "so far as practicable." [1] In holding places belonging to the government he would not go "beyond what . . . [was] necessary." He intended "no invasion, no using of force against or among the people anywhere." [2] If Federal officials encountered determined hostility, there would be no forcing of "obnoxious strangers" among the people. It was not merely a matter of legal authority. He said: "While the strict legal right may exist . . . to enforce the exercise of these offices [in the seceded states], the attempt to do so would be so irritating, and so nearly impracticable withal, that I deem it better to forego for the time the uses of such offices." [3] Even as to the mails, he said they would be furnished throughout the country "unless repelled." [4]

Remembering the importance of requiring the observance of Fedderal laws, he was nevertheless willing, in the existing crisis, that their enforcement be suspended. What about tariff duties, for instance, where United States authority was resisted in the lower South? On this point he carefully studied a plan for offshore collection of duties where ordinary collection at a port might be "impracticable"; even this was dropped, however, while collection (where it would be resisted) at custom houses was also dropped. The matter has been summarized as follows by David M. Potter:

This, then, was the much vaunted "firm" policy of Lincoln. He would assert Federal authority vigorously—but he would not exercise it. He would enforce the laws—where an enforcement mechanism existed. He would deliver the mails—unless repelled. He would collect the duties— offshore. He would hold the forts—at least the ones which Buchanan had held, and which seemed capable of holding themselves. [5]

Why such forbearance? How could firmness be so qualified? What did Lincoln hope to gain by it? He answered this himself: "Of all that . . . a President might constitutionally and justifiably do . . . , everything was forborne without which it was believed possible to keep the government on foot." [6] "Nothing valuable can be lost by taking time. If there be an object to hurry any of you in hot haste to a step which you would never take deliberately, that object will be frustrated by taking time; but no good object can be frustrated by it." [7] "The course here indicated will be followed unless . . . events . . . shall show a . . . change to be proper, . . . and with a view and a hope of a peaceful solution of the national troubles and the restoration of fraternal sympathies and affections." [8]

Lincoln would forbear irritating measures even to the point where his authority would, at places, become well nigh invisible. He would take time, hoping that time would be on the side of the Union and looking forward to a friendly and peaceful solution. This will explain his orders and instructions, his effort to bolster unionism in Virginia, his slowness in sending the Sumter expedition (though he thought surrender of the fort would be "ruinous"),[9] his notification to South Carolina, his adherence to inaugural declarations which stressed the avoidance of bloodshed, his studious distinction between Pensacola and Charleston, his disbelief that provisioning Sumter would bring war.

Lincoln was not among those who considered war inevitable. In the July message he spoke of the issue being referred to the ballot-box as in March he had urged a "peaceful solution." The Confederate commissioners in Washington wrote on March 12, 1861, to Toombs, Confederate secretary of state, that Lincoln had assured a Louisianian that there would be no war and that the President was determined to keep the peace.[10] The Virginians Magruder and Baldwin state that Lincoln rejected the idea that a Sumter expedition meant war.[11] In respect to Sumter Lincoln went no farther than Buchanan, the man who has been so roundly denounced for Northern weakness. Orders for Lincoln's April expedition were no more of a challenge to war than those for Buchanan's *Star of the West*.[12] Even before Buchanan had sent this ship, South Carolinian commissioners had severely abused him. Unless one is to conclude that Lincoln was provocative in his very non-aggressiveness, it is hard to see how the March and April evidence bears out the theory of provocation.

If even so non-hostile an expedition as Lincoln's was *casus belli* to the South (and one must pay high respect to Professor Ramsdell's analysis of Southern sentiment on this point), then indeed was the President in a tight place. Lincoln's prestige was slight even at the North in 1861. In secessionist circles his name was assailed and cursed. His messenger, Lamon, was almost mobbed at Charleston. It is difficult to see what Lincoln could have done in his capacity as President of the United States to satisfy those who considered secession a finality. Among extremists on both sides everything done by the other side in March-April 1861 was given some kind of sinister meaning.[13] The trouble under which the country suffered was not so much an expedition sent by a President; it was rather an ugly deadlock and a background of antagonism. It is a tragic thing that often the boldness of extremists seems actually to be assisted by the very mildness of moderates. Out of the whole pot of trouble of which the Sumter situation was but one ingredient we know that war came. We do not by any means know that Lincoln intended it should come.

V. THE RULE OF LAW
UNDER LINCOLN

THE Presidents that have been outstanding in American history are those that have used—one should say developed—presidential influence. Some of them, at least for significant periods, have been fortunate enough to exert this influence in coöperation with Congress, promoting government in terms of coördination between the executive and legislative branches. Lincoln, being less fortunate, took authority to himself. He did not merely obey—often he did not consult— Congress. He welcomed a congressional recess, and especially a recess of the committee on the conduct of the war. He obtained little genuine coöperation from the Congress which the American people, or the politicians, gave him. Yet he abhorred an impasse. Though an assertive President, he valued compromise and sought human solutions in case of deadlock.

Civil and military relationships under Lincoln were not entirely a matter of what Lincoln thought.[1] There were American traditions to be remembered; farther back there were concepts of long standing drawn from English experience. It is an Anglo-Saxon principle that military power is subordinate to the civil. Down the long stretch of their history Americans have shown an avoidance of a large military establishment, a distrust of excessive military control, and a dislike of those militaristic tendencies that would allow to the army or navy the formulation of fundamental policy. As late as 1910 the regular army of the United States numbered only 80,718, while the national guard (119,660) could hardly have been said to constitute an effec-

THE RULE OF LAW UNDER LINCOLN

tively trained reserve. Peacetime conscription, for many decades a regular practice in Europe, was not used in the United States until 1940, and that could hardly have been called a peaceful year. As yet, neither conscription nor compulsion for general military training has been adopted as a continuing policy in time of peace.

Professor Albert Venn Dicey [2] has shown us that the principle of the "rule of law" is an ancient one in England, going back to the old yearbooks, and he has given it a definite content. In England, he says, it means that no man can be made to suffer punishment or pay damages for any conduct not definitely forbidden by law, that every man's legal rights or liabilities are almost invariably determined by the ordinary courts, that executive officers have a more limited discretion and less arbitrary power than in continental countries, and that no man is above the law, but all are amenable to the jurisdiction of the ordinary civil tribunals, men in office being personally liable for wrongs done, even though acting in an official capacity. He adds that personal rights in England do not derive from a constitution, but inherently exist. Such also is the American concept. Basic civil rights are not brought into being or created, or granted, by a constitution. It is rather that these rights have prior existence; the function of a constitution—or one function—is to protect or guarantee them.

The American ideal, it has been said, is a "government of laws, not of men." Law is above government: government is under law. Martial law, while sometimes used in this country, occupies no recognized niche in our constitutional structure. It is the setting aside of law, not its fulfillment. Even for grave disturbances, as at the time of the Whiskey Insurrection, reliance has been placed upon civil procedure.[3] There is often in the United States a deplorable disregard for law as it restrains individuals, but there is a disposition to subject rulers to legal restraints.

Nor is it conformable to American interpretation to hold that during war legal checks are to be ignored. Even in war, the military authority should be restrained in at least three respects: (1) by treaty obligations, (2) by the laws of "civilized warfare," and (3) by a due regard for civil rights, both in conquered territory and at home. War is not anarchy; and, though the maxim has a kernel of truth, it is not sufficient to say that "necessity knows no law." [4] It is rather the American view that even in war the laws hold. One of the chief principles of the Milligan case is that the Constitution is not suspended during war. (One is speaking here of the relation of war to legality in the long accepted, or conventional, sense. Significant recent developments on the international level are another matter.) [5]

II

This concept of the reign of law is, of course, an ideal. The settled, permanent will of the whole community, as expressed in fundamental law, is believed to be a great stabilizing force, so that in the ordering of the nation's political life every effort should be made to give superior force to mature, sober judgment as against the designs of rulers. It may be that the ideal is never completely realized. In a sense it is always true that we live under a government of men. But during the Civil War there were particular factors which made for an extreme, irregular, and extra-legal use of governmental power.

There was the legal confusion as to what the war was, whether it was a domestic uprising of insurgents or war in the international sense.[1] Was the conflict something like a greatly magnified Whiskey Insurrection, or was it a struggle between governments possessing belligerent powers? According to the Supreme Court it was both.[2] It was a war, and also a rebellion. The Court's view was that the United States had, in seceded territory, both belligerent and municipal powers. As to the attitude of the Lincoln administration on this matter, it held to the insurrectionary concept of the war as a theory; yet in practice the Confederacy was treated as a government with belligerent powers, not as an organization of irresponsible insurgents or pirates. The Supreme Court did not hold that the Confederate States had no rights whatever. The Court held that the governments of the seceded area, state and Confederate, were null in the sense that they could enforce no right as against the United States. It also held, however, that belligerent powers were "conceded" to the Confederacy,[3] and that as to civil and local matters obedience on the part of the Southern people to the authority of the Confederate government, and to that of states within the Confederacy, was both a necessity and a duty. The Supreme Court even declared a contract for the payment of Confederate money enforceable in the courts of the United States.[4] During the war, however, the legal confusion as to the relation of the seceded states to the Union made for irregularity and for a sweeping use of Federal power.

Antiwar activity in the North offered a temptation to arbitrary rule.[5] The schemes of spies, the conspiracies of the Knights of the Golden Circle, the enemy sympathies of "copperheads" were regarded as a serious threat. As a pro-enemy underground such groups accomplished little, but their secrecy made them seem ominous, they served as a political instrument for anti-Lincoln sentiment, and they greatly increased Lincoln's difficulty in the double task of promoting success in a desperate war and at the same time preserving civil liberty.

Another factor working against the strictest reign of law was Lincoln's wide assumption of power. His measures, which rested upon his honest concept of vital public needs, were supported by logic or argument, but it was the argument of emergency; the motives came first. Legal instruments were chosen to fit the purpose. In this Lincoln was not peculiar. Throughout our history it is necessary to look through the legal arguments of our leaders to the broad social purposes they have sought to attain. Constitutional history, in its ultimate significance, thus becomes social history.[6] Lincoln believed that rights of war were vested in the President, and that as President he had extraordinary legal resources which Congress lacked. In vetoing the Wade-Davis bill in 1864, he questioned the constitutional competency of Congress to abolish slavery in the states, though his own emancipation proclamation had been in force for a year and a half.[7] He voiced his broad, free interpretation when he said: ". . . as commander-in-chief . . . , I suppose I have a right to take any measure which may best subdue the enemy . . . ."[8]

The war began with what has been termed a "presidential dicta-

torship." As to executive measures taken between April and July of
1861, when Congress was not in session, such a thing as the call for
militia was not to be questioned if the war was an insurrection; but
certainly the enlargement of the army and navy beyond the limits
fixed by existing law was most unusual, and Lincoln himself frankly
admitted that in this he had overstepped his authority.[9] It was during
this period that the first suspension of the habeas corpus privilege
came.[10] The alleged unconstitutionality of this and other conduct of
President Lincoln was urged to show that the whole process by which
the war began was illegal! The Supreme Court, it is true, upheld the
President and confirmed the legality of early war measures in the
Prize Cases—it could hardly have done otherwise with so vital a
political question—but four dissenting judges held that the President's action alone was not sufficient to institute a legal state of war.[11]

This question of the dictatorship should not be passed over lightly.
Lincoln's defense was two-fold: (1) He insisted that the national
safety imperatively demanded that these vigorous measures be
taken. (2) At those points where he had not exceeded the power of
Congress, he supposed all would be made right by subsequent legislative approval. This second point in his defense, even though conceded in the case of Lincoln, may be questioned as a generalization
or a precedent for other executives. It argues a curious commingling
of legislative and executive functions for a President to perform an
act which he adjudges to be within the competence of Congress and
then, when the measure has been irrevocably taken, to present Congress with an accomplished fact for subsequent sanction. Lincoln himself said, concerning executive steps taken early in the war: "These
measures, whether strictly legal or not, were ventured upon, under
what appeared to be a popular demand and a public necessity; trusting . . . that Congress would readily ratify them. It is believed
that nothing has been done beyond the constitutional competency
of Congress." [12]

This savored of forcing the legislative hand. The possession of a
constitutional power by Congress—e. g., determining the size of the
army, controlling the expenditure of money, or imposing unusual

severities upon the nation—implies the right to withhold the power as well as the right to use it. The agency intrusted with a function of government may be expected to determine the timing, circumstances, extent, and conditions of its use, if and when it is used. This much of legislative discretion is denied when Congress is confronted with a *fait accompli* for subsequent approval.

The fact that Abraham Lincoln could adopt this course in such a way as to avoid offense (at the "bar of history") does not argue that a repetition of this conduct would be advisable. Not every one can wear Lincoln's hat. His case was unique. Many of the situations of the sixties were *sui generis*. No President has carried the power of presidential edict and executive order (independently of Congress) so far as he did.[13] His far-reaching acts have not been treated as patterns appropriate for later imitation. Most of the executive powers under Wilson and under Franklin Roosevelt were conferred by Congress.

It would not be easy to state what Lincoln conceived to be the limit of his powers.[14] Besides exercising extraordinary executive authority, he took over legislative and judicial functions. In anticipation of subsequent ratification he performed acts which he recognized as belonging to Congress. If one were to deal with "presidential legislation" [15] he would find the administration of Lincoln a fruitful field. There were many who thought he was trenching upon the domain of Congress in his edict of emancipation and his suspension of the habeas corpus privilege. The militia act of 1862 [16] did not specifically authorize conscription; the drafts of that year were made in pursuance of executive orders.[17] Thus the first national use of compulsory army service by the United States was a case of presidential conscription. As to the President's performance of judicial functions, wherever martial law was declared, wherever Southern territory was brought under Union control, wherever military justice was enforced, wherever quasi-judicial powers were exercised by executive departments, presidential justice was illustrated; and besides, there were "special war courts" created by President Lincoln with sweeping powers, as, for instance, the "provisional court of Louisiana." [18]

III

In all this wide extension of governmental power, there was a noticeable lack of legal precision. A tendency toward irregularity may be observed as a characteristic of the period, in military and civil administration, in legislation, and in legal interpretation. The generals frequently exceeded their military authority, as when Frémont, in his western department in 1861, assumed to himself "the administrative powers of the State," confiscating property, freeing slaves by proclamation, and ordering that persons taken with arms were to be shot after trial by court martial.[1]

This irregularity manifested itself in state and Federal relations. State governors performed Federal functions such as raising United States volunteer regiments, purchasing arms here and abroad, chartering steamers and railroads for the transportation of troops, and even maintaining Federal troops in the field. Andrew at Boston, or Morton at Indianapolis,[2] were war ministers as truly as was Cameron at Washington, and this elaborate state activity produced much legal confusion.[3] The states spent money, then put in claims for Federal reimbursement.

Such was the laxness of Congress that it passed, for instance, a confiscation law which presumably provided for freeing the slaves of "rebel" owners; but the law specified no method by which any slave could make good that freedom.[4] The slaves were not confiscated; if free they were not "property," and the provision that confiscated property was to be sold would, of course, be inapplicable to emancipated Negroes. The act did not say that the slaves were to be confiscated. It merely declared them free, saying nothing as to how the freedom should be made legally effective. The emancipating feature of the second confiscation act was not enforced.[5] It is mentioned as an example of the unscientific legislation which was characteristic of the period.

This looseness led to some curious legal anomalies. The Southern states were taxed as if part of the United States; [6] yet the property out of which such tax was to have been paid was declared confiscable on the ground that its owners were enemies. Contrary to the prevailing view, the South actually bore the full burden of the direct tax of 1861, through direct payment, forfeitures, or otherwise.[7] In the ratification of the thirteenth amendment in 1865 the action of eight states of the former Confederacy was counted.[8] These Southern commonwealths thus helped to modify the Constitution of the United States; having done so, they were promptly treated by Congress as outside the Union. The Unionist government in Virginia was considered a competent legal body when it was a matter of consenting to the division of the state; later this same government was denied representation in Congress [9] on the ground that "rebel" control of the state prevented free elections. If elections in Virginia were not to be recognized (and for some years beginning in 1863 recognition was denied on this ground to Unionist congressmen from what was called "restored Virginia"), then the process of creating West Virginia is hard to justify.

Other examples could be mentioned. On the whole it appears that legal interpretation in the sixties lacked precision and consistency. Much of the constitutional reasoning of that time was what James Harvey Robinson has called mere "rationalizing"—*"finding arguments for going on believing as we already do."* [10]

IV

How far did the usual checks operate to prevent an extreme use of power? A careful examination reveals little in the form of legislative or judicial restraint. Congress specifically approved the President's course between April and July 1861.[1] As to the habeas corpus question—i. e., the problem of arbitrary arrests—Congress delayed for two years; then it passed an ambiguous law which might equally well have been interpreted as sanctioning or as disapproving the doctrine that the President has the suspending power.[2] The net effect, however, was to support the President; immunity from prosecution was granted to officers if brought into court for acts (such as seizures and arrests) committed in pursuance of presidential orders during the suspension.[3]

It is true that the habeas corpus act of 1863 directed the release of prisoners unless indicted in the courts. This was equivalent to saying that the President's suspension of the privilege, authorized by this act, was to be effective in any judicial district only until a grand jury should act. On paper this law radically altered the whole system regarding political prisoners, making arbitrary imprisonment illegal after grand juries had examined the prisoners' cases. This law of 1863, however, like so much of the legislation of the period, was ineffective. Many arrests were made after the act was passed; a search of Federal court records reveals that the provisions as to furnishing lists to the courts, and judicial release of prisoners not indicted, were not carried out.[4] Congress offered no real obstacle to the use of extraordinary powers by the executive.

How did the courts deal with these matters? There were limiting factors which controlled the judicial branch. The Federal courts did little in dealing with disloyal practices. The President, through the attorney general and the district attorneys, controlled the prosecutions, and where it appeared that treason indictments were being pushed toward conviction the administration showed actual embarrassment at the government's success.[5] Its way of dealing with dangerous citizens was not by prosecution in courts, but by arbitrary imprisonment and equally arbitrary release.[6] The commissary general of prisoners reported 13,535 citizens arrested and confined in military prisons from February 1863 to the end of the war. This record is incomplete and a satisfactory total has never been reached.[7] In the vast majority of cases these persons had no trial, not even a military one. They were arrested, held in prison irregularly with no charge or indictment (often without even a military case being made up), and then released just as irregularly.

This informal conduct on the part of the executive was chosen because the public safety was threatened, while the courts and the statutes were inadequate. Ordinary procedures were not meeting the case. There is a striking contrast between the great number of arbitrary arrests and the negligible amount of completed judicial action for such matters as treason, conspiracy, and obstructing the draft.

As to completed punishment for treason by Federal judicial process,

the main record in United States history has been negative.[8] The
chief points may be quickly noted in a thumbnail survey. Benedict
Arnold was not caught. If caught, he would have been tried by court
martial. Burr was acquitted. Some of the leaders of the Whiskey Insurrection were convicted in the courts and sentenced to death for
treason, but pardoned by President Washington; one Fries was
similarly sentenced and pardoned by John Adams. John Brown's
prosecution was under Virginian, not Federal law. B. F. Butler's
execution of Mumford for treason at New Orleans in 1862 was an
exceptional and high handed procedure that illustrated eccentric
severity rather than regular justice. Though sentenced by a military
commission (for tearing down the United States flag) it cannot be
said that Mumford was treated in accordance with American practice.
Sometimes, in the Civil War, a grand jury indictment for treason
against the United States would not come to trial. After the war,
in 1867, Jefferson Davis was indicted for treason in a Federal court,
but he was never tried.[9] The treason statutes were not effectively
applied under Wilson; offenders accused of disloyalty were prosecuted
under the espionage act of 1917, its 1918 amendment, the trading-
with-the-enemy act, the selective service act, etc., but not under the
law for treason. Completed prosecutions for this or that type of disloyalty were few under Franklin Roosevelt. It was in 1944 that the
Supreme Court of the United States took up for the first time in its
history an actual case of a man brought to trial for treason against
the United States. In this case—*Anthony Cramer* vs. *United States*— [10]
the Court reversed the lower court's judgment of conviction. Not until
the Haupt case (March 31, 1947) did the Supreme Court uphold a
conviction for treason. The mass sedition trial of 1944 stands out as
the chief episode of the Roosevelt administration in its efforts to
prosecute disloyalty of ideas, but in that episode the government's
elaborate efforts broke down in midcourse and the prosecution was
not completed.[11]

Whether the courts could have dealt with the emergency under
Lincoln is another matter. A marshal, executing the order of a court,
cannot call out a posse comitatus as large as an army. Suppression of
insurrection is an executive function.[12] Even where courts are used

it is the executive that prepares and prosecutes the cases. Courts do not go out and find offenders; they do not prepare testimony or arguments. They hear the cases that are brought before them. Midway in a case the executive may discontinue the prosecution. These things in the present age are handled by the executive department of justice with its staff of prosecutors and its FBI, a colossal organization compared to the tiny office of Lincoln's attorney general.[13] In time of war it is customary for government to be greatly expanded.[14] Under Lincoln such expansion pertained almost entirely to the armed forces in one way or another; there was no appreciable expansion of government in the business of preparing and arguing cases in the courts.

It is, of course, true that courts may restrain the executive, being open to citizens for that purpose, but that is a rule of normal procedure requiring executive consent. Such consent may exist willingly, or it may arise from fear of popular disapproval; in either case it presupposes a matured democratic process in a law-minded people. If an emergency exists, such restraints are ultimate, not immediate. They may be applied after a time, but it is a fact of history that during America's wars the courts have done little to restrain the executive.

The Supreme Court of the United States did not, during the war, exert any serious check upon either Congress or the President. In the *Prize Cases,* already noted, the Court approved Lincoln's acts in the early months. Such an extreme measure as confiscation was upheld by the Court.[15] It was not the Supreme Court, but Chief Justice Taney in his capacity as circuit justice, hearing the Merryman petition in chambers, who declared the President's suspension of the habeas corpus privilege to be illegal.[16] His opinion did not become controlling law; it did not even control the Merryman case. In an unpublished and confidential memorandum to Stanton, Attorney General Bates expressed the fear that, if the legality of the President's suspension were brought up in a test case, the Supreme Court would declare against the power assumed by the President; but the issue was never forced.[17] In the Bollman and Swartwout case of the Jefferson period, sometimes cited in this connection, presidential suspension did not come up.[18] After the war, it is true, in the Milligan case,[19] the Court declared a military regime illegal in regions remote from the theater of war; but while the war was in progress the high tribunal had declined to interfere with the action of a military commission in the case of Vallandigham.[20] On the whole, it appears that, while extreme wartime measures were being taken by the executive, neither Congress nor the courts exerted any effective restraint. In the long run fundamental guarantees were not extinguished—the Milligan case established that—but for the emergency men were imprisoned independently of the courts, while governmental officers, by the indemnity act of 1863, were given a privileged place above the law and made immune from penalties for acts that are normally considered wrongful.[21]

V

There is, however, another side to the picture. There were factors which at least partly redeemed the situation. The greatest consideration, perhaps, was the legal-mindedness of the American people; and a very powerful factor was Lincoln himself. His humane sympathy, his humor, his lawyer-like caution, his common sense, his fairness toward opponents, his dislike of arbitrary rule, his disinclination toward military excess, his willingness to take the people into his confidence and to set forth patiently the reasons for unusual acts— all these elements of his character operated to modify and soften the acts of overzealous subordinates and to lessen the effects of harsh measures upon individuals. In the midst of war's severity, though that is not the best setting for such an inquiry, one can perceive Lincoln's liberal mind at work.

Everywhere during the war one finds this tempering of severe rules. Deserters, with but few exceptions, were saved from death. Escape from penalties was made possible by taking the oath of allegiance; ignorance of the law was often accepted as an excuse; even spies were released on the acceptance of stipulated terms. Freedom of speech was preserved to the point of permitting the most disloyal utterances. The case of Vallandigham, an anti-Lincoln politician of Ohio whose offense was that of making a speech considered disloyal, was quite exceptional, and that was but a partial exception. He was sentenced by a military commission to imprisonment, but Lincoln commuted the sentence to banishment within the lines of the enemy. Later in the war, after the anti-climax of his carefully staged return to Ohio via Canada, he was left unmolested, though delivering violent speeches.[1] There was under Lincoln no espionage act or sedition law.[2] Abusive statements, throughout the war, were continually uttered and published.

As to the relation of the government to the press, while a book could be written on the suppression of certain newspapers, the military control of the telegraph, the seizure of particular editions, the exclusion of papers from the mails, and the arbitrary arrest of offending editors, yet it would be easy to exaggerate the effect of such measures.[3] The enumeration of particular instances of newspaper suppression, or rather suspension, creates a distorted impression. In general, the press was unhampered. There was no real censorship. Newspaper correspondents were privileged characters, dining at officers' mess, using army horses and wagons, passing freely through the armies on government passes, and even at times conveying confidential dispatches. The papers were continually revealing military secrets, abusing such generals as Grant and Sherman, playing up inferior men, creating a public clamor which led to ill-advised engagements, and functioning, to use Sherman's words, as "Confederate spies in the Union camp." Their usefulness to the enemy was clearly shown by Lee's perusal of Northern journals. The fact that the newspapers were permitted to do all this, and that powerful opposition organs were left unmolested though breaking down public confidence in the government, is more worthy of comment than sporadic instances of suspension. In the case of the Chicago *Times* the suspension order was issued without Lincoln's knowledge, against his judgment, and was promptly revoked, though this Chicago journal was most virulent in its opposition to the President and all his works. As to the New York *World*, suspended in May 1864 because it had published a bogus presidential proclamation, the period of suspension lasted but three days. While the suspension order was signed by Lincoln and countersigned by Seward, this use of executive severity was promoted and manipulated by Stanton.

Though there were arbitrary arrests under Lincoln, there was no thoroughgoing arbitrary government.[4] The actual effect of executive practice in the suspension of the habeas corpus privilege is to be defined in terms of accompanying procedures, which may vary. Sometimes extreme measures may accompany the suspension, sometimes not. What the suspension usually implies is that persons who commit some offense, or are under suspicion, are summarily arrested, held as political prisoners for a time, and then either released to the civil courts or merely released. To suppose that the suspension of the privilege under Lincoln set aside all law would be a mistake. Even where martial law was declared—over limited areas, such as the District of Columbia—the ordinary courts were to a large extent permitted to function.[5] Martial law, which includes the suspension of the privilege, allows a military regime and theoretically permits the utmost severity, including execution of sentences for which the civil law offers no basis. The extent to which such extreme severities are applied, however, depends upon the orders of the commanding officer, which properly depend upon orders and instructions from Washington.

It should not be supposed that the suspension—i. e., the regime of arbitrary arrests—constituted the last word in extreme executive justice or in harsh treatment of prisoners. Naturally the Lincoln suspension was regrettable—indeed, this precedent was not followed under Wilson nor under Franklin Roosevelt—but the actual treatment of prisoners (arrest, detention, and release) was milder than the rapid completion of all the steps of a severe summary process, including the execution of the sentence. It was even milder than regular civil justice as usually applied in time of war. *The American Bastile*, compiled by John A. Marshall, historian of the association of prisoners of state, is an overstatement as to prison conditions. The imprisonment itself was, of course, a hardship amounting to a punishment, but the men who were tried before juries in the civil courts under Wilson fared worse. Under Lincoln there was no Revolutionary Tribunal to feed an American guillotine. Stanton's secret service was a thing of abuse, but the United States government in Civil War times presented nothing remotely comparable to the procedure of a Himmler.

As to the military trial of civilians, it should be noticed that the typical use of the military commission was legitimate; these commissions were commonly used to try citizens in military areas for offenses that had military significance. Where, as in Missouri, civilians in proximity to the Union army were engaged in sniping or bushwhacking, in bridge-burning or the destruction of railroad and telegraph lines, they were tried by military commission; this has occasioned little comment, though there were hundreds of cases.[6] The prominence of Vallandigham and Milligan should not obscure the larger fact that their cases were exceptional—in other words, the military trial of citizens for conspiracy, disloyal speaking, anti-war agitation, and the like in peaceful areas was far from typical. It was thus a rare use of the military commission that was declared illegal by the Supreme Court in the Milligan case.

Legally the Civil War stands out as an eccentric period, a time when constitutional and legal restraints did not fully operate and when the "rule of law" at least partially broke down. It was a period when opposite and conflicting situations co-existed, when specious arguments and legal fictions were adopted to excuse extraordinary measures. The line was blurred between executive, legislative, and judicial functions, between state and Federal powers, and between military and civil procedures. National functions, as distinct from those of the states, were noticeably extended, especially in the latter half of the war. Constitutional interpretation was stretched. The powers grasped by Lincoln caused him to be referred to as a "dictator." Yet civil liberties were not annihilated and no actual dictatorship was established. The traditional attachment of the American people to the "rule of law" as a principle had its steadying effect. Since the personal element in government was then of unusual importance, it was fortunate that the nation had in the presidency such a personality as Lincoln's. No undue advantage was taken of the emergency to force arbitrary rule upon the country or to promote personal ends. The government did not employ criminal violence to destroy its opponents and perpetuate its power. It is significant that Lincoln half expected to be defeated in 1864. The people were free to defeat him, if they chose, at the polls. The Constitution, while stretched, was not subverted.[7]

In a legal study of the war the two most significant facts are perhaps these: the wide extent of the war powers; and, in contrast to that, the manner in which men in authority were controlled by the American people's underlying sense of constitutional government. Measures taken were recognized as exceptional; they were held to be no more exceptional than the emergency for which they were used. In the net effect it was Lincoln's hope that the nation would not develop a taste for extreme rule any more than a patient, because of the use of emetics during illness, acquires a taste for them in normal life.[8] To use another of Lincoln's similes, the unusual legal processes were like the surgeon's knife; it was a time of cutting in order to save.[9]

Note. The whole matter of "rules of war"—indeed of the legality of war itself—finds a new orientation in 1946. The problem offers too important a challenge for adequate treatment here; yet the significant fact of that reorientation cannot well be ignored. The larger significance of the Nuremberg trial of Nazi criminals—that being one aspect of a vast subject—was well presented by Justice Robert H. Jackson at Buffalo on October 4, 1946. From that speech, which ought to be read in full, the following passages may be quoted:

Our entire cultural inheritance has long been strangely hospitable to the idea that war is an acceptable and honorable means to a people's place in the world. History, literature, drama, sculpture, painting, even music, for many countries vied with each other in glorification of war and of the warrior.

. . . .

Perhaps no branch of Western learning has been more tolerant of war than nineteenth-century jurisprudence. Law . . . embodied more of people's customs than of their ideals. . . . It said that killings in war were not crimes because to kill and maim is part of war, and war itself was a legal activity.

At an earlier time a distinction was made . . . between just wars and unjust wars. . . .

In the eighteenth and nineteenth centuries international law ceased to follow those teachings. . . . As one American authority put it, "Both parties to every war are regarded as being in an identical legal position . . . ." Of course, this

legal doctrine that an invader intent on conquest and pillage stood on the same
basis as a people defending its homeland, did not commend itself to the moral
sense of mankind. But it has exerted a powerful influence on our thinking and
particularly on foreign office thinking, which always tends to the conventional.

. . . .

It is an easy step from believing that war is never illegal to believing that war
is never reprehensible. . . .

Of course, an international law which rested upon such foundations won little
respect anywhere and invited the contempt of evil and aggressive men. To them
it was only a compilation of pious preachments without practical sanctions. It is
no coincidence . . . that both of the World Wars which have been so catastrophic in our times began with men who openly avowed a cynical and contemp-
tuous attitude toward international law.

Justice Jackson then pointed out how these problems were attacked in
the Nuremberg trial and in the agreement signed at London on August
8, 1945, on which that trial was based. He continued:

This agreement regards the citizen or official who commits crimes against the
peace and dignity of international society as answerable to it for the offense, just
as one may be answerable for crimes against the peace and dignity of the United
States or the State of New York.

It departs from the old theory that international law bears only on states and
not on statesman, and that "sovereignty" is a shield against all the world for any
action done under the laws of a state or under its orders.

. . . .

. . . the Nuremberg trial has been a sincere . . . effort by the nations to give
international law what Woodrow Wilson described as "the kind of vitality it can
only have if it is a real expression of our moral judgment." [10]

VI. LINCOLN AND JOHN BRIGHT

A PHILADELPHIA abolitionist was calling one day upon Lincoln. After a while the President "diverted the conversation by saying that he wished to read . . . the most eloquent passage he had ever seen and taking from his pocket book a newspaper clipping proceeded to read the final passage of one of John Brights speeches . . . ." The caller was J. Miller McKim. His account was given to Edward L. Pierce, Sumner's biographer, who wrote the above words to William H. Herndon.[1]

That Lincoln treasured this clipping by carrying it on his person and that he used such superlative praise for any speech are interesting items in themselves. More than that, the incident revealed a deeply significant friendship. While Abraham Lincoln was President he enjoyed a community of understanding with the English leader John Bright, which being interpreted throws a flood of light upon human influences that leaped across the ocean eight decades ago. One is dealing here with a topic of dominant significance for Lincoln, for Bright, and for the essential harmony and unity of Britain and America.

I

Bright and Lincoln never met, for the British leader never visited the United States, thus forgoing not only the ovations he would have received, but also the opportunity to talk face to face with the homely President whose aspirations were essentially his own. His relations with Lincoln were indirect. His American correspondence was with Charles Sumner, who showed the letters to Lincoln; other matters pertaining to the friendship came through Thomas H. Dudley, American consul at Liverpool. This indirectness may have been largely a matter of position in office: Lincoln's foreign relations were handled through diplomatic channels; Bright was so prominent a British leader that direct communication with him by the American President might have been deemed irregular.

Few friendships so indirect have been so real. Its essence is to be understood in terms of the lack of personal contact or face-to-face association. Lincoln and Bright were not alike in manners, habits, background, or personality. Perhaps they might not have enjoyed the same jokes. It is not even claimed that they were identical in social and economic views; the mutuality of their understanding is rather to be regarded as an international link. They are to be remembered, not as men who see each other and grasp hands, but as embodiments of that good will which is above mere difference and is unshaken even by dispute.

It is not to be thought, however, that the relation was distant or altogether impersonal. Mementos and symbols played their part; affection was not absent. A bust of Bright, donated by one Thomas G. Blain of Manchester, was sent to the United States. It had been intended for Lincoln, but was presented after his death to President Johnson as a gift to the American nation.[1] A cane once carried by Lincoln became a treasured heirloom in the Bright home. Goldwin Smith, describing the anteroom leading to Lincoln's office, noted how "a large photograph of John Bright" struck his eye.[2] The story of this photograph, noted in diverse sources—including manuscripts in the Library of Congress,[3] the British Museum,[4] and the Huntington Library,[5]—would make a chapter in itself. The portrait did not come from Bright to Lincoln, but indirectly by the kindness of an English admirer of the two leaders.

There was also the episode of Alfred Rubery—an adventuresome British youth who became the beneficiary of one of Lincoln's most notable pardons.[6] Participating in a privateering escapade against the United States, Rubery had been convicted in a federal court in California and sentenced to a fine of $10,000 and imprisonment of ten years. Interesting himself in the case as that of a young man of his Birmingham constituency who was foolish and thoughtless rather than vicious, Bright brought the matter to Lincoln's attention through Sumner, and on December 17, 1863, Lincoln issued a pardon for Rubery in a formal and carefully worded proclamation (much more than was usual in a presidential pardon), in which he took pains to mention that in addition to other considerations the act of clemency was done "especially as a public mark of the esteem held by the United States of America for the high character and steady friendship of . . . John Bright." On January 22, 1864, Bright wrote beautifully to Sumner expressing both his own appreciation of Lincoln's act and the heartfelt gratitude of Rubery's mother and sister. He referred to the matter as one that "produced a kindly feeling towards the President and towards the . . . United States." Carl Sandburg noted it in his *War Years*. Lincoln, he said, "believed John Bright was entitled to one pardon and no questions asked." [7]

II

The Lincoln-Bright friendship was not related to any particular setting nor confined to a special episode. Its reference was to great and enduring values. Its concern was the essential attitudes of whole peoples towards each other. Its bearing was even broader, for it touched problems of world significance. We are dealing here not alone with men but with nations and destinies. Since it is the weakness of men that they live in the midst of such destinies without rising to a full contemplation of them, the friendship of these great minds has the more meaning because this contemplation was not lacking.

On this side of the Atlantic, in the Civil War period, there were groups who served their own short-sighted ends by misrepresenting and denouncing Britain. Within England also the forming of attitudes towards the American struggle was a matter of classes and groups, or rather of a small element against the great majority. Those groups that were most class-conscious—those whose mental slant was reactionary and anti-democratic—wanted the United States adventure to fail and for that reason favored the Confederacy. Liberals in England, and with them the masses of the people, favored the American Union, despite what Bright called the "folly" of the tariff in contrast to the Confederacy's gesture towards free trade.[1]

In a country such as Britain there are times when the aristocracy, in its reactionary aspects, has to cave in. When the sentiments of millions surge powerfully against the interests of a few, the ultimate result usually is that the few must yield. In an attempt to understand Anglo-American relations during Lincoln's time it would, therefore, be the greatest mistake to place too much emphasis upon the few who opposed democracy, who favored exclusive rights, and who vociferously opposed Lincoln and his cause for that reason. It is stupid to give attention only to this element and to ignore the great English nation. This factor, though insufficiently understood by most people, was stressed in 1863 by a thoughtful Indiana citizen—Bartlett Woods of Lake County—who had formerly lived in England. "The Tories," he wrote, "wish our entire destruction," desiring that democracy in America should fail after eighty-seven years of trial. They could then say to Englishmen who urge universal suffrage and other popular reforms that American disasters prove the weakness of republics. "They will not see that *not Democracy* but *Slavery* is the cause of our trouble." Woods pointed out that nothing but opposition to the American Union cause could be expected from such men. Very significantly, he then continued:

. . . I think from all I see in public prints & by observation that we do not as a people understand England . . . . We magnified Mr. Russell [William Howard Russell whose venomous account of the battle of Bull Run appeared in *The Times* of London in 1861]. We accepted the Times as the Embodiment of England . . . . Our Papers . . . pitched in taking it for granted that nothing but opposition could come from England & made their articles accordingly; these in turn were copied in the Times . . . . Our Papers . . . & our Government . . . ought to have considered the Times as simply representing a Party, Tories, High Church, & State men glad of any opportunity to prove that a Republic is all wrong & that Hereditary aristocracy & a King are necessary to the well being of a Nation—we never should have ignored *the fact* that the mass of the

[British] People are on our side & we should never [have] allowed the Times & that set to have driven us from that Position. . . . Let the Times howl on . . . the Times is not the exponent of *the Power* that does govern in England.

Continuing his argument, Mr. Woods pointed out that various reforms—Catholic emancipation, the reform of Parliament, free trade measures, repeal of the Corn Law, etc.—were opposed by *The Times* and its party; yet they were passed. "[T]he Times," he wrote, "is not the *Great Power* in the Land—We have attached too much importance to it altogether . . . ." Then he added: ". . . Bright and Cobden are a Host in themselves—The People here ought to know their Friends there . . . ." He wanted speeches such as those of Bright and Cobden more widely published in America. He regretted that people "talk here of the Governing classes as being all against us as if there was no People as a power there." "To anticipate opposition is half to make it." [2]

III

It was the great English nation, rather than the few, who had their way. Britain's relation to Washington was not only unbroken, but grew notably more friendly in the latter half of the war. It is important that this fact be understood, the more so since misconceptions in this field of history are all too common. It has even been mistakenly said that Britain "intervened" for the Confederacy! Such statements have appeared in American newspapers. This is the exact opposite of the truth. It is true that there were tensions; there were disputes; on two or three occasions there came what were called "crises." It is precisely in such situations that the friendship of nations is tested. Peace does not depend upon the lack of dispute or difference; it depends upon the basic common sense of statesmen and the fundamental harmony of peoples when faced with disputes and confronted with international problems.

The fundamental question was whether Britain would offend the government of the United States by recognizing the independence of the Confederacy; whether it would attempt mediation between the opposing sides, thus promoting a termination of the war on the basis of a broken American nation; and whether it would throw its military and naval power on the side of disunion. Britain did none of these things. Belligerency of the Southern government was recognized, but never its independence. As to episodes that involved serious tension, there were two: the matter of the *Trent* late in 1861, in which a naval officer of the United States had removed Confederate envoys from a British ship, and the *Alabama*, which, with several other ships, was built in Britain and delivered to Confederate hands with the alleged "connivance" (though it was more like delay or inaction) of the British government. When one speaks of these two matters, one has told the worst; yet both of these issues were peaceably adjusted. The American government released the Confederate envoys, Mason and Slidell, in January of 1862, and, after vigorous protests from Washington, the further delivery of British-built ships for service against the United States was decisively stopped midway in the war. Strenuous efforts of the Richmond government to get additional warships from England were unsuccessful, as in the case of the *Alexandra* and the Laird rams in 1863. The sequel of this signal failure, as also of the British government's refusal to receive Confederate diplomats and deal officially with them, was the total disillusionment of the Confederacy in its frustrated contact with Britain.

This frustration, which is insufficiently understood, amounted to nothing less than a complete breach between Richmond and London, if one can speak of a "breach" between governments that never had regular relations, or anything approaching them. The Southern envoy, Mason, withdrew from England, and British consuls, whose irregular status had caused considerable questioning, were expelled from Confederate cities by the government of Jefferson Davis. This was but a natural result of the aloofness of the British foreign minister towards Southern representatives and the disappointment of Confederate hopes for mediation, recognition, and support. Thus it was not Washington but Richmond that broke with England, and that in 1863, the middle year of the war.[1]

It seemed natural and inevitable that Southerners should command the admiration of many English minds. That admiration has become a long-standing tradition, but it needs to be rightly viewed. Where friendliness to the South was motivated by willingness to see the United States fail as a nation and as a democratic experiment—such motivation being not entirely absent—it became only a complicating wartime factor. This, however, leaves much to be said, for in the long run, in its healthier aspects, British interest in the South has managed to transcend or by-pass the political implications of the American controversy. It is true that Britons have admired Lee and Jackson, but that does not mean that they have turned against Lincoln. In the matter of official relations their unbroken amity since 1815 has been with the United States. In the sense of American reunion that amity may be said to embrace both North and South. When one emphasizes the friendship of the British people for the United States he has in mind the whole nation which preceded and survived the unhappy war. He has in mind the continuing Union.

IV

In the days of America's internal struggle it would be a fair judgment to say that the Anglo-Saxon world presented two prominent liberals: Lincoln in the United States and Bright in England. Bright was an industrialist; yet his great contribution was that of economic liberal and friend of workingmen. With Richard Cobden (the names Cobden and Bright being inseparable) he had promoted a whole school of thought in terms of free trade, opposition to militarism, and relief from those hated "corn laws" which were associated with landed privilege and monopoly.[1] Instead of conceiving of England in terms of the school tie, the aristocracy, the martial spirit, and the Tory's raised eyebrow, he was concerned for the political rights of sturdy millions of fellow humans whose sufferings and aspirations he knew at first hand. He had that feeling for the people which was matched by Lincoln's expressed wish to "lift artificial weights from all shoulders." If this be idealism, make the most of it, was Bright's view. There were times when he felt almost wholly alone. He was caricatured in *Punch* and endured the scorn that progressive men suffer; yet, in considerable part, England did the things he asked. He was more than a voice of protest, though he was often that.

It has been said that he "stood before his audience like a tower," never hiding behind a pulpit, for he thought that "No man can move an audience that does not see his boots." [2] His portraits show a leonine head with a countenance of remarkable handsomeness and distinction. His combination of Quaker simplicity with electrifying eloquence should cause no wonder, for it was said of him, "if he had not been a Quaker he would have been a prize-fighter." [3] His speeches read well today, but to the words themselves one must add the magnetism of his appeal to popular audiences and the effortless ease with which his bell-like voice filled the largest hall. There was the further fact of his religion, for with the devotion of a forthright nature Bright was a Christian and a Friend. In his biography of Bright, George Macaulay Trevelyan writes: "He practised the silence of his sect, and drew thence the strength of his soul, the purity of his heart, and the quality of his speech." As a boy he had sat in the Quaker meeting house at Rochdale, "where silence spoke in the heart." [4] His phrases became popular slogans. One epigram would have the carrying power of a whole discourse, as when he caricatured a few political malcontents under the Biblical analogy of the Cave of Adullam,[5] a comparison which Lincoln also used, or when he remarked with regard to Irish disturbances, "Force is not a remedy." [6]

His public activity was that of reform leader and Member of Parliament; in personal affairs he was owner of a textile mill at Rochdale in industrial Lancashire. In the superficial sense in which economic motive is supposed to color all history, he might have been expected to favor the Confederacy, for he found his business threatened with ruin by the Union blockade which shut off the supply of Southern cotton. It was precisely this economic dislocation, widespread and disastrous in British manufacturing districts, on which leaders of the secessionist government banked in their drive for foreign intervention.

Despite this business motive, Bright emphatically favored the Union cause, including the blockade, because to him it was the cause of broad opportunity and political liberalism. Thousands of English laborers were thrown out of work, including employees of Bright, but British self-help and American good will came handsomely to their relief. Trevelyan records that "all England came to the rescue with abundant generosity"—then he adds that three large ships brought American flour as a token of friendship "tangible to eye and hand and mouth." [7]

The economic thesis of "King Cotton"—the doctrine that this master crop would control the affairs of governments including international relations—broke down, and the colossal tragedy of war between the great English-speaking nations was averted. A significant chapter was added to the history of peace, whose economic basis is more fundamental than the overadvertised material "causes" of war, these often being mere excuses for an aggressive war party whose economics is as unsound as its jingoism. [8]

V

To take the measure of Bright's influence one must remember factors and overtones that escaped formal diplomacy. One cannot adequately write the story of that time without due contemplation of Bright in England writing letters of passionate intensity to Sumner, waiting in suspense for news of Union victory, mustering his superb oratorical power so that the Union cause would be fairly presented and the acts of the Lincoln administration not misunderstood, acting as friend, counsellor, and interpreter. ". . . I write to you," he wrote to Sumner, "with as much earnest wish for your national welfare as if I were a native and citizen of your country." [1] "Don't allow *temper*," he wrote, "in any of your statesmen to turn his judgment." [2] "At all hazards you must not let this matter [the *Trent* case] grow to a war with England, even if you are right and we are wrong." [3] He would not have it said by Americans "that, in the darkest hour of their country's trials, England, the land of their fathers, looked on with icy

coldness, and saw unmoved the . . . calamities of their children." [4]
In the period when tension was most acute because of the *Trent*
controversy, he declared: "I dread the consequences of war quite as
much for your sakes as for our own. So great will be my horror of
such a strife that I believe I shall retire from public life entirely . . .
should war take place between your country and mine." [5]

Bright's letters and speeches in this period are significant, not only
in ardent sympathy for the United States and in the poignantly keen
wish to avoid the barbarous stupidity of war, but also in their reading
of British sentiment. While anti-Lincoln propagandists were over-
stating the alleged British wish to see the Union fail, Bright knew
that such opinion in his country was misleading and unrepresentative.
He never lost sight of the fact that the Tories and the privileged orders
were unfavorably disposed toward the Union cause. As to some in
high places he could "believe anything bad." [6] He referred bitterly
to those British "wretches who, hating your Institutions, except that
one [slavery] of the South, will be glad to make war upon you." [7]
He was particularly caustic toward *The Times* for its anti-American
and anti-Lincoln sentiment. Recognizing the danger of temporary
excitement, he observed that this was "fed, as usual, by newspapers
whose writers seem to imagine a cause of war discovered to be something like 'treasure trove.' " [8] But he strove effectively to disappoint
the enemies of America. He urged moderation on both sides, he did
not consider the British ministry hopeless (though distrusting some),
and he rejoiced when the policy of statesmanlike adjustment and
mutual moderation succeeded.

It is important to note that his comments on the arrogance of the
privileged few among his countrymen can always be more than offset
by his clear seeing appraisal of the friendly attitude of the British
people in general. When Lincoln's emancipation proclamation was
issued in January 1863 he wrote: "Our Southern Newspapers are surprised and puzzled at the expression of opinion in favor of the North.
. . . I think in every town in the kingdom a public meeting would
go by an overwhelming majority in favor of President Lincoln and
of the North." [9]

Liberalism is relative. On some matters Bright was not as far advanced as certain reformers would have wished. It is hard to understand why he opposed those factory laws which were intended to ameliorate the lot of industrial workers. He must not be entirely judged by the stands he took in the earlier period when he was no more than a leader of local importance. At times he spoke the language of his group—that is, of British manufacturers. In common with others of that period he may have been overimpressed with the "classical" economic theory that was then current. Men's minds were hampered and almost imprisoned—sometimes the best minds—by theoretical economics. Readers of the impressive works of Adam Smith, and of his dismal successors, Ricardo and Malthus, were all too likely to come through with a kind of frustration. If you did something for large numbers of workers, they were led to believe, there could be no good permanent result. They would merely produce more offspring; there would be pressure upon the food supply; the "iron law of wages" would be their undoing.

Overawed by *laissez-faire* economics, some of the public men of that day tended to distrust the power of government to promote social and economic improvement. This would be a theme for a whole volume, in which it would have to be shown that progressive men of a later period have turned to a more human interpretation of economics, have seen the abuses of *laissez-faire* in actual practice, and have found the realities of economic experience more significant than the dicta of old-line economic theory.

If Bright did not rise to what would now be considered the full measure of liberalism, it should be remembered that the decades of his political activity had their limitations. One can analyze his public life and find that it did not present all the answers; but one cannot explain away his notable collaboration with Cobden, his work for free trade, his campaign against the corn laws, his resistance to aristocratic tendencies, his upstanding opposition to the Crimean War, his friendliness toward the United States, his admiration for Lincoln, his support of emancipation, his eloquent speeches on "the American question," and his influence in favor of those later reform bills by which the voting right was extended among British working-men.

There were other leaders in Britain who befriended the United States: they included George Thompson of antislavery fame, W. E. Forster, Prince Albert, the Duke of Argyll, Goldwin Smith, Leslie Stephen, the evangelist Spurgeon, Christopher Newman Hall (church leader), and John Stuart Mill. None, however, was so eminent as Bright; none took so much time from a busy life for this "foreign" matter, none brought to it such high-caliber leadership. By his eloquence in Parliament he effectively opposed a motion looking towards a recognition of the Confederacy; by his contact with Sumner he kept in touch with the man who was chairman of the committee on foreign relations of the United States Senate. The importance of this contact was impressively shown on Christmas day of 1861, one of those occasions when deliberation on matters of high policy brought practical results. Lincoln's cabinet met; Sumner was invited in, this being most unusual for one who was not of the cabinet; friendly letters just received from Bright and Cobden constituted a unique feature of this important consultation; the *Trent* affair was settled then and there; the cabinet decided that the envoys must be released and that war with England was to be avoided.[10] Bright's contribution to this fortunate outcome was one of the most significant acts of his life.

VI

That Lincoln was also a liberal is the main point of emphasis in this book. Since, however, a special essay is devoted to this topic, it will not be elaborated at this point. Where Bright favored the rights of workingmen, Lincoln wanted "every man to have a chance." Where the English statesman labored for intelligent international understanding, the American President stressed the essential unity of feeling between laboring men in all nations. Each emphasized the dignity of labor and the need for a broadening of political rights. One could prepare parallel columns to show how their writings and speeches proceeded along similar lines. Avoiding the claptrap of the demagogue, both chose their words carefully when speaking of human rights; what is more, both men were active in the political arena to carry their views forward to fulfillment. Both leaders spoke and acted courageously against tendencies which today we associate with the ugly name of fascism. Both saw the need, not only of enforced order, but of deep inner forces without which freedom cannot be kept. To view these men—and to view them side by side is a liberal education—one must think not only of their eloquent idealism as if that were an ethereal quality or delicate flower; one must remember also the toughness and rude alarm with which both Lincoln and Bright warned against factors of arrogant despotism and terroristic lawlessness. In favoring for his own land those principles that are universally sound, each of these leaders thought of his country's own problems in a broad world setting.

In his magnanimity, friendship for the soldier, humor, tolerance, opposition to oppression, readiness to reason with his people, and careful effort to maintain the Union cause on an enlightened level, Lincoln developed his statesmanship in liberal terms. His regard for Bright was no accident. It signified union of thought. It offered a commentary on political and social attitudes shared by congenial spirits. The sympathy of these men for each other belongs to the history and definition of liberalism.

VII

It was not as if Bright's championship of Lincoln's cause had brought him into opposition to the dominant British leaders of the time. Certainly among the men who kept Britain friendly were Palmerston the Prime Minister and Earl Russell the foreign secretary, both Liberals. To support this statement by tracing the history and development of the Liberal party in Britain would carry us too far afield. One needs to absorb a good deal of English history—political, economic, social, and intellectual—to know all the skeins of influence that have been woven into the sometimes confusing pattern of party organization.[1] Without attempting so elaborate a discussion it is well to remember that one spoke in the old days of Tories and Whigs, in transitional days of Peelites, Canningites, and Radicals, and in later days (broadly the Victorian and Edwardian period) of Conservatives and Liberals. Still later, in the present age, the general picture of party politics has been profoundly altered by the significant rise of the Labor party and the almost complete disappearance of the historic Liberal organization, so that the division now is between the Labor and Conservative parties.

The term "Liberal" on the political front came into use, displacing the old name "Whig," about the time of the agitation for parliamentary reform culminating in the Reform Bill of 1832, or more particularly in the following decade. In England of the 1840's one spoke definitely of the Liberal party or Liberal groups, with Lord John Russell as one of their chief spokesmen. (It is true that Peel, of the Conservatives, had elements of liberalism. It was under his ministry that the corn laws, so burdensome upon the poor, were repealed. Such repeal, however, was accomplished with Liberal votes and against Tory opposition.) In the period of the American Civil War Palmerston and Russell, the one at the head of the administration and the other in charge of foreign affairs, were of the Liberal party, while the Conservatives or Tories, with Lord Derby as their leader, were of the opposition.[2]

As it actually worked out in parliamentary maneuvers, however, not even the Conservative party (whatever may have been the feelings of some of its supporters) went "all out" for a policy of basic hostility to the United States and of support for the Confederacy. Derby, Conservative leader, watchful though he was of an effort to overthrow the existing ministry, approved Russell's policy of non-intervention toward the American struggle.[3] As a matter of serious consideration in Parliament the effort to commit Britain to pro-Confederate intervention simmered down to a hopeless and ineffective motion of "the pseudo-Radical"[4] John Arthur Roebuck (June 30, 1863) in favor of joint British and French recognition of the independence of the Confederacy, which found so little support in debate that Roebuck himself moved its discharge.[5] Trevelyan writes: ". . . Bright poured out on Roebuck a deluge of weighty ridicule from which he never fully recovered. 'He shook him as a terrier shakes a rat,' said one who heard the debate." [6] The fact that the ministry in power favored the preservation of British friendship for the American Union, together with the further significant fact that even the opposition party made no parliamentary move for breaking that friendship, strongly emphasizes the solidity of Anglo-American peace. In stressing Bright, therefore, one must not forget the work of Charles Francis Adams, of Earl Russell, of Lincoln and Seward, indeed of all who controlled events and caused the harmony of nations to become vocal and dominant.

That the masses of the British working people recognized as did Bright the identity of their cause with Lincoln's, was impressively shown in a notable series of popular meetings all over England in January of 1863. The Emancipation Proclamation was the cue for these meetings, which were held in London, York, Halifax, Birmingham, Sheffield, Coventry, Manchester, Bristol, Bath, Glasgow, Cobham, Carlisle, Chesterfield, and in many other places. [7] In all these gatherings, economic liberalism and political democracy were prevailing notes. It is no disparagement of these demonstrations to say that, in hailing Lincoln, British workingmen were promoting their own cause. In reply, Lincoln sent his famous letter to the workingmen of Manchester in which he spoke eloquently of human rights while expressing sympathy for the sufferings which laboring people in Britain were enduring.

People did not realize the part that Lincoln himself had in these assemblages. Through Sumner he had sent to Bright in his own handwriting the draft of a resolution expressing the views which he wished to have adopted in British public meetings. The gist of the resolution was that civilized states ought to deny recognition to a nation constructed with the "fundamental object to maintain . . . and perpetuate human slavery." [8] This Lincoln autograph not only offers another illustration of Lincoln's connection with Bright; it shows what was not known at the time—namely, that in his own discreet manner Lincoln was a conscious factor in the interplay of public opinion between nations. The memorandum through Sumner to Bright would now be called "propaganda," but the shaping of sentiment is the business of statesmen, and such a memorandum was the kind of propaganda that wise leaders do not fail to use.

These popular demonstrations in England, which seemed a kind of tidal wave, are matters of voluminous record. In the National Archives at Washington one finds the original "Address of the Inhabitants of Birmingham to His Excellency Abraham Lincoln, President of the United States of America." It is a gigantic scroll, a huge paper carrying at least ten thousand signatures, in which the men of Bright's constituency conveyed to Lincoln their "deep and heartfelt sympathy" and assured him of the "good wishes of all Men who love liberty." [9]

To know the harmony of views between such a Briton as Bright and such an American as Lincoln is to do more than make clear the solid ground of understanding between two great nations. It is characteristic of Anglo-American collaboration that its objectives do not conflict with the true interests of other peoples. Not only for English-speaking countries but for the United Nations today, the theme that the cause of democracy is of world importance, that it lives because of its deep human significance, and that it is inseparable from its international aspects, presents a stirring challenge.

VII. LINCOLN'S PEACE AND WILSON'S

I

IN THE agelong martyrdom of man there is no sadder tragedy than the Lost Peace that followed the "first World War." Every healthy motive, including national interest, cried to heaven for adjustments that would check aggression. The League of Nations was not so defective that it could not have been used, and in addition there were the Locarno Treaty, the Geneva Protocol, the Kellogg-Briand Pact, the World Court, and many treaties of arbitration. There were also the regular processes of diplomacy. Will it be said that these procedures were imperfect? The answer is that society constantly uses imperfect instruments, and that the alternative—another world war—was so hideous that obstacles to adjustment seem utterly trivial.

Wilson's program of order was lost; rather, it was thrown away. Its strength was sapped in the days when peace-minded nations were easily dominant. When a common front was yet feasible, timid men in this and other countries cast away their own power, trembled at every Nazi bogey, and surprised Hitler himself by the ease of his preposterous maneuvers.

A half century prior to Wilson there had been another peace sabotaged by politics. Abraham Lincoln as President had had the foresight to know that enlightened rebuilding after a war does not merely happen, that it takes planning, and that the time to plan was during the war itself. He regarded this wartime planning, if well conceived, as not only a way of winning the peace, but also a way of both winning and shortening the war.

Lincoln's plan was forthright and practical. It included overthrow of the army and government that warred against the United States, abolition of slavery, pardon for the past, loyalty for the future, reunion, amnesty for Confederates, return of confiscated property, and home rule for the South. The Lincoln scheme for state governments in the South was offhand to be sure, but it offered hope both for the transition to normal polity in a restored Union and for needful adaptation in the decades ahead.[1] At City Point, in late March 1865, Lincoln met with Sherman, Grant, and other high officers, and by Sherman's statement the President was "all ready for the civil reorganization . . . at the South as soon as the war was over." To the citizens of North Carolina he would at once guarantee "their rights as citizens of a common country." As to the existing state governments in the South he would give them temporary *de facto* recognition. As to Jefferson Davis, he would welcome his escape from the country. He wanted Confederate soldiers back in their homes, "at work on their farms and in their shops." [2]

Lincoln's spirit was evident in the convention of surrender at Appomattox, which, in spite of its brevity and military emphasis, contained one important element bearing upon political reconstruction in the provision that "each officer and man . . . be allowed to return to his home, not to be disturbed by the United States authorities so long as they observe their paroles, and the laws . . . where they may reside." [3] This meant that Confederate soldiers so paroled could not be prosecuted in Federal courts for participation in the war; and Grant, making his views known to an attorney general who agreed with him, saw to it that such prosecution was avoided.[4] Even Jefferson Davis was not brought to trial, though he was indicted. A few high Confederate officials were imprisoned under military authority for short periods, released, and from that time unmolested. There was severity in the case of Wirz, the officer who had been in charge of the Confederate prison at Andersonville, but his execution was an exception and it was the decree of a military commission. As to the civil courts, and almost entirely as to the military administration, army officers were unmolested. This nonvindictive policy was largely of Lincoln's doing.

On the day after the surrender Grant urged Lee to go and see Lincoln, offering safe conduct, but Lee declined,[5] partly because Jefferson Davis, though in flight, was still, however ineffectively, President of the Confederacy. The subject should not be dropped, however, without a lingering thought as to the proposal that Lincoln should confer with the highest general of the South, nor without a reflection on Grant's conference with Lincoln shortly before the proposal was made. When Sherman in North Carolina offered fuller terms to Johnston covering political reconstruction, he also was fresh from a conference with the President.[6] It is known that Lincoln, in cabinet meeting on the last day of his life, considered modifications in the specific terms of his plan, and that the plan which President Johnson put into effect in 1865 was essentially Lincoln's.[7] As to carpetbag rule in the South, Lincoln repudiated the idea emphatically as "disgusting and outrageous" in a letter to Shepley, military governor of Louisiana in November, 1862.[8] In the matter of pardon, which was executive, generosity was applied by both Lincoln and Johnson.[9]

II

The overthrow of Lincoln's plan by partisan radicals, in the vindictive period of exploitation and abuse that has been miscalled "reconstruction," cannot be reviewed here, though its sordidness should be remembered for those twinges of conscience that are good for the soul.[1] But if Appomattox had its illiberal aftermath, the sequel of 1918 was vastly more tragic. Near the end of his life, on November 10, 1923, Woodrow Wilson delivered an address for the Armistice Day of that year. His program had been shattered and his health broken. His words come with overwhelming poignancy to a generation that has witnessed in the second World War the result of discarding his principles.

The memories of the armistice, said Wilson, "are forever marred . . . by the shameful fact that when the victory was won . . . by the . . . ungrudging sacrifices of our . . . soldiers—we turned our backs upon our associates and refused to bear any responsible part in the administration of peace, . . . and withdrew into a sullen and selfish isolation which is deeply ignoble because manifestly cowardly and dishonorable." Wilson added that each passing year "has made the exceeding need for such services as we might have rendered more and more evident and more and more pressing . . . . And now . . . the whole field of international relationship is in perilous confusion." [2]

A great difficulty in dealing with Wilson is that so much must be done by way of clearing the air. Wilson is remembered, not genuinely by authentic history, but by what his enemies have said of him. Fame has been kinder to Lincoln, whose memory has been shaped by friends or even extravagant eulogists. If one were to do to Lincoln what has been done to Wilson—i. e., remember him by what opponents, including men of his own party, have said—the picture would be amazingly different from the present concept. This subject has been treated above.[3] The verdict of "the ages" for Lincoln is secure, but the molding of his fame has been in friendly hands. Some men, such as Lincoln, have had their meed of fame, some have not. In the case of Wilson a reconsideration is essential as a matter of simple justice and straight thinking.

To clear the air it is necessary to reëxamine certain stereotyped notions. Among these are the concepts that Wilson was an impractical idealist, that he deceived the country into war after promising to keep out,[4] that he made this or that mistake (there are several almost universally enumerated), that he betrayed Germany, and that it was his peace, not the people's, that he was promoting.

What of this visionary idealist? He rose to the top of his profession, mastered the workings of government, put through reform laws in New Jersey to the dislike of practical bosses, formed his own precedents in presidential dealing, made notable adjustments in banking, currency, the tariff, taxation, labor legislation, and trust control, attained election and reëlection against hard-headed opposition, and so ordered his relations with Capitol Hill that coöperation between the legislative and executive branches became a notable fact during his administration.

Wilson respected Congress and became the leader of legislation to a degree that completely belies the superficial concept of an inept professor who issued fine sayings while living in the clouds. Over and over again important laws enacted under Wilson were "administration measures" initiated by presidential influence, drawn up with his informed coöperation, and put through Congress under his leadership. In legislative matters Wilson led the way, appeared before Congress if necessary, called a special session where needed, and made public appeals to carry his point.

It is well to emphasize Wilson's first administration, concerning which public memory seems somewhat less than perfect.[5] Things were done in that period that have affected American economic life ever since. The achievements in those earlier Wilson years, involving such major reforms as the Federal Reserve System, the Underwood tariff, and the Clayton act, hardly confirm the concept of Wilson as an ineffective dreamer in the White House. In both his administrations the President was sustained by Congress in a long list of acts, including such matters as canal tolls, the tabling of the McLemore resolution, steps toward preparedness, the averting of a railroad strike in 1916, the breach with Germany, senate cloture, the declaration of war, and a complex array of wartime enactments touching manpower, finance, disloyalty, espionage, enemy property, organization of industry, shipping, and indeed all that pertained to military and economic mobilization. When in January 1918 "practical" men proposed a war-cabinet plan that would have served partisan ends by taking war functions out of the President's hands, Wilson not only thwarted the scheme; he requested more power (in the Overman Act of 1918) and got it. When the dust of this unhorsing episode had cleared, Wilson was in the saddle.[6]

These things were done within the pattern of democracy. Free elections occurred under Wilson; opposition newspapers flayed him severely in editorials, cartoons, and misleading articles. No dictator allows such things to be printed. Accomplishments from 1913 to Wilson's physical collapse in 1919 required a leader who could bring things to pass. After Wilson's breakdown senatorial approval was withheld in the vital matter of the League of Nations, but that was the exception. It was, of course, a momentous exception, but that does not invalidate the record of the years before 1919. Much of the trouble, though not all, was the lack of a two-thirds vote. In March 1920 ratification of the Treaty with the League was voted by forty-nine senators and opposed by thirty-five in a sorry tangle in which some of the supporters of the League voted nay in the hope of a later vote free from hampering reservations.[7]

It has been said that Wilson and his followers kept the United States out of the League of Nations rather than make concessions, that they are to blame for what has been aptly called the "Great Betrayal." [8] The cause of the League in America, it is said, was killed in the house of its friends.

One can answer this accusation by reference to the record of those times, though many of the significant points seem to have been almost forgotten. When Wilson consulted the Senate in late February 1919 the sequel on his part was the inclusion of clarifying clauses in the covenant as requested; the sequel on the part of senators was the stinging round robin presented by Lodge in March 1919,[9] which amounted to a virtual declaration of war upon the League and the President. This was at a time when the work of the Peace Conference was still to be done, and when, as shown by a newspaper poll, American opinion strongly favored the League.[10] That very opinion was a kind of key to anti-Wilson "strategy."

Those who put the blame upon Wilsonians ought to read Lodge's own book, The Senate and the League of Nations. There he shows that, in organizing the incoming Republican Senate in the spring of 1919, he worked hand-in-glove with total foes of the League, such as Borah.[11] Recognizing the strength of American sentiment for the League, its foes plotted to kill it by indirection. Reservations were so worded as to be unpalatable to League supporters. The foreign relations committee of the Senate was packed with enemies of the League.[12] This is amazing when it is remembered that even in the Senate the element that fully opposed the League amounted to a small fraction of that body. It was not merely that the foreign relations committee, as set up in 1919, did not represent the attitude of the nation; it was not even representative of the Senate. Of the ten Republicans on the committee every one had signed the "ultimatum" (round robin of March 1919) except Brandegee of Connecticut, who was known to be an irreconcilable.

"Strategy" in the upper house was a matter of talking the subject to death, over-investigation, long delays, complicated amendments, reservations, and like maneuvers—precisely the kind of obstruction that perfectly suited the anti-League purpose. Indeed it has been confessed that "reservations" were a trick to prevent ratification. When senators in sympathy with League objectives voted against Lodge's formula of ratification with ponderous reservations, they did not expect adjournment. They expected another parlimentary step, hoping it would be in accord with public opinion.

Perhaps both sides played politics, but it is pertinent to ask who shaped the parliamentary situation. If Lodge genuinely desired his hampered ratification to be adopted, which is by no means evident from the whole record, he was by his own statement quite content with the minority outcome which made anti-League isolationists jubilantly happy.[13] If, in the leaderless period of Wilson's illness, the President's followers were wary of "coöperation" on a pattern set by Lodge in consultation with irreconcilables, it was Lodge and the Republicans who commanded Senate maneuvers from 1919 to 1921. Theirs was the party fully in power in the years following; had they wanted to support international order under the League—avoiding the "Great Betrayal"—they could assuredly have done it under Harding. Leading Republicans in October 1920—a most impressive roster of distinguished men—had in fact asked that Harding be elected for that very purpose! [14]

A queer factor has arisen in the discussion of these matters. Even those who now admit the mistake in the rejection of Wilson's program sometimes pin the blame upon the broken President. In years that should have been fruitful for peace the United States drifted down the anti-Wilson road through international anarchy to Hitler and world disaster. To blame Wilson and his followers for this outcome, against which Wilson issued earnest warnings, would be an over-refinement of misrepresentation. It is in the nature of a dismal post-mortem now to ask who produced the result, but certainly one cannot overlook the responsibility of the Senate, of those who organized the Senate, and of Wilson's successors. Foreign policy always—certainly the most fundamental and vital aspects of it, which we have in mind here—requires following through. The League of Nations did not suddenly cease to be a pressing international problem in March of 1921.

The notion that Wilson betrayed Germany [15] was one of the theme songs of that famous historian, Adolf Hitler! The idea was that Germany was so much in favor of Wilson's program that they surrendered on Wilson's pledge that the Fourteen Points would be established; then an opposite peace was made, and Germany was tricked. But the Fourteen Points were announced in January 1918, and in March 1918 Germany forced upon Russia the treaty of Brest-Litovsk, under which Russia was to lose a half-million square miles and sixty-five millions of population, yield the Ukraine, give up important manufacturing districts and coal deposits, and be subjected to a huge indemnity. That did not look much like the Fourteen Points. In the same month Germany, having disposed of the Eastern front, made a terrific thrust toward Paris in the hope of an aggressive conquest victory in the war. Such a victory, if it had come, would have had little resemblance to Wilson's program.

That is only part of the story. Another point is found in a recent book by a French-American, Mr. Maurice Léon (*How Many World Wars?*),[16] in which the author bitterly denounces Wilson for being too lenient on Germany, when, as Mr. Léon thinks, the Allies ought to have permanently occupied the Rhine bridgeheads (Foch's idea) as a way of preventing a resurgence of aggressive German militarism. Wilson, says Léon, rejected Foch's plan and induced Clemenceau to be satisfied with a substitute—a treaty of assistance between Britain, France, and the United States as a check to German attack. The treaty was not ratified; France was cheated (as Léon states); in 1929 the bridgeheads were surrendered in reliance upon Locarno; the blitzkrieg was perfected under the second Reich; and the dogs of war were loosed.

Germany did not grasp the Fourteen Points by genuinely accepting them when they were announced, but quit the war in November 1918 because of military defeat. Even Bernstorff thought that Germany made a serious mistake in not rising to the opportunity it had in Wilsonian terms, instead of attempting total victory in opposite terms.[17]

III

It shows little understanding, however, to begin and end with the Fourteen Points. To say this is not to imply that the points were repudiated as much as has been supposed. They were not fully implemented, of course, but to a considerable extent they were embodied in the Treaty. The point is, however, that the Fourteen Points do not give the most significant expression of Wilson's program. The history of those points is that they were announced at a time when leaders of various Allied countries—Lloyd George and others—were stating their war aims rather specifically, as to peoples under Austrian rule, restoration of Belgium, and many such matters.[1] These were Allied aims. To end the war these aims, so the governments said, had to be achieved. It was because Wilson was a spokesman for the Allies that he issued a combined statement of objectives, covering a rather wide range of topics, including elements of European adjustment. Only one of the Fourteen Points pertained to a world organization for peace, though in Wilson's mind that point was greater than all the rest.

Even more than the Fourteen Points, therefore, one should study Wilson's notable speeches on world problems, especially those of January 22, 1917 ("peace without victory"—Germany's opportunity to accept a liberal peace if that was its purpose); of July 4, 1918, a notable speech at Mount Vernon announcing four points; and of September 27, 1918, opening the fourth Liberty Loan campaign. These speeches ought to be required reading today. On September 27, 1918, Wilson stated the issues:

Those issues are these:

Shall the military power of any nation or group of nations . . . determine the fortunes of peoples over whom they have no right to rule except the right of force?

Shall strong nations be free to wrong weak nations and make them subject to their purpose and interest?

Shall peoples be . . . dominated, even in their own internal affairs, by arbitrary and irresponsible force or by their own will and choice?

.   .   .   .

Shall the assertion of right be haphazard and by casual alliance or shall there be a common concert to oblige the observance of common right? [2]

Wilson's four points, announced at Mount Vernon, which looked to a permanent regime of order, and which were more important than the fourteen, were as follows: reduction to impotence of any power that could disturb world peace; free popular acceptance of territorial and other settlements; respect for the common law of civilized society; and such an organization of peace as would check aggression and promote peaceable and judicial adjustment. Then he reduced the four points to one point. He said: "These . . . objects can be put into a single sentence. What we seek is the reign of law, based upon the consent of the governed and sustained by the organized opinion of mankind." [3]

That an American leader should have attained such clarity might well have been a point on which Americans could take pride. If we are a nation grown up, it is precisely this type of world influence that we should foster. In the program which he launched despite great odds Wilson deserved well of his country. Perhaps we are far enough away from those times to admit that now. Wilson's words and presence sent a thrill through his own and other lands. Their appeal was universal, but at the same time sturdily American. His ovations were real tributes; they were never the synthetic response to a demagogue's tricks.

The League of Nations has been misrepresented by those who should have been its friends. We have this and that superficial concept. It has been urged that international order and self-determination are contradictory; in fact it is only by coöperation to prevent aggression that self-determination for nations can exist. There is the old chestnut that the League "had to fail" because it was all bound up with the *status quo*. But law and order at home upholds the *status quo*, in individual possessions and personal rights, as against criminal intervention. Law and order anywhere does that. Civilized society requires that a "status" or existing order be set up which is indeed subject to modification, but which is protected against terroristic, violent, or unilateral overthrow. The time came when, to enslaved millions and to plundered nations under Hitler, the *status quo* of the 1920's (or of 1938) looked like heaven. Denunciatory association of the League with the *status quo* has been a trap to fool liberals—i. e., to get liberals to assail the League. The purpose of the Treaty and the League was not to freeze Europe into an unalterable pattern—not at all, as the trend of events proved—but to have a public law and an international agency so that reasonable modification in the future could be peaceably achieved.

It was unmistakably obvious that Wilson and his friends looked for orderly revision. This was one of the main objectives in Wilson's drive to bring about, not merely a peace treaty, but a treaty into which the League would be interwoven. And what of Wilson's opponents? They are estopped, as the lawyers would say, from denouncing the punitive clauses of the Versailles Treaty because, while rejecting its curative element, they adopted its harsh features in the curious German-American treaty of 1921. By that treaty the successors of the Wilson administration adopted for application to the United States the portions of the Treaty of Versailles which pertained to war guilt, reparations, German colonies, the German army and navy, conscription (which was declared abolished), munitions, air power, inter-Allied commissions of control, complex measures of finance, shipping, railroads, debts, industrial property, German rivers, and other like matters.[4] What they did not adopt was the League. If it was the restrictive terms of Versailles that hindered, the Harding administration gave those terms its blessing, while there was no warmer friend of orderly change than Wilson.

IV

It is true that the Treaty of Versailles contained severe terms against Germany. It is also true, however, that failure of the treaty did not come because harsh terms were rigorously enforced. At least as early as February 1936, relaxation of the settlement was the recognized pattern of things in Europe. In an article in the New York *Times* of February 26, 1936, the commentator "Augur" observed that progressive relaxation of the terms of Versailles had reached the point where "by continuous nibbling" the Germans had "succeeded in doing away with the major part of the restrictive provisions of the peace treaty." [1] In this process the Allies' trump card was tossed away. As the obvious *quid pro quo* the most elementary statesmanship ought to have obtained in return an unequivocal guarantee of peace. Bargaining with Hitler was a matter of giving everything, including full control of the situation which the Allies had, and getting precisely nothing.

There is the stereotyped idea that Germany had to present a violent challenge to the other powers, that the Reich had no future in peaceable revision. There was the Nazi pose of defying the Allies! It is about like saying that the Germans defied Chamberlain's umbrella. The main point in British-German relations in the 1930's was that the Britons regarded Germans as good scouts and tried to get along with them. It is a fallacy to suppose that Hitler struck because the existing order was anti-German. As to the Rhineland in 1936, the reason he struck, or rather strutted, was that the Allies allowed him to. Revision was actually under way, but Hitler did not want peaceable revision. What he dreaded was not that France and Britain would keep Germany crushed, which they were by no means doing, but that Germany could rise within the pattern of the League, which would have left Hitlerism flat. It was the good in the Versailles settlement that Hitler despised. The League could have had no clearer tribute than the raving enmity of the aggressor. For a realization of what Hitler did to his country one must consider how far Germany could have gone in peaceable development and in revision if the all-out effort misapplied to colossal aggression had been devoted to a program of reason and international coöperation.

Versailles was no prisonhouse in actual practice.[2] The Allies permitted reparations to be dropped, huge loans to be supplied to the Central powers, Rhine bridgeheads to be relinquished, the Rhineland zone to be remilitarized, and control of German rivers to be relaxed. The Saar was reclaimed within the pattern of the treaty itself. Germans had valid reason to make a distinction which, if made, would have given Europe a hopeful outlook. They had precept and example to distinguish between escaping the treaty and blasting the peace. They could have worked toward change with Allied coöperation without plunging Europe and the world into war. True policy for the Allies was to permit modifications, as Wilson intended and as actually happened, but only on the condition that the peace of Europe be not destroyed. For the defeat of this true policy the steady weakening of the League, along with the discrediting of Wilson, was one of the chief contributing factors.

V

For the United States isolation has never been a reality. A detached position has never been even approached. It is rather that nationalist groups in this and other countries, with an inadequate view of real national interest, have killed hopeful movements for peace. Whatever has been the particular international program emphasized at a given time, that is the thing that such groups have opposed, whether it was the League, the World Court, the Geneva Protocol, or even such a mild proposal as that the United States should not actually help an aggressor if other nations were trying to check him and thus prevent war.

From the days of Barbary pirates, through Perry's Japanese expedition, the Algeciras conference on far-off Morocco, and the whole post-Wilson story, the patent fact has always been that the United States exists in a world of other nations. Even in the 1920's, with the sanction of Wilson's opponents, Uncle Sam was closely tied up with

European affairs in Dawes-Young finance, in enormous banking advances to Italy and Germany (those well-known "have-not" countries), and in American treaty approval of Versailles terms which carried us far into the internal affairs of Germany.

If one judges success by what is achieved, one may measure failure by the greatness of what is thrown away. The opportunity that was offered in 1865 in Lincoln's terms is the gauge both of Lincoln's peace and of anti-Lincoln failure. So also one may assess Wilson's program and the anti-Wilson debacle by the possibilities of 1920 contrasted with the consequences since 1938.

Emerging from World War I, the nations were (by contrast with Munich and beyond) supremely fortunate in two respects. (1) An organization of international security was a going concern; (2) Germany, within German boundaries, was under a reasonable government. Instead of crying for perfection, or asserting that the League had to fail, one stands aghast at opportunities that existed in Wilsonian terms. For approximately two decades after 1918, or at least until 1936, power was available for the cause of world order; and not only power, but a world organization that needed only to be used. Hitler was like a bogus prizefighter who usurped the championship when the title could not have been taken except by the holder refusing to defend it.

Hitler did not go into Austria until Chamberlain had dropped Eden. Each subsequent aggression was preceded by a sign that defenses on the peace front were unmanned. To have a peace front that did not include the nation that was economically the most powerful of all—the United States—was not feasible, and for this reason the Nazis placed a high value upon American isolationism. Where some assertion of international right might have checked them without war, they saw on American shores a neutrality act cooked precisely to their taste.

The way to have defended America was not to predict falsely that Americans would be indifferent in the face of a colossal blackout of human values, but to have given notice that the United States would stand with other nations in a peace front, instead of stupidly waiting till it became a war front. Had this been done in the days before the debacle of appeasement was hatched, when the strength of Russia could have been enlisted to prevent a Munich surrender, and when the upholding of Czechoslovakia (with its Skoda works and its Central European location) was of great importance, Hitler's bluster might have been laughed off, and the war averted. Prevention of war was both a higher motive and a truer self-interest than encouragement of the warmaker.

It is not that Americans have in truth been without international concern. In the face of Nazi conquest the American people never were indifferent. Had they been, their aloofness would have required no legislative neutrality act; it has long been a recognized procedure for a President to proclaim neutrality. Since they were not indifferent, nor immune from violent consequences, the neutrality act (or acts, of the 1930's) joined the limbo of laws that failed because they did not harmonize with actuality.[1] It is also the limbo of appeasers who thought that Hitler would be satiated so soon as the collapse of international solidarity was evident—"realists," some people called them! A nation highly sensitive to the international climate was cast in a misleading anti-international role in such a vital matter as war prevention, while being nevertheless drawn into complicated foreign transactions. The reason why this policy has broken down is that it has always involved a kind of pretense; it has never stood four-square. America could not fail to be affected by a terrific war of the Nazi type. One can no more base successful international policy on isolationism than he can work out astronomical calculations on the child's concept that the moon is larger than the star. Realities cannot be ignored. Human interdependence cannot be violated with impunity.

VI

Did Lincoln's pronouncements have an impact upon the South comparable to the effect of Wilson's utterances upon the German will to fight? (The thought in raising this question is that both Lincoln and Wilson were war leaders who developed their peace policies during the war. There is, of course, no intention at any point in this essay to suggest any comparison of the German program with that of the Confederates.) Writers on Wilson's speeches as propaganda, from Lasswell,[1] Bruntz,[2] Creel,[3] and Mock [4] to George Sylvester Viereck [5] and the orders of the German army, agree as to the effectiveness of Wilson's statements in depressing the German warmaking spirit and vitalizing the will to overthrow the Hohenzollern government. Viereck called Wilson's eloquence a "powerful battering ram"; [6] Lasswell spoke of it as unequaled.[7] As to Lincoln, it can be shown that he hoped his plan would rally the South, but it is hard to prove that his wish materialized. Southern defeatism and peace societies found their activating forces elsewhere than in Lincoln's program. Jonathan Worth of North Carolina did not think well of Lincoln's plan; it probably created as much antagonism as support within Confederate lines.[8] The Southern answer came chiefly, not in response to Lincoln's appeals while the war was on, but in the ready acceptance of what was called presidential reconstruction by Johnson's reorganized state governments, under genuine Southern control, in 1865.

What then? To get the significance of Lincoln's announcements, such as his speech of April 11, 1865, one must note that their appeal was less to the Southern than to the Northern mind. For the South the very ending of the war, the obvious collapse of the Confederacy, and the example of Lee, with other factors, could be counted on for the desired mental climate.

The real tug was for Lincoln to rally his own government, especially Congress, and a re-reading of his speeches shows far more of a laboring with his own people than with his friend the enemy. What Lincoln tried to do in his last speech, with an earnestness that seems pathetic despite the triumph in the air, was to mold his own people into some unified understanding of peace and restoration. What hurt him was not the postwar South. It was that "loyal people" in the North, as he said, differed among themselves.[9] It was for this, not for any personal feeling, that he deplored the attacks that he knew to be directed against himself in connection with his plan as to Louisiana. It was for this that he did his best in this last speech to discard immaterial points and pin emphasis upon bringing the states again into "their proper practical relation with the Union." [10] In this he was like Wilson, who did more abroad, but whose greatest difficulty was at home. The main problem both for Lincoln and for Wilson was internal unity for the perpetuation of peace.

The blight that spread over the South after Lincoln was not without its effect upon the North. After eight decades one still sees the consequences of an unenlightened policy of post-Civil-War reconstruction. If the road to reunion was not blocked, it was diverted by serious detours, and it stopped short of its true goal. Bad as this was, the blight after Wilson was more tragic. American nonparticipation in efforts to prevent war put an obstacle in every movement toward security. Over and above stipulations was the matter of impetus, drive, and resolution. Sincere adoption of Wilson's program would not have stopped with paper provisions. The essence of the program was not to write a covenant as an end in itself, but to supply constructive energy, as well as legal machinery, for peace. It was not to produce a utopia, but to achieve the indispensable minimum of international security. Statesmen of the New World, regretting Europe's squabbles, have often assumed for themselves just such a power for international sanity. It is a New World principle, and it comes with better grace to recognize this principle than to cast the slur upon Europe.

Wilson was not asking the impossible. He was not advocating foolish, faraway ventures. The probability was that under Wilson's program American armies would not actually have been required for foreign duty. The United States has never had to fight a war in order to uphold the Monroe Doctrine, yet the doctrine has been unfailingly upheld. It is because of the opposite program that enormous foreign operations were again required.

It is the isolationists who have produced for America the greatest entanglement in international affairs; in their case, however, it is a matter of stumbling, not planning. If the nations, the United States with others, had gone in for so much international solidarity as would have prevented the Axis war, international commitments could have been kept at a moderate level. Under the Wilson program an enormous army would not have been required. It was the breakdown of international peace that required such a force. It was after isolationism and appeasement had done their work, permitting another world war to come (though it is abundantly evident that Hitler could have been stopped without war), that a vast and far more difficult American effort on the front of world affairs became unavoidable. It is in the promoting of Wilson's essential policies today—in the prevention of war and the removal of thoughts of coming war—that statesmen must find relief from excessive and provocative military establishments.

Isolationists have not helped the nation to escape international obligations. They have proved that such obligations cannot be escaped. Coöperation with other nations is not the costly thing, nor the un-American thing. Wilson's international planning was as American as Theodore Roosevelt's support of the second Hague Conference, or William Howard Taft's approval of the League to Enforce Peace.

Nonparticipation signified more than a repudiation of Wilson. It denoted the rejection of the ardent advice of those Americans of both parties whose competence entitled them to leadership in world affairs. What happened was as if Americans were rewriting Gresham's law to make it read: bad politics drives out good. It was more than a discarding of the League. It carried over to the rejection of other remedies, till the negative attitude of the United States became a kind of impotence, as well as a hopeless barricade. Even the World Court was rejected, though every President favored it, and though it was approved by the House in 1925 by a vote of 303 to 28,[11] and was actually adopted by the Senate in 1926 by a vote of 76 to 17.[12] (Trouble arose over the Senate's fifth reservation in the formula of adoption, and it was ruled that this country had not effectively ratified, but the Root formula would have covered that point.) Nonparticipation in international security went farther than even its sponsors, save a very few die-hards, intended. It was only a small minority of bitter-enders who had their way. It is no wonder that foreign policy in the United States in the 1920's has been characterized as the "Great and Solemn Muddlement." [13]

VII

In the case of both Lincoln and Wilson the President had a constructive plan in which restoration was to be promoted, with guarantees to consolidate the beneficial results of victory. In each case partisanship wrecked the program. Under Lincoln and Johnson as under Wilson there was a disastrous deadlock between President and Congress. (In the case of Wilson it was a depârture from the pattern of executive-legislative coöperation that prevailed for the most part from 1913 to 1919.) There was in each instance a fateful congressional election whose effect was felt in later years: 1918 may be matched against the "critical year" 1866.[1]

It was a reactionary or negative choice that was made in the rejection of Lincoln's as of Wilson's plans. In each episode the rejection was bound up with a whole complex of reactionary attitudes. In each instance the negative plan broke down in practice. In the period when post-Lincoln—and anti-Lincoln—policies showed their fruit, which was chiefly in the Grant era, there was in the conquered South no consistent and constructive policy that was inaugurated, promoted, and carried through to completion under Northern radical direction. Constructive development in the South, in this era, was largely a matter of Southern effort uninspired by Northern politicians, or achieved in spite of them. That, of course, is a mild way of putting it. The full story of reconstruction abuse cannot be summarized here. If one takes only the case of Louisiana in the Grant era he finds bogus governmental devices, election frauds, intimidation, and questionable use of Federal troops. One state government was declared to be in power by the Grant group, another by the anti-Grant faction. This was done by fictitious election returns.[2] By 1876 the collapse of the Republican program of "reconstruction"—its breakdown in fact—was obvious for every state except Florida, South Carolina, and Louisiana. Its collapse in those remaining states was recognized by Hayes as he took office with disputed title in 1877. As to the period after Hayes there were Northern contributions to the South, but they were not in the Wade-Chandler spirit; nor can one overlook the part that Northern business interests had in supporting those tendencies that are associated with Southern Bourbons.

So with post-Wilson isolationism. After 1918 as after 1865 the negative politicians were caught short with no plan of their own. Peace caught them unawares. The floundering from the Knox peace resolution to the amazing German-American Treaty of 1921 may be compared to the circumlocutions of post-Civil-War days by which the legislative pattern of carpetbag rule was not completed till three years after Appomattox.

Lincoln and Wilson had similar views as to America's larger responsibility. Each thought that democracy in the world, with peace and order, was at stake. Lincoln's statement that the issue embraced "more than the fate of these United States," and other like statements, may be compared to Wilson's concern for democracy in world affairs. There were Lincolnian parallels to Wilson's spirited refusal to belittle America, or to say that this nation could not carry its responsibilities.

We hear much of Wilson's mistakes. He has been criticized for going to Paris, and for not appointing a Republican on the Peace Commission. (He did appoint Henry White, but someone who was more of a Republican than White seems to have been desired.) One should watch his pleadings here. What in particular was the disaster that happened because of Wilson's mistakes? Would that disaster be the nonratification of the treaty with the League? Would it be the failure of the United States to support an effective program for peace? You cannot have it both ways. One who opposed the League, or blandly accepted its downfall, could hardly argue that Wilson was at fault because by his mistakes the League covenant was not ratified! If, however, friends of the League rebuke Wilson for going to Paris, perhaps they have not sufficiently considered the difficulty of getting the League at all without Wilson's presence. It may be contended with some reason that Wilson would have done well to appoint Root or Taft, though Root was deemed reactionary and Taft had little influence in his own party. It is only those who favor the League, how-

ever, who could so contend, because Root and Taft turned out to
be League supporters. As to Lodge, Wilson can be pardoned for not
appointing a man who worked so thoroughly and bitterly against the
President's objectives. While Wilson was in Paris, Lodge circulated
the above-mentioned "round robin" to get a controlling minority of
incoming senators to block the League; [3] he tried unsuccessfully to
use White to the same end; [4] when it was all over, he said he was well
satisfied that ratification had failed.

What is failure? Some might say that Thad Stevens, Ben Wade, and
their like "succeeded." They overthrew Lincoln's peace. They
launched their vindictive program. They got the votes. They pil-
loried Andrew Johnson. But their program had its uneasy day and
collapsed. If a man fails precisely because he has his way, that is failure
indeed. If on the other hand a man has a goal which, if achieved,
spells success, and for which he accomplishes far more than the odds
against him seem to allow, his steps toward that goal deserve to be
remembered.

Wilson did not fail to make his contribution. As to those negative
men who checked him, defeat of international order was inherent in
their very aims. Certainly no such far-reaching program as that of
Wilson—as well as Taft, Root, and other Republicans—could have
succeeded without American continuity in its support. Hampered
though he was by opposition, Wilson gave his successor the makings
of a constructive program. It is not that his effort fell short of his duty.
The League was in fact set up. It was that others had a part to play,
and that in what they did, and left undone, they laid the foundation
for disaster.

However painful it may be in our own day to read of the sanity
that might have been, Wilson's statements, and Lincoln's also, should
be restudied for their supreme practical importance. Whether the
application of historical understanding to present-day problems is
strictly a "matter of history" may be left to those who wish to debate
such things. Applied understanding of history is a matter of human intelligence. Statesmanship may gain much by consideration of what is
past. Failure in statecraft may come by lack of such consideration.

History is no merely academic subject. It is far from satisfactory to study Lincoln and Wilson, to show the conclusions that arise from such a study, and then to relegate such conclusions to academic history as if they did not matter. Lincoln's policies did not lose validity in 1865, nor Wilson's at the time of his collapse in 1919 or death in 1924. In later years it has always been needful for their statements to be brought into discussion, not to be twisted as to meaning, but to be understood and put to use. If anti-Lincoln partisans produced a period of unfortunate reaction in post-Civil-War days, that may serve as a warning for today. If isolationists had the wrong answers between 1919 and 1939 (and later), their answers since 1945 may be usefully contrasted with present-day applications of Wilson's policies.

In the period since the Axis war men of the anti-Wilson type have become promoters of reactionary intervention abroad, of imperialism, and of a bigger and by no means better militarism. If in this tendency isolationists produce a greater entanglement, they are true to form; they have done that before. To ignore this would be to leave the whole subject in midair. To achieve tremendous coöperation in war and then throw it away in peace—to do that again—would be unthinkably tragic. War constitutes the negation of international unity, the complete affirmation of militaristic and exclusive nationalism. Where perfect unity is unattainable, a kind of working unity is necessary. One takes international affairs at a certain stage, looking forward to a later, and, if God wills, a better stage. Much can be done by expecting improvement, not deterioration, in international relations.

To ask only for easy tasks in peace, after doing the "impossible" in war, would be a kind of flabby defeatism. Where international problems are difficult, the challenge to statesmanship is all the greater. International order is not to be achieved by emphasizing national exclusiveness, by promoting talk of coming war, by imagining a particular nation in the role of future enemy, by brandishing the atomic bomb, by excessive fortification, by subjecting foreign policy to undue military influence, or by denying those measures that make for helpful relations on the economic front. It is not to be achieved by discrediting those at home who advocate such measures. The object is not to be attained by assuming that peace among nations must wait upon the impossible day when all countries shall be alike in their economic, social, or political patterns. Unity is more important than uniformity. One may disapprove of a foreign regime and yet realize that avoidance of world catastrophe is the momentous issue.

Over and over Wilson stated his concept. The United States must play its part by agreeing to "join the other civilized nations of the world in guaranteeing the permanence of peace." "The power of the United States is a menace to no nation or people." "The people of the United States . . . are ready to put their own strength, their own highest purpose, their own integrity and devotion to the test." [5]

The world-embracing feature of Wilson's plan was in terms of the hard realities of his time, and of ours also. He proposed total peace. He knew that world peace is indivisible. He knew that the way to deal with war is to prevent its breaking out.

As was said in *The Federalist,* statesmen must choose "the greater, not the perfect, good." [6] The saying fitted those days when the American nation, having failed under its League (the Confederation was a "League of Friendship"), wisely tried again and succeeded. It is not a matter today, any more than under Wilson or Lincoln, of finding a formula so perfect that commentators cannot criticize it. It is a matter of looking at a shattered world, realizing that saving procedures were blindly discarded in the 1920's and 1930's, and resolving that international blindness shall not be permanent.

Comparison of Lincoln and Wilson in its current application would suggest abatement of hatred, emphasis upon a continuing process of orderly life, readiness for revision within the pattern of peaceful security, enduring solidarity among the United Nations, and nonpartisan coöperation at home between the Capitol and the White House. Peace plans of Lincoln and of Wilson are like a photograph of a far-focused view, marred and distorted because by double exposure there has been superimposed upon the true impression a close-up of a politician with an ax to grind.

The highest thing in statesmanship is not confusion, partyism, or disruption. Problems of another peace are upon us, and as Herbert Agar has well said, it is "a time for greatness." [7] In remembering Lincoln and Wilson it is appropriate to recall their ideals, to ponder the essence of things for which they strove, and to reflect upon the cost that has been paid for rejection of their programs. With unprejudiced historical insight it may be possible to recapture the significance of Wilson's "organized opinion of mankind" [8] and of Lincoln's "just and lasting peace among ourselves, and with all nations." [9]

VIII. LINCOLN THE LIBERAL
STATESMAN

I

TO WRITE of Lincoln's fundamental views requires a good deal of caution. It is the commonest thing to see the mind of Lincoln fitted into a preconceived pattern. Sometimes this is done by an elastic or strained interpretation of what he actually said, sometimes by pure conjecture as to what he "would have" said or done on some matter far beyond his time. Writers look into the body of Lincoln's utterances, or skim the surface, for the most diverse purposes. Obviously, not all the Lincolns we have presented to us can be genuine.

Lincoln has been presented to us as a conservative. In an able and eloquent paper his political philosophy has been analyzed in terms of expediency with more than a touch of opportunism.[1] There is validity in thinking of him as conservative if one does not leave it there, but conservatism in the usual sense did not by any means encompass the horizon of his thought. There was, of course, moderation in his preference for orderly progress, his distrust of dangerous agitation, and his reluctance toward ill digested schemes of reform. More especially, he was conservative in his complete avoidance of that type of so-called "radicalism" which involved abuse of the South, hatred for the slaveholder, thirst for vengeance, partisan plotting, and ungenerous demands that Southern institutions be transformed overnight by outsiders. One of the tragic mistakes which Southerners made in an era of incredible blundering was to suppose that this type of intolerant radicalism was typical of the North. Antislavery ideals had their noble aspects. Only the best leadership could have adequately promoted them; but, historically speaking, abolitionist excess was not the sentiment of any substantial Northern element. That was shown even in war time by the congressional election of 1862.

It was because of Lincoln's more tolerant attitude toward the South that he was nominated by the Republican party in 1860 at a time when even the conservative Seward was rejected under the mistaken impression that he was too radical. It needs to be understood, however, that the word "radical" in the days of the Civil War and reconstruction was not a generic term. It had a meaning not discernible in the word itself. It was a specific designation of a particular group —Stevens, Chandler, Wade, et al.—whose dominance in the Federal government set the stage for one of the most abusive periods of American history. These men, considered realistically and taken as a group, were the opposite of liberal. As indicated in an earlier essay, they were in fact reactionary. This was evident from their opposition to civil rights, their denunciation of the Milligan decision of the Supreme Court, their denial of autonomy to Southerners, their extreme partisanship, and their friendliness toward exploitive capitalism.

One can ignore this, or deny it. A fabricated, rose-colored portrait of these radicals can be presented, but only if one distorts history. Thaddeus Stevens of Pennsylvania, for example, had, and still has, a reputation for egalitarianism and sympathy for the common man. He has been called the "Commoner" and has superficially been accepted as such. It is a different matter if, in studying this complex personality, one looks at the record instead of the stereotyped portrait. Stevens's dominance over the House of Representatives in Lincoln's day was arrogant, factional, and dictatorial. As Richard Nelson Current has pointed out, he "was not only the embodiment of Pennsylvania capitalism himself but also a go-between for others of that ilk, one whose function it was to convert the votes of the many into the policies of the few." Treating his rise to political power in prewar times, Mr. Current writes: "Lacking the humanitarian impulse, he stood stubbornly for 'vested rights' as against what he called 'the wild visions of idle dreamers,' 'the revolutionary and

agrarian folly of modern reformers.' " [2] His "Commoner" label was
a handy thing. The reputation of the alleged friend of the people
served perfectly to rake in thousands of votes, while maneuvers behind the scenes made use of these votes for special interests that were
exclusive and predatory.

It is clear from convincing masses of contemporary evidence—including voluminous unpublished sources known to specialists—that
these men who opposed Lincoln were "radical" in the sense of being
drastic or violent, not in the sense of being liberal. To combat such
men was in truth a mark of liberalism. In Lincoln's case particularly
it should be so understood, from earlier stages of rampant sectionalism, on through the wartime days of radical intrigue, and down to
the ugly and menacing deadlock by which the vindictives wrecked
Lincoln's program for the postwar years.

In all such matters Lincoln emerges as a moderate, but that made
him none the less a liberal. Liberalism is associated with democracy
and democracy requires moderation. It is among enemies of democracy, as we know by bitter experience in our day, that we find violence,
unbridled extravagance of statement, torture, terrorism, fanaticism,
and criminal atrocities. Lincoln believed in planting, cultivating, and
harvesting, not in uprooting and destroying. He believed in evolu-
tionary democratic progress.

It is possible to take his economic views and, by a superficial showing, argue Lincoln's "conservatism" with reference to such matters
as the national bank or the protective tariff. His favoring of the bank
—the famous "Bank of the United States" so productive of discord
in the Jackson era—was due largely to his attachment to the Whig
party. As to the tariff, nearly everything he said on that subject could
be classified under the head of tiresome or labored economics. Some
of Lincoln's writings or speeches show that he either missed the point
as to the working of the tariff or permitted himself to indulge in those
meaningless verbalisms or homely illustrations which were characteristic of protectionist politicians; in Lincoln's case, however, there
seem to have been twinges of conscience which coarser men lacked.
Speaking at Pittsburgh on his presidential journey in February 1861

he related the tariff question to the lack of "direct taxation" and remarked that it "is to the government what replenishing the meal-tub is to the family." [3] These phrases would apply to a tariff for revenue rather than for the protection of manufacturers. Yet his remarks on that occasion were supposed to be an endorsement of the Republican protectionist position.

After reading Lincoln's papers and speeches generally, with their clarity and pithy effectiveness, one turns to this Pittsburgh speech with a sense of let-down or disappointment. Trying to fit himself into the Republican tariff pattern, the more so because of his Pennsylvania audience (where among dominant party men the tariff was a specialty and questions concerning slavery unimportant), he fell into a lameness of statement and a confession of ignorance that were quite uncharacteristic. Republican protectionism was not his forte. Indeed his private correspondence shows that he had doubts on this subject which he did not wish to become public. [4] The party was making a strong appeal to manufacturers, but Lincoln did not want to repel men who believed in freedom of trade or who disliked excessive favors to special groups. One suspects, not without reason, that Lincoln had an un-Republican fondness for freer trade himself.

The subject of the tariff is an example to show the manner in which Lincoln's "conservatism" can be overstated or superficially presented. What is needed is something deeper than superficial indications. It is partly a matter of the use of terms. What does "conservatism" mean? If it means caution, prudent adherence to tested values, avoidance of rashness, and reliance upon unhurried, peaceable evolution, Lincoln was a conservative. If, however, the dignified word "conservative" comes to us with an alloy as with the word "politics," if it has a reactionary connotation, if it casts an aura of respectability over tendencies that are exploitive and unprogressive, or if it signifies indifferent apathy toward human problems, then one can say with complete confidence that Lincoln was no conservative.

To think of Lincoln's conservatism is to think of selected facets of his policy. But the deeply searching mind of Lincoln had more in it than static acquiescence. It had motivating sympathy, awareness of

social needs, enthusiasm for effective democracy—qualities appropri-
ately denoted by the word liberal. If in procedure he wanted to be
sure of his ground, in the content and purpose of his program he
wanted liberal causes to succeed. If his conservatism was a kind of
brake or saving common sense, liberalism was his vital spark.

The surest way to judge him is by those statements in which he
appeared at his unhampered best. In expounding the protective
tariff for the special benefit of manufacturers he fumbled and limped;
but, as William H. Herndon said, it was far different when he dealt
with fundamental human rights. In one of Herndon's manuscripts
we have this description: "If he was defending the right—if he was
defending liberty—eulogizing the Declaration of Independence, then
he extended out his arms . . . as if appealing to some superior
power for assistance and support; or that he might embrace the spirit
of that which he so dearly loved. It was at such moments that he
seemed inspired, fresh from the hands of his creator. Lincoln's gray
eyes would flash fire when speaking against slavery or spoke volumes
of hope and love when speaking of Liberty—justice and the progress
of mankind." [5]

II

It would not be going far wrong to say that the liberal credo was the
key to Lincoln's views of man and the state. His basic ideas were those
of Thomas Jefferson. He owed little to Hamilton who wanted a government to please the moneyed interests. Human rights meant more
to him than profits. He was not content with lip service to the Declaration of Independence. He took its doctrines seriously in their stress
upon equality of men. He cherished Anglo-Saxon muniments of
civil justice. On one occasion he spoke out for woman suffrage far
ahead of his time. Believing as he did in the broadening of political
rights, he did not stop there but urged that such "rights" be carried
forward in governmental achievement and human betterment. His
thought went out to the less privileged, to the "prudent, penniless
beginner." [1] The grasping rich who gained by the misfortunes of
their fellow men, or who thought of war as an opportunity for prof-

iteering, had his contempt, but repeatedly he expressed the wish that every poor man should have a chance.

Just how far Lincoln "would have" gone in extending the functions of government, and in using the government to promote the welfare of the country, is difficult to say; but there is ample evidence that his philosophy of man and the state did not begin and end with *laissez faire*. He vigorously favored what were called "internal improvements"—that being the term used in his day for large appropriations by the Federal government for various kinds of public works all over the country. He also favored such expenditures by the states. In the late 1830's when Illinois was launching upon a grandiose program for improvements in every county Lincoln was one of the most active legislative promoters of the plan. In Congress ten years later he argued elaborately in favor of such governmental expenditures. In this argument he took up, point by point, the objections of those who urged that such a system would "overwhelm the treasury," would provide merely local benefits with the use of general funds, and would be unconstitutional. He summed up the position of his opponents in the phrase "Do nothing at all, lest you do something wrong." This, he said, applied "as forcibly to . . . making improvements by State authority as by the national authority; so that we must abandon the improvements of the country altogether, by any and every authority, or we must resist and repudiate the doctrines of this message [an anti-internal-improvement veto message by President Polk]." Lincoln plainly stated that he favored the latter alternative.

Warming to his theme, Lincoln showed that improvements in the 1820's had by no means overwhelmed the treasury, even in "the period of greatest enormity." He showed that "No commercial object of government patronage can be so exclusively general as to not be of some peculiar local advantage." Then he added: ". . . if the nation refuse to make improvements of the more general kind because their benefits may be somewhat local, a State may for the same reason refuse to make an improvement of a local kind because its benefits may be somewhat general." Such an argument "puts an end to improvements altogether." In this we have a typical Lincolnian argument. We recall the circuit lawyer in Illinois, analyzing the position of the opposing side and exposing the weakness of that position. He dealt with the constitutional objection at some length by quoting Kent and Story, clinching it with the following conclusion: ". . . no one who is satisfied of the expediency of making improvements need be much uneasy in his conscience about its constitutionality." Summarizing his whole position, he said: ". . . let the nation take hold of the larger works, and the States the smaller ones; and thus, . . . what is . . . unequal in one place may be equalized in another, extravagance avoided, and the whole country put on that career of prosperity which shall correspond with its extent of territory, its natural resources, and the intelligence and enterprise of its people." [2]

On other matters Lincoln showed how far he was from the concept of a do-nothing government. He favored government help for the promotion of education. He earnestly advocated an elaborate scheme of state-enacted emancipation with Federal sponsorship and compensation. It was under him that the department of agriculture, destined to become one of the most active of government agencies, had its beginnings. As President he signed the homestead act of 1862, a measure of far-reaching government aid to the rural home maker. By that measure Uncle Sam gave away a vast amount of land in order to encourage a democratic system of individual land tenure. The act did not accomplish all that was hoped, because of exploitive tendencies in the post-Lincoln decades, but it assuredly did not proceed on the fundamental assumption that government should forever let the nation's economy alone. Lincoln's disapproval of that do-nothing theory was expressed in a fragment on government attributed to the year 1854. "Government [he said] is a combination of the people of a country to effect certain objects by joint effort. . . . The legitimate object of government is 'to do for the people what needs to be done, but which they can not, by individual effort, do at all, or do so well, for themselves.' There are many such things . . . ." [3]

III

In any survey of Lincoln's beliefs and thought-patterns it is important to emphasize the supreme quality of tolerance. Innocent of that holier-than-thou attitude which made extremists of his day particularly irritating, he realized that slavery was a moral question—an institution which he hated—yet at the same time he recognized the moral sense of the Southern people.[1] In personal matters he would deftly put in the tolerant touch. Writing in 1840 to a man who imagined he had been attacked and insulted, he was careful to assure the gentleman: "I entertain no unkind feelings to you . . . ." [2] Any personal altercation he considered regrettable. Often in his correspondence one finds the conscious effort to avoid wounded feelings. He summed up the matter as follows:

> When the conduct of men is designed to be influenced, persuasion, kind, unassuming persuasion, should ever be adopted. It is an old and a true maxim "that a drop of honey catches more flies than a gallon of gall." So with men. If you would win a man to your cause, first convince him that you are his sincere friend. Therein is a drop of honey that catches his heart, which, say what he will, is the great highroad to his reason, and which, when once gained, you will find but little trouble in convincing his judgment of the justice of your cause, if indeed that cause really be a just one. On the contrary, assume to dictate to his judgment, or to command his action, or to mark him as one to be shunned and despised, and he will retreat within himself, close all the avenues to his head and his heart; and though your cause be naked truth itself, transformed to the heaviest lance, harder than steel, and sharper than steel can be made, and though you throw it with more than herculean force and precision, you shall be no more able to pierce him than to penetrate the hard shell of a tortoise with a rye straw. Such is man, and so must he be understood by those who would lead him, even to his own best interests.[3]

It is worth while to linger a moment on this passage if one would understand Lincoln. In large part it is a key to his public and private relations. The emphasis is upon friendly approach, upon showing a man that you are his friend. You do not win a man by showing that he is wrong and you are right, by seeking to "command his action" or by setting him down as one to be despised. Your effort should not be to dictate his thought or coerce his judgment. The heart is "the great high road to reason." Gain access to a man's heart first; after that you may convince his judgment. Make sure that your own cause is just, but remember that if a man retreats "within himself" he will not be won over even by the purest truth. Your success does not depend only on the hardness of your lance, the precision or force of your throwing. You might wish it otherwise. You might prefer that naked truth and rightness of clear reasoning should come first and emotions be disregarded, but such is man. You must know what manner of animal he is. You must deal with human nature. If you are to lead you must understand those you are seeking to lead.

Lincoln was not justifying the idea that emotion rather than reason should take command in the formation of a man's attitudes. On other occasions he stressed the importance of clear thinking. In the passage before us he was not hedging on the bedrock value of solid judgment. He did not say that reason was of secondary importance, but that the heart was the "high road to reason." To get acceptance of a position based on tested thinking was his purpose, but he did not want the accomplishment of that purpose prejudiced by the wrong approach. He wanted truth to prevail, but he was thinking in terms of human relations, in which tact and winsome understanding were, by his observation, trump cards.

This attitude is the opposite of the fanatic. Such a man may be righteous, but his righteousness tends in the direction of the witch burner. Those who oppose him are evil; they must be destroyed, or at least suppressed. In that suppressive crusade one's language becomes extravagant; zeal overreaches itself; the lance of argument is thrown as if the Almighty himself were hurling a thunderbolt to strike down the evil doer. One's own motives are pure; the opponent must therefore be a sinister person; there must be no compromise with him. You withdraw from him. You spurn his friendship. Your speeches and articles are presented not so much to your opponent; he is hopeless; they are presented to your own audience; your opponent is treated as a third person. The more you can put him in the wrong the better you are pleased. You stand at Armageddon and you battle for the Lord, but you are the recruiting officer who enlists the Lord's services. Public affairs must be viewed in terms of clash, struggle, and crisis, rather than adjustment. To state these contrasting attitudes is to show that Lincoln stood not with the fanatic but with the friendly persuasive statesman.

Lincoln's liberal minded tolerance was evident in his friendly attitude toward foreigners. One must recall the factors working against such tolerance in his day. Men who came from other lands—they came in immense streams in the 1850's—were confronted with difficult conditions.[4] America beckoned but Americans often repelled.

It is not sufficient to say that hostility to foreigners was prevalent in that period. It was rampant. The nativism of that time was characterized by an assumption of racial superiority and a policy of exclusiveness in favor of old-stock Americans. It is amazing how far this movement extended, particularly within the Whig party, in which Lincoln was a vigorous leader. On the political front the evasive nickname for these nativists was "Knownothing"; as of 1856 theirs was the "American" party; before that party was formed they had gone so far in organization on the state level as to control some of the key commonwealths. When the Whig caucus of the New York legislature met in February 1855 it was stated by the *Evening Post* that of the eighty senators and assemblymen present "sixty at least" of these Whigs had taken the Knownothing oath and joined the order.[5] The mysterious secrecy of the order and the unblushing casuistry of their reasoning enabled them to pay as much or little attention to these oaths as they chose. If it became necessary for political purposes to evade their pledges they could absolve themselves with the greatest of ease. Lines of retreat were prepared in their rear. They could even deny membership. Their "principles," which "smell mouldy and unwholesome in the dark and damp," [6] were not often ventilated.

In Massachusetts, by the election of 1854, the Knownothing party elected the governor (Henry Joseph Gardner), all the state officials "all but two members of the legislature and every member of Congress from Massachusetts." [7] According to George F. Hoar, Gardner played the game of flattery and demagoguery, using men "who were odious or ridiculous among their own neighbors, but who united might be a very formidable force." He rose to power by organizing "the knave-power and the donkey-power of the Commonwealth." [8] Two names will illustrate the powerful hold which this anti-foreign group had upon leading men of that period—Samuel F. B. Morse, one of the most outstanding nativist propagandists of his time, and Millard Fillmore, ex-President of the United States, who became the candidate of the American party in 1856.

Lincoln was like Fillmore in Whig allegiance; he was like both Fillmore and Morse in ancestral American background; he was, however, firm and outspoken in his opposition to nativism. Writing to his friend Joshua F. Speed in 1855 he said: "I am not a Know-nothing; that is certain. How could I be? How can anyone who abhors the oppression of negroes be in favor of degrading classes of white people? . . . When the Know-nothings get control . . . I shall prefer emigrating to some country where they make no pretense of loving liberty . . . ." [9]

He vigorously opposed anti-alien tendencies in Massachusetts. He was careful to say that he had never been in an American or Know-nothing lodge.[10] In 1858, in a slightly known message to a committee of Chicago Germans, he offered the following sentiment: "*Our German Fellow-Citizens:*—Ever true to *Liberty,* the *Union,* and the *Constitution*—true to Liberty, not selfishly, but upon *principle*—not for special *classes* of men, but for *all* men . . . ." [11] He made a contract with Theodore Canisius for the control of a German-American newspaper at Springfield. In a letter to Canisius in 1859 he wrote: "Understanding the spirit of our institutions to aim at the elevation of men, I am opposed to whatever tends to degrade them. I have some little notoriety for commiserating the oppressed negro; and I should be strangely inconsistent if I could favor . . . curtailing the . . . rights of white men, even though born in different lands, and speaking different languages from myself." [12]

As President he showed the same tolerance. When General Grant issued an order expelling "all Jews" from the lines of his military department early in 1863 (the purpose being to exclude peddlers), Lincoln revoked the order. It was explained to Grant that he did this because the order "proscribed an entire religious class, some of whom are fighting in our ranks." [13] These are but a few examples; others could be added. Lincoln's Americanism was not a matter of prejudice, of witch hunting, or hatred directed against particular groups or classes of men.

It is instructive to compare Lincoln's record as to Knownothingism with that of the alleged equalitarian and "Commoner," Thaddeus Stevens. Lincoln was clear cut against the Knownothings and against anti-foreign intolerance. Stevens courted the nativists; the roping in of their votes appealed to his politician mind. When the Republican national convention in 1856 indirectly condemned nativism by a declaration in favor of "liberty of conscience and equality of rights," Stevens tried unsuccessfully to have these words withdrawn. Realizing that the Knownothings were politically powerful in Pennsylvania, he did not want to alienate their support and for this reason he favored the colorless McLean of Ohio for presidential candidate instead of Frémont, who was not a Catholic, but against whom the cry of Catholicism had been raised. After the presidential nomination of 1856 had been made, including Fillmore for the "Americans," Stevens (as we learn from reading the biography by Richard Nelson Current) worked hard to enlist the support of Knownothing editors for the Republican ticket. In this he succeeded, not without a brazen use of money. He himself stated that he "expended $4,000 in securing presses." One "American editor," he said, "was to change his course and have $350." Mr. Current remarks: "Old Thad was the sort who believed an honest man to be one who, once bought, would stay bought . . . ." [14] All this was in 1856, but the day was to come when Lincoln as President, in his unhappy relations with Congress, would have to deal with the domineering and intriguing Stevens as Republican leader (or boss) in the House of Representatives.

Lincoln's broad tolerance was shown in his speech on temperance. He had nothing of the self-righteous unction so common among temperance reformers. Far from denouncing the drunkard, he showed

that in his own growing years intoxicating liquor was "a respectable
article of manufacture and merchandise." "From the sideboard of
the parson [he said] down to the ragged pocket of the houseless loafer,
it was constantly found." [15] To berate habitual drunkards as utterly
incorrigible was repugnant to his sense of human decency. He considered such an attitude "fiendishly selfish." It was "like throwing
fathers and brothers overboard." He himself was not a drinker, but
taking drunkards as a class he believed that "their heads and their
hearts will bear an advantageous comparison with those of any other
class." Proneness to this vice he believed characteristic of generous
people. As to those who had not fallen victims to drink, he thought
they might have been spared "more by the absence of appetite than
from any mental or moral superiority." [16] It should be added that
Lincoln spoke vigorously for temperance. The point emphasized
here is his manner of doing so. Temperance in his judgment was not
promoted by any type of intolerance, nor by unfriendliness toward
"a large, erring, and unfortunate class of . . . fellow-creatures." [17]

IV

Lincoln repeatedly spoke in terms of friendliness to labor. Hard
work had been his portion in pioneer days. While very young, as he
states in his autobiography he "had an ax put into his hands . . .
and from that till . . . his twenty-third year he was almost constantly handling that . . . useful instrument." [1] More than once
he identified himself with workingmen. He referred to himself as a
"penniless boy, working on a flatboat at ten dollars per month." [2]
At New Haven, Connecticut, on March 6, 1860, he said: "I am not
ashamed to confess that twenty-five years ago I was a hired laborer
. . . ." [3] With no thought of denying legitimate profits, he disliked
the concept of labor being in a dependent position with reference to
capital. One can quote several passages on this point. The following
is typical:

The world is agreed that labor is the source from which human wants
are mainly supplied. . . . By some it is assumed that labor is available

only in connection with capital—that nobody labors, unless somebody else owning capital . . . induces him to do it. . . . They further assume that whoever is once a hired laborer, is fatally fixed in that condition for life; . . . . That is the "mud-sill" theory. But another class of reasoners [Lincoln associated himself with this group] hold . . . that . . . these assumptions are false, and all inferences from them groundless. They hold that labor is prior to, and independent of, capital; that . . . capital is the fruit of labor, and could never have existed if labor had not first existed; that labor can exist without capital, but that capital could never have existed without labor. Hence they hold that labor is the superior— greatly the superior—of capital.[4]

These words having been uttered in 1859, Lincoln returned to the theme in the same words in his first annual message to Congress in December of 1861, where he spoke unfavorably of "the effort to place capital on an equal footing with, if not above, labor." Speaking now from the presidential chair, he said: "Labor is prior to, and independent of, capital. . . . Labor is the superior of capital, and deserves much the higher consideration." Fairness toward both labor and capital was his aim. He said: "Capital has its rights, which are as worthy of protection as any other rights. Nor is it denied that there is, and probably always will be, a relation between labor and capital producing mutual benefits. . . . No men living are more worthy to be trusted than those who toil up from poverty . . . . Let them beware of surrendering a political power . . . which, if surrendered, will surely be used to close the door of advancement against such as they, and to fix new disabilities and burdens upon them, till all of liberty shall be lost.[5] He did not want laborers "tied down" or "obliged to work under all circumstances." He wanted labor peace, but he favored the right to strike.[6]

It is not to be supposed that Lincoln had any antagonism toward capital. That was not the point. "[W]hile we do not propose any war upon capital [he said], we do wish to allow the humblest man an equal chance . . . with everybody else." [7] Often he recurred to this idea of equality of opportunity. Remarking that his own lot was "what might happen to any poor man's son," he said: "I want every man to have a chance—and I believe a black man is entitled to it—in which

he can better his condition . . . ." [8] It was to produce such a result that he favored the cause of the Union. Describing it as "a
people's contest" he declared: "On the side of the Union it is a struggle
for maintaining in the world that form and substance of government
whose leading object is to elevate the condition of men—to lift artificial weights from all shoulders; to clear the paths of laudable pur-
suit for all . . . ." [9]

In the dark days of the war it gave Lincoln heart for his task to believe that labor's welfare would be promoted by the cause for which
he struggled. One of his finest presidential papers was his letter to
the workingmen of Manchester, England, in response to a laudatory
address which had been sent to him at the time of the New Year,
1863.[10] When honorary membership in the Workingmen's Association of New York was tendered to him in 1864 he indicated his grateful acceptance in a speech especially directed to the cause of labor.
Repeating his comments as to labor and capital already given in his
message to Congress of December 1861, he showed the breadth and
international application of his principle in these words: "The strongest bond of human sympathy, outside of the family relation, should
be one uniting all working people, of all nations, and tongues, and
kindreds. Nor should this lead to a war upon property, or the owners
of property. Property is the fruit of labor; property is desirable; is a
positive good in the world. That some should be rich shows that
others may become rich, and hence is just encouragement to industry
and enterprise. Let not him who is houseless pull down the house of
another, but let him work diligently and build one for himself, thus
by example assuring that his own shall be safe from violence when
built." [11]

V

Lincoln is known, as much as anything else, for a basic Americanism. At the outset of his presidency he showed the utmost fervor in
emotionally underlining "our national fabric, with all its benefits, its
memories, and its hopes." [1] Here was national pride historically buttressed, reason enlivened by feeling, present loyalty linked with folk

memory. He once said: "I love the sentiments of those old-time men . . . ." [2]

Yet these thoughts were qualified. They were not naively simple. He did not forget national shortcomings. They brought a sense of humility, though he believed that the United States had the best government in the world. He said as a young man: "We find ourselves in the peaceful possession of the fairest portion of the earth . . . under . . . a system of political institutions conducing more essentially to the ends of civil and religious liberty than any of which the history of former times tells us." [3] That this was not thoughtless boasting was shown by other statements in which he warned against lawless and antisocial tendencies into which his countrymen were prone to fall.

Not oratorical exaggeration, but clear-headed logic, characterized his thinking on American institutions. The pillars of the national temple, he thought, should be "hewn from the solid quarry of sober reason." Passion would be our enemy. "Reason—cold, calculating, unimpassioned reason—must furnish all the materials for our future support and defense." [4] Lincoln's head and heart were in balance. His emotions might glow, but his well considered judgment would take command. In reading his writings one finds a constant blend of stirring inspiration with steady reflection.

There is, perhaps, a kind of earth-bound quality in the philosophy of most Americans. Ready pragmatism is more to their liking than the unballasted flights of the mystics. America is of the West, not the East. This attitude of hard practicality—of impatience for "success" and "results"—is impressively evident in scientific achievement, industrial organization, managerial talent, and technological accomplishment. Sometimes, however, the same quality—or a coexisting quality—is expressed in a careless and unambitious acceptance of things as they are so far as governmental and social institutions are concerned, sometimes in impatience toward those who sincerely labor to improve social conditions. Faults of American democracy as imperfectly practised—rampant partisanship, interracial maladjustment, uninspired "politics," pressure lobbying, congressional inefficiency, and deadlocked government—are too often endured with indifference. The public conscience is never dead, but it is often dormant, inarticulate, or frustrated. The active electorate may be only a fraction of the people. Appeals to prejudice, sometimes on a shockingly low level, may carry an election. The "anti-" agitator (anti-labor, anti-Negro, anti-British, etc.) may win by a kind of default—that is, by the absence of an outstanding candidate to represent the more intelligent element. American democracy has not been in danger from those who would "subvert" it nearly so much as from those who give it superficial adherence and lip service while ignoring its pressing problems.

Lincoln had given thought to certain aspects of this problem, or related problems, as they arose in his time. His Americanism was no mere badge or slogan. He was never the professional patrioteer. Our democracy, he urged, is in danger from within; its threat is a kind of "suicide." In addressing the Young Men's Lyceum at Springfield in 1838, he specified contemporary factors that caused him great distress: "the increasing disregard for law which pervades the country," the breakdown of that "strongest bulwark of any government"— namely, "the attachment of the people," and the tendency of the "best citizens" to become alienated from a government that permits abuses to exist.[5]

In Lincoln's attitude toward these matters of law and order one finds the kind of liberalism that is deeply thoughtful rather than superficially optimistic. He faced unpleasant facts. Speaking of mob rule he said that the process went on "from gamblers to negroes, from negroes to white citizens, and from these to strangers, till dead men were seen literally dangling from . . . trees upon every roadside."[6] The thought that men should be impatient of government disturbed him. Bad laws, he thought, ought to be repealed, but while on the books they "should be religiously observed."[7] To give up enforcement of laws because people resisted, disobeyed, or disregarded them he considered highly unfortunate.

He pleaded for eternal vigilance in this matter. "There is no grievance [he said] that is a fit object of redress by mob law." Government in former days had "many props"; in his day he feared that the fruits of government achievement, having been appropriated, were less appreciated. Democracy was an experiment. The very impulse to make the experiment succeed was a stay, a prop, and a chance for deathless distinction. The game having been caught and the crop harvested (at least in the attainment of independence), he hoped that the constant, day-by-day preservation of democratic standards would be as much of an object as their early establishment. To this end he said:

> Let reverence for the laws be breathed by every American mother to the lisping babe that prattles on her lap; let it be taught in schools, in seminaries, and in colleges; let it be written in primers, spelling-books, and in almanacs; let it be preached from the pulpit, proclaimed in legislative halls, and enforced in courts of justice. And, in short, let it become the political religion of the nation; and let the old and the young, the rich and the poor, the grave and the gay of all sexes and tongues and colors and conditions, sacrifice unceasingly upon its altars.[8]

In such warnings and pleadings there was sternness in Lincoln's tone. He did not burble about democracy. To describe him briefly, he could be called a tough minded, liberal realist. He was, of course, a man of ideals. His leadership would not have been worth much otherwise. But it is in fact our liberals who have been the tough minded men. It is only a misconception to suppose that liberals have been soft minded, nor is it true that they have been removed from practical reality. Sometimes we call the wrong ones "realists." Foolish and uncritical acceptance of stereotyped ideas or slogans is not unknown among "conservatives." Sometimes those who oppose liberal views, or who have appeased reactionaries, have fallen prey to arguments or blandishments which are shockingly unreal and flimsy.

VI

In the matter of Negro rights Lincoln's position must be viewed in relation to the background of his time. He opposed intermarriage of the races, resenting the very suggestion. Such intermarriage, however, was not an issue. It was only a bogey or scarecrow intended to mislead and becloud the less intelligent popular mind. Lincoln was cautious as to political and social equality, though he vigorously objected when the Supreme Court issued its opinion in the Dred Scott case to the effect that a Negro, even though a citizen of a state, could not be a citizen of the United States. In the debate with Douglas (1858) he did not favor Negro voting, but that is not to say that he was opposing any actual movement to establish Negro suffrage; there was no such movement. It is more to the point to note that as the nation's leader he became increasingly liberal and that in the latter part of his presidency he took a more advanced position as to the franchise. Writing on March 13, 1864, to Michael Hahn, governor of Federally occupied Louisiana, he asked "whether some of the colored people may not be let in—as, for instance, the very intelligent, and especially those who have fought gallantly in our ranks. They would probably help, in some trying time to come, to keep the jewel of liberty within the family of freedom." [1]

Often he praised the colored soldiers and emphasized their vitally important contribution to the Union cause. He showed friendliness to the Negro. He wanted him treated as a man. He confessed a sensitiveness on this subject. He could not bear to see Negroes sold at auction, nor strung together "like so many fish upon a trot-line." He argued: "If the negro is a man, why then my ancient faith teaches me that 'all men are created equal,' and that there can be no moral right in connection with one man's making a slave of another." He added: ". . . no man is good enough to govern another man without that other's consent." [2]

The following passage, which seems to have been but slightly quoted, illustrates Lincoln's sympathy for human beings held in bondage:

. . . In those days [i. e., earlier days of the republic] our Declaration of Independence was held sacred by all, and thought to include all; but now, to aid in making the bondage of the negro universal and eternal, it is assailed and sneered at and construed, and hawked at and torn, till, if its framers could rise from their graves, they could not at all recognize

it. All the powers of earth seem rapidly combining against him. Mammon
is after him, ambition follows, philosophy follows, and the theology of
the day is fast joining the cry. They have him in his prison-house; they
have searched his person, and left no prying instrument with him. One
after another they have closed the heavy iron doors upon him; and now
they have him, as it were, bolted in with a lock of a hundred keys, which
can never be unlocked without the concurrence of every key—the keys
in the hands of a hundred different men, and they scattered to a hundred
different and distant places; and they stand musing as to what invention,
in all the dominions of mind and matter, can be produced to make the
impossibility of his escape more complete than it is.[3]

To make Lincoln out as a practical contender for full equality
would be unhistorical, however strong might be the impulse of liberals so to represent him. Very few in his day, in any part of the country,
were contenders for complete equality to be applied in their own
localities. Even Kansas, famous for antislavery emphasis, proved in
many of its laws and social attitudes to be an anti-Negro state. The
Negro suffrage amendment did not come until five years after Lincoln's death; the full observance and implementing of that amendment has never come. There were things Lincoln could do and things
he could not. There was, as he said, the "argument of necessity." [4] On
moral grounds, he favored the ideal of equal rights. He believed that
an ideal, though unrealized at the time, could point the way toward
future reality. He would not deny the humanity of the Negro. He
spoke eloquently of a "sense of justice and human sympathy continually telling you that the poor negro has some natural right to
himself." He spoke in stinging denunciation of "those who deny it
and make mere merchandise of him." [5]

Racial bigotry did not control Lincoln's mind. Slavery was legal in
his day, till by the hand of war and constitutional amendment it was
abolished. Bad laws, he felt, ought to be observed till repealed. Despite many difficulties presented in a slaveholding nation, and in a
Northern society that fell far short in interracial relations, he did
what he could in his own day to elevate the status of the Negro, to
present his case at the bar of humanity, and to urge his claim for sympathy and fair treatment. Lincoln was no Don Quixote. He had to

deal in practical terms. Gradualism was essential in his method. He had elements of conservatism as well as liberalism. Steps to elevate the race could not all be taken at one jump. The country had far to go on that road; it still has far to go. No man of genuine feeling can contemplate without painful emotion the long story of the Negro's ordeal, nor deny to him the credit that attaches to his record as faithful servant and loyal soldier. It is in the Lincoln tradition to give the Negro his just place in American social history and to recognize his values in American folklore and culture. These values appear in a hundred varied forms, from strutting cake walk and hilarious minstrelsy to those deeply melodious spirituals through which, rather than through degrading self pity, the age-long memories of a submerged people find undying expression.

<h1 style="text-align:center">VII</h1>

Elsewhere the author has treated Lincoln and slavery, and that treatment will not be repeated here. Before the presidency his approach was quite different from that of the abolitionist. During the presidency the working of his policy was, or seemed, slow. It did not always seem like kingdom come. It was hedged in by circumstances, by the paramount urgency of the Union, by political factors, constitutional restrictions, congressional non-coöperation, border-state reluctance, regard for Southern property rights, the need for proper timing, military considerations, and attention to the realities of Southern home economy.[1] To some his emancipation proclamation had a ringing, messianic fervor; to others it seemed a terroristic invitation to a war of races (a mistaken concept); to still others it appeared utterly futile.

It is essential for the present purpose to note elements of Lincoln's liberalism in his attitude toward human bondage. He kept saying that slavery was an evil, however much its eradication might be impeded by the Constitution, by state rights, or by the existing state of society. His humane sympathy for the slave was combined with that readiness to understand Southern conditions which was ever his characteristic.[2]

Though he confessed that he found no easy answer to the problem of doing away with slavery,[3] he looked forward to such an answer in the future and in the meantime he wanted to resist its spread. He wanted no slavery in the territories and he wanted Illinois kept free. Recalling that we once considered it "a self-evident truth" that all men are created equal, he deplored the degradation of the public conscience to the point where, having "grown fat," we called "the same maxim 'a self-evident lie' " and made the "Fourth of July . . . a great day —for burning firecrackers." [4]

Frequently he showed that he did not want sectional strife because of slavery—that was not the intention of his house-divided speech [5] —but with equal frequency he showed that in his concept slavery was morally wrong. Tolerant though he was, he wanted no apathetic indifference where moral wrong existed. Though not a hater of men, he said:

This declared indifference . . . for the spread of slavery, I cannot but hate. I hate it because of the monstrous injustice of slavery itself. I hate it because it deprives our republican example of its just influence in the world; enables the enemies of free institutions with plausibility to taunt us as hypocrites; causes the real friends of freedom to doubt our sincerity; and especially because it forces so many good men among ourselves into an open war with the very fundamental principles of civil liberty, criticizing the Declaration of Independence, and insisting that there is no right principle of action but self-interest.[6]

In the same vein, in the year of his nomination for the presidency, he said: "We think slavery a great moral wrong, and while we do not claim the right to touch it where it exists, we wish to treat it as a wrong in the Territories, where our votes will reach it. We think that a respect for ourselves, a regard for future generations and for the God that made us, require that we put down this wrong where our votes will properly reach it. We think that species of labor an injury to free white men—in short, we think slavery a great moral, social, and political evil, tolerable only because, and so far as, its actual existence makes it necessary to tolerate it . . . ." [7]

If he envisaged "irrepressible conflict," it was not that he preached the need of war between North and South, but rather that ideas were in conflict. "Now these two ideas—the property idea that slavery is right and the idea that it is wrong—come into collision, and . . . produce that irrepressible conflict which Mr. Seward has been so roundly abused for mentioning." He added: "Now I don't want to be misunderstood . . . . I don't mean that we ought to attack it where it exists." If he saw a snake in the road he would seize the nearest stick and kill it; but if it were in bed with his children or his neighbor's children, he would be cautious. "If there was a bed newly made up, to which the children were to be taken, and it was proposed to take a batch of snakes and put them there with them, . . . no man would say there was a question how I ought to decide!" [8]

He deplored as fallacious the assumption that " 'In the struggle between the white man and the negro' . . . either the white man must enslave the negro or the negro must enslave the white." This sort of contention he regarded as a misleading catch phrase. "There is no such struggle [he said]. It is merely an ingenious falsehood to degrade and brutalize the negro. . . . This good earth is plenty broad enough for white man and negro both, and there is no need of either pushing the other off." [9]

In the phraseology of the Constitution he noted that references to slavery were "ambiguous, roundabout, and mystical"; never was the institution mentioned directly by the word "slavery" or "slave." Why didn't they use the word? "They expected and desired that the system would come to an end, and meant that when it did the Constitution should not show that there had ever been a slave in this good free country of ours." [10] Historically, the name of Lincoln is the one most prominently associated with the abolition of slavery in the United States. Contemporary limitations and legal complexities of his policy are not commonly understood in the popular mind, but it is with valid and well earned distinction that he remains the Emancipator.

VIII

No problem of modern civilization is more urgent than reorientation of outlook and of policy in the matter of war making. The pledges that have been made in establishing the United Nations, and the principles that have been implemented in the Nuremberg trial, have placed war makers in the category of criminals. In terms of international commitments as they now exist, there is no honorable way by which one nation, by its own unilateral action, may *begin a war*. By principles now solemnly declared there are only two conditions in which one of the United Nations can be honorably at war—by defense against attack, or by action envisaged by the United Nations charter. Such action could legitimately be taken only to check an aggressor. Perhaps the full implications of existing commitments are yet to be realized, but aggressive war, as shown at Nuremberg, is a recognized crime—indeed the highest of crimes.

For this reorientation, and for the revulsion toward war which it involves, one may rightly invoke the spirit and also the words of Lincoln. Nothing was more foreign to his nature than the character of the warlord. He dared to speak out against President Polk for the conduct of his administration at the beginning of the Mexican War. In his Mexican speech he said that "a nation should not, and the Almighty will not, be evaded." As to Polk he said: "he feels the blood of this war, like the blood of Abel, is crying to Heaven against him."

Though many historians would be less severe on Polk, these words of Lincoln may now be seen to have a timeless importance as a denunciation of war itself. It is in this sense that one may now read in this same speech Lincoln's stinging reference to "the exceeding brightness of military glory,—that attractive rainbow that rises in showers of blood—that serpent's eye that charms to destroy." [1] In the *Trent* affair, by reasonable international adjustment instead of warlike truculence, he produced tremendous international as well as American gain. Earlier in that year, 1861, in the July 4 message to Congress, he wrote eloquently that "ballots are the rightful and peaceful successors of bullets." He added, in a context which showed that he was thinking of a world-wide principle, that success in the appeal to ballots instead of bullets would "be a great lesson of peace: teaching men that what they cannot take by an election, neither can they take it by a war; teaching all the folly of being the beginners of a war." [2]

IX

Though primarily interested in popular rights on these shores, Lincoln showed a vigorous sympathy for democracy in other lands. He declared that when he saw a people borne down by tyranny he would do all in his power to raise the yoke. He showed both his lack of isolationism and his sympathy with movements for free institutions in Europe in connection with the Kossuth affair. Here was a question of liberalism abroad which was too hot for the American state department, but it was a subject on which Lincoln did not hesitate to express himself.

Louis Kossuth was a revolutionary leader in Hungary, a defiant opponent of the conservative Metternich, and a spearhead of the movement which culminated in the anti-Hapsburg declaration of Hungarian independence in April of 1849. In September of that year a meeting was held in Springfield, Illinois, to express sympathy for the cause of Hungarian freedom. Lincoln was the spokesman of a committee of four to voice the sentiments of the meeting. The resolutions which he reported extended to the revolting Hungarians "our highest admiration . . . our warmest sympathy . . . [and] our most ardent prayers for their speedy triumph and final success." [1] Success did not come. In that mid-century period liberal revolutionary aims were aflame in many parts of Europe, but they were quenched and reaction lived on. Had these aims succeeded as Lincoln hoped—had Austria-Hungary and the German states (to mention examples) been able to use and encourage, instead of ruthlessly suppressing, their democratic-minded elements—a colossal amount of future grief would have been avoided. Lincoln was no specialist on European matters, but there was more than localism and nationalism in the wide reach of his democratic thought.

In writing a eulogy a man may give a key to his own sentiments. If one is studying Lincoln's thought and faith he cannot ignore the elaborate eulogy of Henry Clay which he delivered in the Illinois state house in 1852. There is much of Lincoln's own ideal in the following statement:

Mr. Clay's predominant sentiment, from first to last, was a deep devotion to the cause of human liberty—a strong sympathy for the oppressed everywhere, and an ardent wish for their elevation. With him this was a primary and all-controlling passion. Subsidiary to this was the conduct of his whole life. He loved his country partly because it was his own country, and mostly because it was a free country; . . . he burned with a zeal for its advancement . . . because he saw in such the advancement, prosperity, and glory of human liberty, human right, and human nature. He desired the prosperity of his countrymen . . . chiefly to show to the world that free men could be prosperous.

.   .   .   .

Mr. Clay's efforts in behalf of the South Americans, and afterward in behalf of the Greeks, in the times of their respective struggles for civil liberty, are among the finest on record, upon the noblest of all themes, and bear ample corroboration of what I have said was his ruling passion —a love of liberty and right, unselfishly, and for their own sakes.[2]

It is obvious that no man could have uttered those words with such a glow of enthusiasm and with such genuine appreciation unless he himself had been a man of liberal views. If in that period Lincoln had been conservatively apathetic toward human liberty in other lands, his eulogy of Henry Clay would either have omitted such a passage entirely or he would have presented it without enlisting his own ardor and with less emotional emphasis.

When Lincoln thought of self-government he thought not alone of America, but of the human race. In a passage of unusual literary embellishment he referred to "our political revolution of '76" as having "given us a degree of political freedom far exceeding that of any other nation of the earth." "In it," he said, "the world has found a solution of the long-mooted problem as to the capability of man to govern himself. In it was the germ which has vegetated, and still is to grow . . . into the universal liberty of mankind."[3] In speaking of temperance he hailed it as "a noble ally . . . to the cause of political freedom; with such an aid its march cannot fail to be on and on, till every son of earth shall drink in rich fruition the sorrow-quenching draughts of perfect liberty." He linked the factor of moral self-control with governmental self-rule. "How nobly distinguished that people who shall have planted and nurtured to maturity both the political and moral freedom of their species." In eulogizing Washington he spoke of the might of his name "in the cause of civil liberty, . . . [and] in moral reformation." [4] His bond of sympathy for John Bright, treated in another essay, shows that his view of democracy was international, not nationalistic; cosmopolitan, not provincial.

This world view as to democracy was so strongly underlined by Lincoln that it is fair to regard it as the pivotal factor in his political philosophy. At Gettysburg, with the ghastliness of the war before his eyes and with the butchery still in progress, he spoke not of immediate issues or war problems; nor did he show even a trace of bitterness. The Gettysburg occasion as he viewed it was a high challenge. To meet this challenge, nothing less would serve than a concept so fundamental that it offered a key to the age in which he lived, or rather to the whole sweep of American history in a setting of world history. It was the exaltation of the theme—democracy as a world factor—that gave serenity and timeless significance to this dedicatory vignette. In phrases that were unforgettable he paid tribute to the dead. Then he associated the deepest of patriotic emotions with his dominant political idea—that is, the imperative obligation to make democracy succeed and thus prove to other nations that the American experiment of government by the people is no failure.

Early in the war he said to John Hay that he considered that to be the central idea in the struggle—"the necessity that is upon us, of proving that popular government is not an absurdity." [5] Addressing Congress on July 4, 1861, he pointed out that the issue "embraces more than the fate of these United States." It was, he said, a question of concern "to the whole family of man." [6] With an eye to that larger meaning he wrote to Congress, December 1, 1862: ". . . we cannot escape history. We . . . will be remembered in spite of ourselves. . . . In giving freedom to the slave, we assure freedom to the free . . . . We shall nobly save or meanly lose the last, best hope of earth." [7]

X

Lincoln had rough sailing in his administration. He had a war to wage on a tremendous scale, with inadequate equipment and faulty organization. More than that, he had a mission to perform—not only to lead a nation to victory at arms, not only to save the Union cause, but to shape that cause in terms of adequate ideals and human values. He did not end with ingrowing thoughts of America. He looked to far horizons. Substantially to advance the cause of free government in the world was his fundamental goal.

In struggling toward this goal he had to endure inefficiency, factional bickering, repeated Union defeat, shameful greed and profiteering, defection behind the lines, and alarming division within his own party. There were times when the military machine, because of the inefficiency of central army control at Washington, almost broke down. His cabinet was an ill-assorted group of men who distrusted each other and were targets of constant attack by Congress or the newspapers.

We think of Lincoln rising to meet the fearful responsibilities of state, and that he did; but a typical picture of the time would show him trying unsuccessfully to dodge a horde of office seekers crowding through his door or waylaying him on the street. It is hard to see how he found time for his larger duties, considering the unending pressure of those who wanted a high judicial office, but who might be willing to serve their country as deputy collector or second assistant paymaster. Military men brought him not merely their problems, but also their petty jealousies. If he told Secretary Stanton to do a thing, it might be that the secretary would do the opposite, or perhaps nothing at all. Lincoln is said to have remarked that he had "not much influence with this administration," [1] meaning his own. Whether or not he said it, the statement had significance. He had to endure the intrigues of cabinet members, and the interference of congressmen whose committee on the conduct of the war was a factor in Union failure and an instrument of inquisitorial abuse.[2]

In meeting these conditions Lincoln became a practitioner of government as a human art. He somehow held his cabinet together. He had a way with governors. In 1862 it might almost have been said that the governors "ganged up" on him. There was a conclave of state executives whose purpose was to criticize and perhaps to do something worse. Some of the papers referred to it as a conspiracy to force the President to resign. The governors met at Altoona, then in Washington; but they found it was Lincoln who held the trumps.[3] They came to assail him, but the interview was so managed that it left Lincoln in command. He had a way with senators. He did not have their coöperation, but he avoided an explosion. A group of Republican senators descended upon him in December 1862 breathing threats; but by shrewdness and tact he turned this senatorial upheaval into a triumph of presidential prestige.[4] He had a way with visiting delegations. He would listen, or perhaps he himself would do the talking, he would tell an amusing story, would bow them out, and act on his own larger judgment. In an age of confusion he kept a clear head. He took the broader view. He saw enduring values, was impatient of unenlightened politics, and refused to surrender to cynicism.

Undoubtedly an important element in Lincoln's statesmanship was mastery of language. Somewhere back in early self-training there was a study of the forms and substance of speech not for their own sake, not just to win applause, but because Lincoln had an object to accomplish, a message to convey, and he realized the effectiveness of the written and spoken word in reaching and controlling men's minds. With Lincoln as with Woodrow Wilson the art of language was a means to an end. In stating a law case, Lincoln had a knack of brushing away technicalities and getting at the core of the subject. Few men could match him in the prairie years as a stump speaker. The people delighted to hear him. Most of the speeches common in his day were rhetorical and florid after the manner of Sumner; they were one with the fashion plates which showed elaborately dressed women and grandiloquently attired men. But Lincoln's speech was not like the Godey fashion plate; it had little in common with Sumner's rhetoric. There was in his diction something suggestive of the King James version of the Bible, something also of Shakespeare, and much that was just Lincoln. What made him a master of words was fitness to the occasion, a readiness of epigram, a cogency of speech that served well in place of adornment, a sense as to how adornment itself should be used, and the ability to take the simplest words and give them the greatness of inspired dignity.

At his second inaugural he made no effort to review the events of his administration, but delivered a brief address which ranks among his greatest papers. He refused to blame the South for the war, and counseled his countrymen to judge not that we be not judged. "With malice toward none"; he said, "with charity for all; . . . let us strive on to finish the work we are in; to bind up the nation's wounds; . . . to do all which may achieve and cherish a just and lasting peace . . . ." In the cacophony of war the note he struck was that of conciliation, of friendliness, of peace and charity. He avoided the language of contemporary preachers, but in his life and utterance he gave sincere expression and devotion to the Christian faith.

He could turn a trick by a good humored story. Your self-important soul, or your strutting dictator, does not often smile. In Lincoln the priceless element of humor was an index to the shape and quality of his mind. To his overburdened spirit,—amid strain and fatigue so overwhelming that, as he said, the remedy "seemed never to reach the tired spot" [5]—laughter was a saving blend of play, restorative relaxation, and mental hygiene. It supplied a sense of proportion. At times it was a refreshing pause. On a very solemn occasion in cabinet meeting when the emancipation proclamation was coming up, he got a big laugh out of Artemus Ward, much to the disgust of his humorless secretaries.[6] He liked Petroleum V. Nasby (David Locke). His humor was down to earth, yet in point and originality it was above the level of his time. His stories, verbal sallies, and quips of expression are a rich part of the American tradition. In treating Lincoln's laughter alongside his religion, Carl Sandburg shows that, in enjoying fun, he was no mere joker or buffoon. The man of backwoods pioneer origin must have courage, and humor is part of that courage. "This side of him [writes Sandburg] was momentous in one respect at least. It had brought him to folk masses as a reality, a living man . . . . Did he truly have something of the cartooned figure of Uncle Sam, benign, sagacious, practical, simple, at times not quite beyond taking a real laugh for himself and the country? Whatever the elements of this trait, it rested on American material, connected with an immense variety of American circumstances and incidents, and had become inevitably associated with Lincoln's name and personality." [7]

Lincoln's greatness arose from a combination of qualities in a balanced personality. One could never define his conduct as springing from mere automatic reaction. It came rather from informed study and mature reflection. Mere slogans and stereotypes did not impress him. He was a simple man—he was unpretentious in manner and straightforward in expression—but he was never naïve. He could be enthusiastic, but he was never extravagant. He combined humanitarianism with practical common sense. He attained a position of lofty eminence and moved among the great without making other men feel small. He was a sturdy individual; this, however, should be understood not as a denial of needful social coöperation, but rather in the Robert Burns sense of emphasis upon human worth. He could assert himself without becoming a dictator. He had ambition, but without selfishness. He had that largeness of soul that we call magnanimity. If a colleague, a subordinate, or a cabinet member were attacked, he would take the blame upon his own shoulders. Sometimes he would write a letter as an outlet for overwrought feeling, think it over, realize that it might wound the recipient, and then withhold it.

He encouraged the North without abusing the South. Though a war leader he wanted no perpetuation of war attitudes in peace time. He opposed the abuses of militarism. It is of present significance that in 1848 he had uttered a crushing denunciation of what would now be called "preventive war." [8] The "war mind" never possessed him. His main feeling toward the war was deep regret that the avoidable tragedy had happened, a sense of mystery as to the ways of Providence, a realization that the scourge was as much a punishment of the North as of the South. He wanted the war to end with the surrenders. As the men after Appomattox went back to their plowing, he wanted healing and restoration. Coarser men took the saddle and Lincoln's plan of reconstruction was defeated, but Lincoln would have brought the South back if possible without bitterness and without treating Southerners as inferiors.

The Lincoln record is no mere success story of a railsplitter who became President, a prairie lawyer who reached world fame. One might wonder just how he became to the majority of his countrymen the embodiment of the American genius. Perhaps the inner source of his strength has not been fully plumbed. It might be hard to answer where and how he learned statecraft, but statesmen even yet will do well to take him as guide and mentor. In each new recurring crisis—in colossal wars that have shaken the world—men continue to carry the appeal to the spirit of Lincoln. Only in poetry does his ghost stalk at midnight, but his inspired words and the rugged vigor of his ideals seem today to have a greater vitality than during the vexed years of his presidency.

ANNOTATIONS

I. MOOT POINTS IN THE LINCOLN STORY

Page

1   [1] Washington's advice that we avoid questions that are specifically European was by no means a counsel of isolation or a warning that we should not deal with European countries on matters common to Europe and ourselves. In "George Washington and 'Entangling Alliances,'" *So. Atl. Quar.*, XXX, 221–229 (1931), the present author has attempted briefly to show how, along with the misrepresentation of Washington, pernicious and irrational inferences have appeared voluminously in editorials, commentaries, cartoons, politicians' speeches, and the like.

2   [2] Elsewhere the author has discussed "The Historian as Revisionist." *Ind. Hist. Bulletin*, XV, 90–101 (1938).

2   [3] W. H. Hoyt, *The Mecklenburg Declaration of Independence.*

2   [4] "Journal of a French Traveller in the Colonies, 1765," *Amer. Hist. Rev.*, XXVI, 726–747 (1921), especially pp. 726–729, 745.

2   [5] *Lincoln the President: Springfield to Gettysburg*, I, preface; "The Historian as Revisionist," cited above.

3   [1] We have the following recollection by Noah Brooks on the subject of rail-splitting: "We were once talking about woodcraft, and the President said that, although he had had undue credit for rail-splitting, he did know how to fell a tree . . . . He said that he did not remember splitting many rails in his life. In fact, rail-fences were not in his line at all . . . ." *Washington in Lincoln's Time*, 303. It is sometimes supposed that Lincoln identified and authenticated certain rails as having been split by himself; the occasion was the state Republican convention at Decatur, May 9, 1860. That is what he avoided doing. Paul M. Angle, *Lincoln, 1854–1861*, 332.

3   [2] John G. Nicolay and John Hay, eds., *Complete Works of Abraham Lincoln*, I, 262. Hereafter cited as *Works*.

4   [3] Arno B. Reincke, *He Could Take It! Best Wishes for the New Year 1934.* In this booklet an advertising man showed how the example of Lincoln cheered a friend in depression days. Reprinted at various times. See *Reader's Digest*, Jan. 1939. For variants, see Jay Monaghan, *Lincoln Bibliography, 1839–1939*, II, 339 (no. 3451).

4   [4] Harry E. Pratt, *The Personal Finances of Abraham Lincoln.*

5   [5] Harry E. Pratt, "Lincoln's [Illinois] Supreme Court Cases," *Illinois Bar Journal*, XXXII, 23–35 (1943).

207

5   6 For interesting details in the reaper case, including the incredible snub-
bing that Lincoln received by men whom he considered fellow counsel (particularly Stanton), see Robert Henry Parkinson, "The Patent Case that
Lifted Lincoln into a Presidential Candidate," *Abr. Lincoln Quar.*, IV, 105–
122 (Sep. 1946). For a general account of the well known episode see Beveridge, *Abraham Lincoln*, I, 575 ff.

5   1 The Ann Rutledge subject is treated critically, with full documentation,
in *Lincoln the President*, II, 321–342.

6   2 Interview of William H. Herndon with Isaac Cogdal, no date, Herndon-
Weik Collection, Lib. of Cong.

6   3 *Mark Twain's Autobiography*, with an introduction by Albert Bigelow
Paine, I, 2.

7   4 In a forthcoming book Mr. David Donald, research associate of the University of Illinois and former fellow of the Social Science Research Council,
will present a thorough and significant study of Herndon as a man, partner,
and biographer.

8   5 Herndon underlined the following statement: *"Mrs. Lincoln's domestic
quarrels in my opinion sprang from a woman's revenge which she was not
strong enough to resist."* (Nothing is said here about marrying her husband
for revenge; indeed the revenge *motif* is a bit vague.) Herndon to Charles H.
Hart, Nov. 26, 1866, Hart MSS., Henry E. Huntington Lib.

8   6 *Herndon's Life of Lincoln*, with introduction and notes by Paul M. Angle,
182. Space is lacking for a disquisition on Herndon's interpretation or theo-
rizing concerning Mrs. Lincoln's motives toward her husband. Referring to
"that fatal New Years Day in 1841," he wrote: "Love fled at the approach of
revenge" (*ibid.*, 182). The evidence on the broken engagement (not a bride-
groom's absence on a wedding night) is none too revealing as to Mary's feelings, but such evidence as we have does not support the idea that her attitude was that of revengeful bitterness.

8   7 *Ibid.*, 350.

9   8 *Ibid.*, 350. Herndon is quoting a letter written to him by Mary Owens
Vineyard, for which he gives the date of May 22, 1866; the copy in the
Lamon MSS., Huntington Library, gives May 23, 1866. For Mary Owens,
see *Lincoln's Other Mary*, by Olive Carruthers, appendix by R. Gerald Mc-
Murtry. The main body of this book gives the story in novel form; the ap-
pendix supplies the documents.

9   9 A. Lincoln to "Dear Mary," Washington, April 16, 1848, original MS.
owned by Oliver R. Barrett, Chicago. See *Lincoln the President*, I, between
pp. 72 and 73. For Mary's letter to "My Dear Husband," Lexington, Ky.,
May 1848 (significant for its glimpses of a normally and happily wedded
pair), see Sandburg and Angle, *Mary Lincoln, Wife and Widow*, 188–190.

10   10 John E. Washington, *They Knew Lincoln*. Faithful research (especially
concerning Mrs. Keckley), and interviews with lowly people who had something to transmit but otherwise no historian to hear, give value to this book
as a matter of record. Beyond all this is an indefinable overtone—a quality
akin to folklore, an unstudied, emotional eloquence with the lilt and pathos
of a Negro spiritual. In the introduction Carl Sandburg writes: "So we have
verities, myths, ghosts, dreams, fantasies, adorations. White House servants,

Page

waiters, doorkeepers, the barbers William Johnson and Solomon Johnson, who shaved Lincoln in Washington, and the barber William Fleurville, who shaved Lincoln in Springfield, they come alive and real . . . ."

10   [11] Mary Todd Lincoln to Mrs. Albert S. White, Chicago, May 2, 1868. Sandburg and Angle, *Mary Lincoln, Wife and Widow*, 281.

10   [12] For a study that is a combination of the medical and historical, see William A. Evans, *Mrs. Abraham Lincoln: A Study of Her Personality and Her Influence on Lincoln*.

11   [13] Mary Lincoln to Noah Brooks, Chicago, May 11, 1866. Noah Brooks, *Washington in Lincoln's Time*, 124.

12   [1] E. E. Sparks, ed., *The Lincoln-Douglas Debates of 1858* (Ill. Hist. Coll., III), 161. In referring to Sparks, here and elsewhere in this book, the printing used is that of the Illinois State Journal Company of Springfield. If one uses the printing by the University of Chicago Press, a slightly different pagination will be found at many points. For a scholarly analysis of these variants, see the article by Marion Dolores Bonzi, in *Abr. Lincoln Quar.*, IV, 140–144 (1946).

13   [2] It is always a question how far an author can go in following the labyrinthine avenues of Supreme Court pronouncements, or vagaries, in the Dred Scott decision. It is usually assumed that the Court's doctrine and reasoning opposed only the kind of law that Lincoln favored (though Republican congressmen did not vote for the Lincolnian type of law in 1861). It should be added that the trend of Taney's reasoning—that slavery ought to be federally protected in the national territories—was also, as a matter of theory, opposed to the Douglas type of law—i. e., the Kansas-Nebraska act, by which a territorial legislature could have prohibited slavery. Yet Taney did not go all the way with his own peculiar reasoning. If a particular statute or part of a statute is declared unconstitutional, that must be done specifically, and Taney did not say that the Kansas-Nebraska act of 1854 was unconstitutional. There was point in Douglas's saying that the Supreme Court doctrine was "abstract" so far as application to an existing statute was concerned. It declared the Missouri compromise act of 1820 unconstitutional, but that act had been repealed. It did not overthrow the existing national law as to slavery in the territories (that of 1854) under which slavery could be voted up or down by a territorial legislature. That law continued until Congress, ignoring the Supreme Court's doctrine, abolished slavery in the territories in 1862. The Dred Scott decision does not stand forth in history as a shining example of judicial review. Among constitutional authorities today it would be hard to find those who would justify it.

14   [3] *Lincoln the President*, I, 185–186, 375–379.

14   [1] Albert J. Beveridge, *Abraham Lincoln, 1809–1858*, II, 80.

15   [2] One does not need to quote enemies of abolition here, and that enmity is not the sense in which the present author wishes his statements to be understood. Contemporary lack of enthusiasm for abolition is shown clearly enough by competent scholars friendly to the humanitarian motives of the crusade but aware of history. When abolitionists first demanded immediate emancipation they meant "immediate emancipation, gradually accomplished," but the public understanding was that they favored an immediate

Page

program "by which the slaves are to be turned loose without any restraint whatever." Thus they were credited, or blamed, for more of radicalism than they intended. Non-Garrisonian abolitionists suffered from the "unfortunate repute" of that sincere but distrusted agitator. As for Garrison himself, it should be remembered that the "reputation of the *Liberator* was made by its enemies and not by its subscribers." Its subscribers were few. It was mailed to an "exchange list" of periodicals. The Northern ones mostly "ignored the paper"; "Southern editors, with slaveholding constituencies already 'in a state of phrensy' . . . , quoted it with enthusiasm." This was the easier because Garrison's editorial style was "supremely quotable," though made up of "rancorous denunciations and brawling, ferocious abuse." "Burdened with the epithet of 'Garrisonism' and crippled by its misunderstood motto of immediatism, the [antislavery] society made small progress among the antislavery public of the North." Gilbert H. Barnes and Dwight L. Dumond, eds., *Weld-Grimké Letters*, intro., I, vii–viii.

17   ³ Lincoln added: ". . . Judge Douglas has heard me say it . . . as good as a hundred times; and when it is said that I am in favor of interfering with slavery where it exists, I know it is unwarranted by anything I have ever intended, and, as I believe, by anything I have ever said." *Works*, III, 34 (speech at Chicago, July 10, 1858).

17   ¹ Chauncey S. Boucher, "*In Re* That Aggressive Slaveocracy," *Miss. Vall. Hist. Rev.*, VIII, 13–79 (1921).

17   ² Having mentioned that he became of age about the time the Free Soil party was born, and believing the Republican organization to be the continuation of that earlier party, Hoar wrote: "In a very humble capacity I stood by its cradle. It awakened in my heart in early youth all the enthusiasm of which my nature was capable, . . . which from that day to this has never grown cold." George F. Hoar, *Autobiography of Seventy Years*, I, 132.

18   ³ *Ibid.*, I, 131.

18   ⁴ "The concept of natural rights was still important in nineteenth century thought, but Weed had no interest in it as a basis for argument on behalf of Negroes, foreigners, or anyone else. Neither was he one . . . to tempt popular wrath merely for the sake of a moral precept. His first reaction to Seward's 'higher law' and 'irrepressible conflict' speeches was one of criticism, . . . for it was his obvious conviction that they were not good politics. He never saw the wisdom of Lincoln's emancipation policy, and he believed that black-white equality was forbidden 'by laws higher even than political constitutions.' " Glyndon G. Van Deusen, "Thurlow Weed: A Character Study," *Amer. Hist. Rev.*, XLIX, 435 (1944). See also *Thurlow Weed: Wizard of the Lobby* (1947), by Mr. Van Deusen.

18   ⁵ In *The First Lincoln Campaign* Reinhard H. Luthin has shown the diverse appeals by which Republicans made their drives for votes in different states or localities. "Minnesota [he writes] was more concerned over free land than slavery" (p. 116). "In Pennsylvania and New Jersey the issue was the tariff" (p. 221). Thus the principle of opposition to the spread of slavery in the territories was not everywhere stressed, though it was emphasized in parts of New England and of the Northwest. Other items in the Republican assortment were temperance, "Americanism" (with its emphasis upon racial su-

periority and inequality), opposition to Catholicism, prejudice against immigrants, the Pacific railway, the overland mail, and in California "the personal feud between Senators Gwin and Broderick over patronage" (pp. 220–221).

19   6 *Cong. Globe,* 36 Cong., 2 sess., 1003 (Feb. 18, 1861).

19   7 *Ibid.,* 1005.

19   8 Blaine, *Twenty Years of Congress,* I, 271–272.

20   9 Samuel S. Cox, *Eight Years in Congress, from 1857 to 1865,* 204, 206.

20   10 Joshua Giddings to Charles Sumner, Dec. 3, 1860, Sumner MSS., Harvard Univ.

20   11 Salmon P. Chase to Governor John A. Andrew, Jan. 26, 1861, Andrew MSS., Mass. Hist. Soc.

21   12 For Lincoln's reference to Stephen, Franklin, Roger, and James (Douglas, Pierce, Taney, and Buchanan) as if there had been a deep laid plot concocted by these four men, see *Lincoln the President,* I, 106–108.

21   13 E. E. Sparks, ed., *Lincoln-Douglas Debates,* 163, 164.

21   14 *Lincoln the President,* I, 228–230.

22   15 Sparks, *Lincoln-Douglas Debates,* 149–152, 159 ff.

22   16 *Lincoln the President,* I, 113. One of the least inspiring aspects of the contest of 1858 was the relation of Illinois Republicans to that faction of the Illinois Democrats which supported Buchanan, with his proslavery tendency, and which savagely opposed Douglas. To remember this bit of "practical" politics is to take away much of the aura that might attach to the Republican opposition to slavery. However much an enthusiast might wish to show that Lincoln was unconnected with these maneuvers, the evidence points the other way. One need not quibble as to whether there was any formal "alliance," which Lincoln denied, but it is known that the Republicans and the Buchananites worked together. Harry E. Pratt writes: ". . . he [Lincoln] had at least three conferences with John Dougherty, the Buchanan candidate for State Treasurer and leader of the party in the State. At these meetings they mapped out the strategy of the campaign against . . . Douglas." (Pratt, *Concerning Mr. Lincoln,* 12.) Lincoln's partner, Herndon, writing to Trumbull, July 8, 1858 (*ibid.,* 13–15) mentioned a conversation of Lincoln with Dougherty. Reporting what Lincoln said to him, Herndon wrote: "He [Dougherty] told Lincoln that the National Democracy [i. e., the Buchanan faction] intended 'to run in every county and district a National Democrat for each and every office.' Lincoln replied to this by saying—'If you do this the thing is settled—the battle is fought.' This you may depend on. The National Democrats are fighting . . . on the sly . . . ." See also George Fort Milton, *The Eve of Conflict: Stephen A. Douglas and the Needless War,* 302, 345.

23   1 "For all classes of laborers—men, women, and children—public opinion [in the North, particularly in New England] approved the 'sun to sun' system of labor. . . . long hours were the rule, leisure was little appreciated, and health was sacrified . . . ." (Helen L. Sumner, in John R. Commons, ed., *History of Labor in the United States,* I, 174.) In return, the Northern worker received "usually but a frugal existence with no provision whatever for possible misfortune" (A. C. Cole, *The Irrepressible Conflict,* 150). Com-

paring working conditions in the North and South, a Boston minister concluded that the slave received wages "in a better form"—that is, "in provision for . . . support for the whole of life, [and] with permission to earn something . . . according to the disposition of the masters and the ability of the slaves"—than did his Northern free counterpart. (Nehemiah Adams, *A South-Side View of Slavery . . . in 1854*, 51.) From the same data George Fitzhugh, pro-Southern sociologist, argued that "capitalists, in free society, live in ten times the luxury . . . that Southern masters do, because the slaves to capital work harder and cost less, than negro slaves." (*Cannibals All! or, Slaves without Masters*, 29.) These considerations and viewpoints were parts of the contemporary scene. Of course they are not offered as a defense or in any way a justification of slavery, but slavery was not the only deplorable condition that existed in American society. Fitzhugh, who was an apologist for the slaveholding class, is by no means presented here as one who gave a fully rounded picture. The point is rather that as to Northern factories there were actual conditions which were properly the targets of social criticism. See Harvey Wish, *George Fitzhugh: Propagandist of the Old South.*

23 [2] Dwight L. Dumond, *The Secession Movement, 1860–1861*, 116.

24 [3] Howard C. Perkins, ed., *Northern Editorials on Secession*, I, 31.

24 [4] *Ibid.*, I, 54.

24 [5] *Ibid.*, I, 119.

24 [6] Charles W. Ramsdell, "The Natural Limits of Slavery Expansion," *Miss. Vall. Hist. Rev.*, XVI, 168, 171 (1929).

25 [7] A. C. Cole, in *Amer. Hist. Rev.*, XXXVI, 767 (1931).

25 [1] Recent careful scholars have placed less emphasis upon Garrison, whose actual following was slight, and more upon those who promoted the movement, again without large influence, on the western front. Arthur and Lewis Tappan, Theodore Dwight Weld, Angelina Grimké Weld, Sarah Grimké, Charles G. Finney, and the "Lane rebels," have received special attention. The "Lane rebels" were a group of students at Lane Seminary, Cincinnati, whose antislavery society publicly denounced slavery and urged the elevation of the colored race. They were viewed as dangerous agitators and their organization was abolished by the Seminary trustees. In the vast literature concerning abolitionism the following titles are representative of recent scholarship: G. H. Barnes, *The Antislavery Impulse, 1830–1844*; Dwight L. Dumond, *Antislavery Origins of the Civil War in the United States*; G. H. Barnes and D. L. Dumond, eds., *Letters of Theodore Dwight Weld . . .* [etc.]; D. L. Dumond, ed., *Letters of James Gillespie Birney, 1831–1857*; Avery Craven, *The Coming of the Civil War* (chap. vi); Robert P. Ludlum, "Joshua R. Giddings, Radical," *Miss. Vall. Hist. Rev.*, XXIII, 49–60 (1936). The sympathetic biography of Theodore Parker by Henry Steele Commager should be noted; also the critical work of James C. Malin in analyzing the John Brown legend. One can gain an insight into the sources for abolition by studying the voluminous notes in Barnes's *Antislavery Impulse.* The Boston Public Library contains a notable collection of antislavery manuscripts.

27 [2] Lincoln did not consider the Civil War "inevitable." See p. 116.

Page
27   ¹ Definition of "rebels," or interpretation as to rebellious status applying to Southerners in particular legal situations, is too complicated for treatment here. Many pages would be needed to present all the complexities and contradictions to be found in governmental attitudes and court pronouncements. On the one hand it was held that insurrection and war do not loose the bonds of society and that ordinary acts of Southern states for maintaining police regulations, punishing crime, etc., were binding upon the people of those states. On the other hand the United States Court of Claims ruled, in connection with postwar Southern claims for restoration of captured property, that residence in an insurrectionary district was *prima facie* evidence of a rebellious character; the claimant would have to prove loyalty for the whole period of the war; the burden of proving disloyalty did not rest upon the government. *Constitutional Problems Under Lincoln*, 237–238, 336. On the effect of pardon in this connection, see *ibid.*, 338–340. Full documentation on this subject—Union rulings as to the status of Southerners—would require voluminous citation. See *Civil War and Reconstruction*, 372, 482 n.; *House Report No. 262*, 43 Cong., 1 sess., 6 ff.

27   ² The author has treated these acts of Congress elsewhere. *Constitutional Problems Under Lincoln*, 357–365; *Lincoln the President: Springfield to Gettysburg*, II, 131–137; *The Civil War and Reconstruction*, 480 ff.

28   ³ Alexander H. Stephens, *A Constitutional View of the Late War Between the States*, II, 611.

29   ⁴ "His [Lincoln's] own opinion was, that as the Proclamation was a *war measure*, and would have effect only from its being an exercise of the war power, as soon as the war ceased, it would be inoperative for the future. . . . So far as he was concerned, he should leave it to the Courts to decide." Lincoln's oral statement at the Hampton Roads Conference, February 1865, is thus recorded by Alexander H. Stephens (*War Between the States*, II, 611). See also *Lincoln and the South*, 98–99, where it is shown that Lincoln contemplated the possibility that his emancipation proclamation might be "declared void by . . . the Supreme Court."

29   ⁵ Lincoln made this proposal to his cabinet, seeking their approval of a recommendation he wished to make to Congress. Not only as to financial compensation to slaveholders, but as to other matters—reduction of the armies, pardon, restoration of property, and general executive liberality—he showed a generous policy for ending the war. On the manuscript containing his proposal he wrote the endorsement: "February 5, 1865. To-day these papers . . . were drawn up and submitted to the Cabinet and unanimously disapproved by them. A. Lincoln." Nicolay and Hay, *Lincoln*, X, 133–137. According to John P. Usher, secretary of the interior, as quoted by Nicolay and Hay (*ibid.*, X, 136), the President noted that the war was costing three millions a day "besides all the lives," and showed deep disappointment at the cabinet rejection of his generous proposal.

29   ⁶ Stephens, *War Between the States*, II, 617.

30   ¹ Paul M. Angle, *A Shelf of Lincoln Books*, 66.

30   ² Louis A. Warren, *Lincoln's Parentage and Childhood*. "He [Warren] showed that in the thirty-four years of Thomas Lincoln's residence in Kentucky there was 'not one black mark against his name,' that he was a sober

Page

citizen of good repute . . . , and that the childhood environment of his son was not a squalid one." Angle, *A Shelf of Lincoln Books*, 69.

30 ³ An example of inventing statements and putting them into Lincoln's mouth is his alleged declaration concerning steel rails. In October of 1936 he was quoted by a political leader as follows: "If we buy steel rails from foreigners, they have the money and we have the rails, but if we buy steel rails here, we have both the money and the rails." There are three defects in that so-called quotation. (1) Lincoln did not say those words. (2) The first Bessemer plant in the United States was erected in 1867, two years after Lincoln's death. Modern steel production in this country dates from that year. (3) The statement shows a misunderstanding of international trade. If we buy certain things from abroad, these imports will stimulate a foreign market for American raw materials and manufactured goods. International trade is a two-way street. No country as great as the United States can remain economically isolated. New York *Times*, Oct. 9, 1936, p. 20, c. 7; J. M. Camp and C. B. Francis, *The Making . . . of Steel* (4th ed., Pittsburgh, 1925), 263; F. W. Taussig, "Abraham Lincoln on the Tariff: A Myth," *Quar. Jour. of Economics*, XXVIII, 814–820 (1914).

30 ⁴ The *Day-by-Day* volumes are as follows: Harry E. Pratt, *Lincoln, 1809–1839;* Harry E. Pratt, *Lincoln, 1840–1846;* Benjamin P. Thomas, *Lincoln, 1847–1853;* Paul M. Angle, *Lincoln, 1854–1861.* The usefulness of these books, with their excellent introductions and complete coverage of Lincoln's whereabouts (within the limits of historical knowledge) is familiar to Lincoln scholars. They cover the whole of Lincoln's life except the presidency. The preparation and publication of these studies is an example of the valuable work done by the Abraham Lincoln Association of Springfield, Illinois.

30 ⁵ Angle, *Shelf of Lincoln Books*, 5. For a one-volume selection of Lincoln's works presented with illuminating comment and high editorial competence, see *Abraham Lincoln: His Speeches and Writings,* edited by Roy P. Basler. In this edition there has been great care to obtain faithfulness to the originals, where available. In view of the defects and incompleteness of the Nicolay-Hay edition and the advance of Lincoln scholarship, it is of interest to know that at present the Abraham Lincoln Association of Springfield is preparing a new edition of the works of Lincoln. It will be some years before this ambitious project is completed.

30 ⁶ Angle, *A Shelf of Lincoln Books*, 8–9.

30 ⁷ In a letter to Nicolay, John Hay wrote, as to McClellan: "It is of the utmost moment that we should *seem* fair to him, while we are destroying him." Quoted in Tyler Dennett, *John Hay: From Poetry to Politics,* 139. For the unfairness of the Nicolay-Hay treatment of John A. Campbell in his postwar role, see *Lincoln and the South,* 130–132. One could mention many other examples to show the slanted interpretation of these biographers.

31 ⁸ Quoted in Angle, *Shelf of Lincoln Books*, 43.

31 ⁹ "The most disagreeable thing about him [Stanton] was the extreme virulence with which he abused the President, the administration, and the Republican party. . . . He never spoke of the President in any other way than as 'the original gorilla,' . . ." *McClellan's Own Story,* 152. Stanton's letters to Buchanan in 1861 (MSS., Hist. Soc. of Pa.) confirm this statement.

Page

The more one studies Stanton the more he realizes his antagonism to the things for which Lincoln stood.

31   [10] *Lincoln the President*, II, 112–113.

31   [11] "The Diary of a Public Man: Unpublished Passages of the Secret History of the American Civil War," *No. Am. Rev.*, vol. 129, pp. 125–140, 259–273, 375–388, 484–496 (1879). For an excellent critical edition see *The Diary of a Public Man . . .* , prefatory notes by F. Lauriston Bullard, foreword by Carl Sandburg (privately printed, Abraham Lincoln Book Shop, Chicago, 1945).

32   [12] A full-length biography of Benjamin F. Butler is being prepared by Professor Louis Taylor Merrill of Beloit College. On the relation of Butler to the vice-presidential nomination in 1864, see Professor Merrill's article in the *Miss. Vall. Hist. Rev.*, Mar., 1947.

32   [13] For a competent, detailed, critical treatment of the many baffling problems concerning the Bixby letter, see *Abraham Lincoln and the Widow Bixby*, by F. Lauriston Bullard. This excellent study illustrates the notable progress of Lincoln research in recent times.

33   [14] William E. Barton, *A Beautiful Blunder: The True Story of Lincoln's Letter to Mrs. Lydia A. Bixby*. The "blunder" was that faulty army records as to the Bixby boys were transmitted to Lincoln. The letter, though occasioned by these records, has validity aside from them.

33   [15] In "An Analysis of Lincoln's Funeral Sermons," by Jay Monaghan, *Ind. Mag. of Hist.*, XLI, 31–44 (1945), one finds a survey of over four hundred printed sermons on the occasion of the assassination. The emphasis in most of these sermons was upon vengeance and hatred.

34   [16] J. G. Randall, "Lincoln in the Rôle of Dictator," *So. Atl. Quar.*, XXVIII, 236–252 (1929).

34   [1] Alice Felt Tyler, *Freedom's Ferment*. Thought currents, humanitarian strivings, theological and philosophical developments, eccentricities such as those of the Mormons and Millerites, social crusades, and idealistic utopian experiments in the earlier half of the nineteenth century are ably presented in this volume.

35   [2] For additional comment on Lincoln's strong sentiment against slavery, see chap. viii, pp. 195–197.

II. A BLUNDERING GENERATION

Page

This essay was first published in the *Mississippi Valley Historical Review*, XXVII, 3–28, being the presidential address before the Mississippi Valley Historical Association at Omaha on May 2, 1940. It has been slightly revised.

36 [1] Joseph Hergesheimer, *Swords and Roses*, 297, 299.

36 [2] *Ibid.*, 267.

37 [3] Howard K. Beale's "What Historians Have Said About the Causes of the Civil War" (*Theory and Practice in Historical Study: A Report of the Committee on Historiography* [Social Science Research Council *Bulletin* No. 54], 55–102) is unequaled for scholarly coverage of this complex subject and for compression of elaborate research in brief form.

37 [4] Joseph K. Barnes, ed., *The Medical and Surgical History of the War of the Rebellion* (Washington, second issue, 1875), Pt. 1, Vol. I, Append., 2.

37 [5] *Ibid.*, Append., 1.

37 [6] *Ibid.*, Append., 2.

37 [7] *Ibid.*, Append., 7.

37 [8] *Ibid.*, Append., 3.

37 [9] *Ibid.*, Append., 99.

37 [10] *Ibid.*, Append., 146.

37 [11] *Ibid.*, Append., 137.

38 [12] *Ibid.*, Intro., xxxiii.

38 [13] *Ibid.*, Intro., xxxiii, xxxiv, xxxvi; Charles G. Souder, Medical Corps, U. S. Army, to the author, November 17, 1939.

38 [14] Of 360,000 Union deaths (round numbers), 110,000 resulted from battle, over 224,500 from disease, and nearly 25,000 from miscellaneous causes including suicide. United States Adjutant General's letter to the author, November 3, 1939. Suicides are mentioned by J. J. Woodward who wrote the introduction to Barnes, *Medical and Surgical History*, Pt. 1, Vol. I, xxxvii. Woodward also (intro., xlii) states that there were 285,545 men discharged from the Union army for disability. The adjutant general mentions 223,535 discharged for "physical disability" (letter to author, November 3, 1939). Union soldiers who became prisoners numbered nearly 195,000; Union deserters, not counting draft dodgers, may be conservatively estimated at about 200,000. J. G. Randall, *Civil War and Reconstruction*, 432, 439; Fred A. Shannon, *Organization and Administration of the Union Army, 1861–1865*, II, 179 n. It thus appears that approximately a million were among the dead, disabled, deserting, or imprisoned. A careful statistician has stated: "It is doubtful if there were 2,000,000 individuals actually in [Union] service during the [Civil] war." William F. Fox, *Regimental Losses in the American Civil War, 1861–65*, 527.

38 [15] Lewis H. Steiner, "Account of the Field Relief Corps of the U. S. Sanitary Commission of the Army of the Potomac," *Sanitary Commission, Pamphlet No. 72* (New York, 1863), 6.

38 [16] H. W. Bellows, "Notes of a Preliminary Sanitary Survey of the Forces of the United States in the Ohio and Mississippi Valleys near Midsummer,

Page

1861," *Sanitary Commission, Pamphlet No. 26,* (Washington, 1861), 15.

39   [17] "In army practice, attempts to save a limb which might be perfectly successful in civil life, cannot be made . . . . Conservative surgery is here an error; in order to save life, the limb must be sacrificed." Frederick L. Olmsted, "Report of a Committee of the Medical Members of the Sanitary Commission on the Subject of Amputations," *Sanitary Commission F* (Washington, 1861), 5.

39   [1] In postwar reminiscence the Union soldier might hold forth on the subject of the war as a purifying force and a builder of character where the same individual during the war recorded his feeling of disgust with what was around him, of degradation, and of the tearing down of character.

41   [1] Concepts as to cultural conflict were presented at the meeting of the American Historical Association at Washington in December 1939. See "Educating Clio," *Amer. Hist. Rev.,* XLV, 505–532 (April 1940).

45   [1] Ulrich B. Phillips, ed., *The Correspondence of Robert Toombs, Alexander H. Stephens, and Howell Cobb,* in *Annual Report, 1911,* Amer. Hist. Assoc., II, 469.

47   [2] "They say Virginia 'has no grievance . . . .' " Mary B. Chesnut, *A Diary from Dixie,* 50 (May 9, 1861).

47   [1] Graham Wallas, *Human Nature in Politics, passim.*

49   [2] These matters are treated by the writer in "The Civil War Restudied," *Jour. of So. Hist.,* VI, 439–457 (1940).

49   [3] Cabinet opinion on Sumter is here treated as of March 15, 1861. Two weeks later there was a somewhat different cabinet alignment.

50   [4] *Lebensraum* as a motive for producing a war is meaningless unless one links it with the following factors: the demand of an aggressive nation to own and rule where its nationals live; repudiation of the idea that Dutch can live with Swiss (to take a non-provocative example) except under Dutch domination; denial of *Lebensraum* to rudely dispossessed people even in their own country; and the sordid ideological justification of such denial on the ground that the intruding race with the bigger guns is superior by nature and has superior rights.

52   [1] Benét did it in the invocation of *John Brown's Body.* Frederick Jackson Turner, whose writings have commanded enthusiastic admiration among American historians (even though some have dissented), gave a distinguished interpretation of qualities and forces that we call American. On the broad canvas of the *War Years* (I, 8 ff. and *passim*) Sandburg presents the great American panorama. The writings of Vernon L. Parrington, Ralph H. Gabriel, and Merle Curti offer illuminating surveys of the American mind. To give the bibliography of this challenging subject is not the purpose here, but one should not neglect the presidential address of Arthur M. Schlesinger, Sr. before the American Historical Association, Dec. 30, 1942 (*Amer. Hist. Rev.,* XLVIII, 225–244). It bears the arresting title: "What Then Is the American, This New Man?" In the Fox-Schlesinger series, *A History of American Life,* the volumes by Carl Russell Fish, Arthur C. Cole, and Allan Nevins are concerned with the generation which included Lincoln, and which, in surviving him, gave further manifestation of its leading characteristics.

Page

52   ² For evidence that Lincoln's thought was not limited to politics one should read those passages in which he contemplated the world about him. In an early address before the Young Men's Lyceum of Springfield in 1838 he looked upon "the great journal of things happening under the sun" and in that broad setting he analyzed America's past triumphs and existing problems. Two decades later, in a lecture on "Discoveries, Inventions, and Improvements" (1858–1860) he thought of "Young America" while standing in wonder of human achievement down the ages—of the habit of observation and reflection, of invention, of language, of "the capacities of the tongue," the "exchange of thoughts." The broad intellectual sweep of these two speeches would serve as the theme for a book on the mind of Lincoln. For the lyceum address, see *Works*, I, 35 ff.; for the lecture, *ibid.*, V, 99 ff. The date 1837, given for the lyceum address by Nicolay and Hay, is an error. It was delivered in January 1838. For comment on these two addresses, see *Lincoln the President*, I, 19 ff.

53   ³ Charles S. Sydnor, "The Southerner and the Laws," presidential address before the Southern Historical Association, Lexington, Kentucky, November 3, 1939, *Jour. of So. Hist.*, VI, 3–23 (1940).

54   ⁴ Henrietta M. Larson, *Jay Cooke, Private Banker*, 189.

54   ⁵ It would now be called that; in Civil War days it was the R. G. Dun rating.

55   ⁶ William P. Fessenden to Hamilton Fish, Jan. 10, 1860, Hamilton Fish MSS., Lib. of Cong. Seward had spoken of "irrepressible conflict" in 1858 and this expression was linked with the violence of the John Brown raid in 1859. He was abroad in 1859, returning in December of that year. His return was the occasion of enthusiastic "welcome home" celebrations in his own state. When he arrived in Washington in January 1860 the Republicans gave him a hearty greeting, his house was a center of friendly hospitality, and delegations from some of the states came to pay their respects to the man who seemed likely to become the Republican candidate for President. Frederic Bancroft, *Life of William H. Seward*, I, 508–510.

55   ⁷ Lt. H. N. Holbrook, 5th Massachusetts Volunteer Militia, to "Dear Brother James," Washington, D. C., April 28, 1861. (For the use of this manuscript letter the writer is indebted to its owner, H. E. Pratt, former executive secretary of Abraham Lincoln Association.)

55   ⁸ Chesnut, *Diary from Dixie*, 3.

55   ⁹ Ralph L. Rusk, ed., *The Letters of Ralph Waldo Emerson*, V, 332.

55   ¹⁰ Edward W. Emerson and Waldo E. Forbes, eds., *Journals of Ralph Waldo Emerson*, IX, 325.

55   ¹¹ *Ibid*, IX, 411, 429.

55   ¹² *Ibid.*, IX, 459.

55   ¹³ *Ibid.*, IX, 572.

56   ¹⁴ *Ibid.*, IX, 461.

56   ¹⁵ *Ibid.*, IX, 462.

56   ¹⁶ David S. Jordan and Harvey E. Jordan, *War's Aftermath: A Preliminary Study of the Eugenics of War*.

57   ¹ Merle E. Curti, *The American Peace Crusade, 1815–1860*; Arthur C. F. Beales, *The History of Peace*, 53 and *passim*.

57   ² *Advocate of Peace* (Boston and Washington), May-June, 1861, p. 258.

Page

59   ³ *U.S. Stat. at Large*, XIII, 9 (sec. 17).

59   ⁴ Edward N. Wright, *Conscientious Objectors in the Civil War;* Rufus M.
     Jones, *The Later Periods of Quakerism*, II, 728–753; Rufus M. Jones, ed.,
     The Record of a Quaker Conscience: Cyrus Pringle's Diary; Randall, *Civil
     War and Reconstruction*, 416–419; *Constitutional Problems Under Lincoln*,
     260–263.

60   ¹ George Winston Smith, "Union Propaganda in the American Civil War,"
     Social Studies, XXXV, 26–32 (Jan. 1944). Dr. Smith is the author of "Gen-
     erative Forces of Union Propaganda: A Study in Civil War Pressure Groups,"
     unpublished doctoral dissertation, University of Wisconsin, 1939.

60   ² William B. Hesseltine, "The Propaganda Literature of Confederate Pris-
     ons," *Jour. of So. Hist.*, I, 56–66 (1935).

61   ³ *Works*, X, 80.

61   ⁴ Randall, *Civil War and Reconstruction*, 638–639. See also Frank Freidel,
     "The Loyal Publication Society: A Pro-Union Propaganda Agency," *Miss.
     Vall. Hist. Rev.*, XXVI, 359–376.

62   ⁵ Published tickets often carried the name "Union" or "National Union"
     party, but a printed circular in Massachusetts urging the formation "of a
     Union Club . . . in every town" is headed: Headquarters Republican
     State Committee . . . Boston, Sep. 26, 1864." Supporting Lincoln and
     Johnson, this circular said "We should be put in . . . correspondence with
     working Republicans of every town in the State." Andrew MSS., Mass. Hist.
     Soc., XXVIII, no. 90.

62   ⁶ MS., New York Pub. Lib.

63   ⁷ *Works*, VII, 119.

63   ⁸ "The . . . question of profit controls all . . . ." *Ibid.*, IX, 10.

63   ⁹ *Ibid.*, IX, 157.

63   ¹⁰ Arthur C. Cole, *The Irrepressible Conflict, 1850–1864* (Arthur M. Schle-
     singer and Dixon R. Fox, eds., *A History of American Life*, VII).

64   ¹¹ The author wishes to give acknowledgment to his students in the Har-
     vard summer session of 1939, especially to Paul Driscoll on the "last ro-
     mance," to Elizabeth Mohr on peace, and to Frederick S. Allis, Jr., on Emer-
     son.

III. THE UNPOPULAR MR. LINCOLN

This essay was first published in the *Abraham Lincoln Quarterly*,
II, 255–280 (1943). Annotations have been added, and the text has
undergone considerable revision.

Page
66   ¹ *Memoirs of Henry Villard* . . . , I, 152.

66   ² *Charles Francis Adams, 1835–1915: An Autobiography*, 74–75, 79, 80, 82.
     (The Adams here quoted was the brother of Henry and the son of the
     United States minister to Britain.)

66   ³ Albany (N. Y.) *Atlas and Argus*, Feb. 15, 1861, p. 2, c. 4.

66   ⁴ For a short account of Lincoln's change of schedule and his night ride into
     Washington, with contemporary cartoons, see *Lincoln the President*, I, 286–
     291.

67   ⁵ Col. J. B. Shaffer to B. F. Butler, Washington, Jan. 25, 1863, *Private and
     Official Correspondence of General Benjamin F. Butler* . . . , ed. by Jessie
     A. Marshall, II, 589–590.

67   ⁶ Count Adam Gurowski to Governor John A. Andrew, Washington, Oct.
     27, 1862, Andrew MSS., Mass. Hist. Soc.

67   ⁷ John Jay to Charles Sumner, Katonah, N.Y., Sep. 12, 1862, Sumner MSS.,
     Harvard University.

67   ⁸ A. J. Betts to E. B. Washburne, Durand, Ill., Jan. 29, 1862, Washburne
     MSS., Lib. of Cong.

67   ⁹ Benjamin R. Curtis (formerly of the United States Supreme Court) to
     "Dear Greenough" (probably Wm. W. Greenough), Washington, Jan. 1,
     1863, B. R. Curtis MSS., Lib. of Cong.

67   ¹⁰ P. W. Chandler to John A. Andrew, Dec. 16 [1862?], Andrew MSS., Mass.
     Hist. Soc.

67   ¹¹ James C. Conkling to Lyman Trumbull, Springfield, Ill., May 31, 1862,
     Trumbull MSS., Lib. of Cong.

67   ¹² P. A. Allaire to Lyman Trumbull, Aurora, Ill., Dec. 10, 1861, *ibid.*

67   ¹³ S. G. Arnold, Editor, *North American*, to Salmon P. Chase, Newark, Ohio,
     Sep. 12, 1862, Salmon P. Chase MSS., Lib. of Cong.

67   ¹⁴ Count Adam Gurowski to John A. Andrew, Washington, Aug. 5, 1862,
     Andrew MSS., Mass. Hist. Soc.

67   ¹⁵ Wendell Phillips to Charles Sumner, June 29, 1862, Sumner MSS., Har-
     vard Univ.

68   ¹⁶ John Russell to Lyman Trumbull, Bluffdale, Greene Co., Ill., Feb. 4,
     1862, Trumbull MSS., Lib. of Cong.

68   ¹⁷ J. D. Andrew to Gov. John A. Andrew, headed "National" (probably
     Washington), Aug. 30, 1862, Andrew MSS., Mass. Hist. Soc. Written shortly
     after McClellan had been demoted and Halleck made general in chief.

68   ¹⁸ These statements by Chase are in copies of letters dated Aug. 1 and Aug.
     5, 1862, Chase MSS., Hist. Soc. of Pa. (The one of Aug. 1 is to Major General
     E. D. Keyes; other recipient uncertain.)

68   ¹⁹ Francis Gillette to Salmon P. Chase, Hartford, Conn., Sep. 15, 1862, Chase
     MSS., Lib. of Cong.

Page
68 20 H. C. Bowen to Salmon P. Chase, *The Independent*, New York, Sep. 13, 1862, *ibid.*

68 21 William H. Herndon to Lyman Trumbull, Springfield, Ill., Nov. 20, 1861, Trumbull MSS., Lib. of Cong.

68 22 Richard Yates to Lyman Trumbull, Springfield, Ill., Feb. 14, 1862, *ibid.*

69 1 *American Annual Cyclopaedia*, 1862, 792.

69 2 Boston *Daily Advertiser*, Feb. 26, 1863. The writer of this article added: ". . . he [Stevens] has attacked it [the Lincoln administration] openly, with the vehemence, and . . . ferocity, which is apt to characterize his action in moments of deep excitement."

71 3 Joshua R. Giddings to George W. Julian, Montreal, Jan. 28, 1862, Giddings-Julian MSS., Lib. of Cong.

71 4 Giddings to Julian, Jan. 18, 1863, *ibid.*

71 5 Benjamin F. Wade to Zachariah Chandler, Sep. 23, 1861, Chandler MSS., Lib. of Cong., quoted in T. Harry Williams, *Lincoln and the Radicals*, 41.

71 6 Statement of Senator Graham N. Fitch of Indiana, *Cong. Globe*, 36 Cong., 1 sess., 2403.

71 7 MS. Diary of Gideon Welles, Dec. 5, 1866, quoted in Howard K. Beale, *The Critical Year*, 14.

71 8 Williams, *Lincoln and the Radicals*, 64.

72 1 John Russell to Lyman Trumbull, Bluffdale, Greene Co., Ill., Dec. 17, 1861, Trumbull MSS., Lib. of Cong.

72 2 Cyrus Pitt Grosvenor (quoting Chase's own words) to Salmon P. Chase London, July 28, 1862, Chase MSS., Lib. of Cong.

72 3 Alphonso Taft to Salmon P. Chase, Cincinnati, Ohio, Aug. 26, 1862, *ibid.*

73 4 Count Adam Gurowski to Gov. John A. Andrew, May 7, 1862, Andrew MSS., Mass. Hist. Soc.

73 5 J. H. Bryant to Lyman Trumbull, Princeton, Ill., Dec. 8, 1861, Trumbull MSS., Lib. of Cong.

73 6 John Mantelieu to E. B. Washburne, Freeport, Ill., Jan. 15, 1864, Washburne MSS., Lib. of Cong.

73 7 Israel Holmes to Senator J. R. Doolittle, Portage, Wis., Aug. 6, 1862. Newspaper clipping, Doolittle MSS., Lib. of Cong.

73 8 J. H. Geiger to Salmon P. Chase, Columbus, Ohio, July 26, 1862, Chase MSS., Lib. of Cong.

74 9 The following passages, typical of many, will illustrate the unsettled and alarming state of opinion in certain circles.
". . . Perhaps it is thought there are no more John Browns. They may not appear if the war is conducted in earnest, but . . . before I will consent to fight for the Union with one hand stretched out to sustain slavery I would put a torch and a knife into the hands of every black man and bid him God speed in the fight for his liberties." General Joseph R. Hawley to Gideon Welles, New Haven, Conn., Sep. 17, 1861, MS., Ill. State Hist. Lib. A parallel statement in a letter of the time read as follows: ". . . I . . . fear that . . . if the resources of the Republic are frittered away in the silly desire to conciliate *loyal slaveholders*, they [the people] will take the law into their own hands . . . —My only hope then will be that the Lord will send us another Cromwell to lead his Puritans." P. A. Allaire to Lyman

222 NOTES

Page

Trumbull, Aurora, Ill., Dec. 10, 1861, Trumbull MSS., Lib. of Cong.

74   10 George B. Loring to B. F. Butler, Salem, Mass., Aug. 26, 1862, *Private and Official Correspondence of . . . Butler,* II, 223–225.

74   11 *Ibid.*

74   12 B. W. Richmond to Salmon P. Chase, Hq., Mil. Dist. of Washington, Sep. 14, 1862, Chase MSS., Lib. of Cong.

74   13 F. Gillette to Charles Sumner, Hartford, Conn., Sep. 15, 1862, Sumner MSS., Harvard Univ.

74   1 James L. Sellers, "James R. Doolittle," *Wis. Mag. of Hist.,* XVII, XVIII (several articles, 1933–34).

75   2 David Davis to Simon Cameron, Lincoln, Ill., Oct. 13, 1861, Cameron MSS., Lib. of Cong.

75   3 Joseph Medill to Lyman Trumbull, Tribune Office, Chicago, July 4, 1862, Trumbull MSS., Lib. of Cong. Medill seemed to feel that the Constitution was being invoked to protect rebels; this was in connection with the confiscation bill then pending in Congress. National conscription had not yet been adopted, and Medill thought there would be a "feeble response" to the recent call for 300,000 troops "to serve [as he said] under proslavery generals to fight for 'Union and Slavery.' "

75   4 Williams, *Lincoln and the Radicals,* 303. On this point one should also read Phillips's abusive speeches.

76   5 "Is it true that the President listens to his wife who has so many Southern relatives, and is induced to deal gently with the 'iniquity' in Consequence?" P. A. Allaire to Lyman Trumbull, Aurora, Ill., Dec. 10, 1861, Trumbull MSS., Lib. of Cong.

76   6 ". . . I find that nearly a majority of the men who voted for Uncle Abe are beginning to come out against him . . . . They curse Lincoln & call him a Damed [*sic*] old traitor & they curse our Cabinet & all the Congress . . . ." W. C. Dunning to E. B. Washburne, Byron, Ill., Jan. 10, 1862, Washburne MSS., Lib. of Cong. (The writer of this letter referred to himself as "a strong friend of Honest Old Abe.")

76   7 W. L. Garrison to Oliver Johnson, Boston, Sep. 9, 1862 (Copy), Garrison MSS., Boston Pub. Lib. In this same letter Garrison wrote: "I am growing more and more skeptical as to the 'honesty' of Lincoln. He is nothing better than a wet rag . . . ."

77   1 In the matter of Stuart's election one should distinguish between the candidate's attitude as defined by himself and the manner in which his election would inevitably be regarded. Stuart was the Democratic candidate; Swett, as Republican, made a point of upholding the President; Swett's defeat and Stuart's election could not fail to injure the President's prestige. Stuart had not, however, presented himself as an anti-Lincoln man. He had expressed confidence in his former partner and declared: "I would rather aid him than embarrass him . . . ." For the election of 1862, see *Lincoln the President,* II, 232–237. See also Harry E. Pratt, "The Repudiation of Lincoln's War Policy in 1862—Stuart-Swett Congressional Campaign," *Jour. Ill. State Hist. Soc.,* XXIV, 129–140 (1931).

78   2 *Diary of Orville Hickman Browning (Ill. Hist. Coll.,* XX), I, 600–601 (Dec. 18, 1862).

Page

79   1 Henry J. Raymond to Simon Cameron, National Union Executive Committee, New York, Aug. 19, 1864, Cameron MSS., Lib. of Cong.

79   2 Same to same, Aug. 21, 1864, *ibid.*

79   3 This correspondent of Cameron wrote: ". . . my friend Barr has just returned from N. Y., where he saw Col. Shaffer (of Ill.) and the Col. sent me word . . . that he had just seen Mr. Raymond . . . who told him that the game was up—that there was no chance whatever for Mr. Lincoln. Shaffer said he replied that while there was life there was hope. 'By God, sir,' said Raymond, 'there is no life. Mr. Lincoln will do nothing. . . . [etc.]'" Russell Errett to Simon Cameron, Pittsburgh, Aug. 25, 1864, *ibid.*

80   4 Whitelaw Reid to Anna E. Dickinson, Sep. 11, 1864, Anna E. Dickinson MSS., Lib. of Cong.

80   5 Henry H. Elliott (Unionist leader in New York) to Gideon Welles, New York, Aug. 31, 1864, Welles MSS., Lib. of Cong.

80   6 Amasa J. Parker to Samuel J. Tilden, Albany, N.Y., July 7, 1864, Tilden MSS., N. Y. Pub. Lib.

80   7 George W. Julian to Charles Sumner, Sep. 4, 1864, Sumner MSS., Harvard Univ.

80   8 Cephas Brainerd to Charles Sumner, Sep. 13, 1864, *ibid.*

80   9 "A council was held last eve'g, of gentlemen who enjoy leading positions in the loyal political organizations of this state; and upon full deliberation, all of them came to the conclusion, that it was useless and inexpedient to attempt to run Mr Lincoln, in the hope of victory . . . . A National Convention was therefore called to meet at Cincinnatti [*sic*] on the 28th Sept to consult upon the affairs of the country, and, if need be, to nominate some candidate who can unite the entire loyal vote." George Wilkes (of *Wilkes' Spirit of the Times*) to E. B. Washburne, New York, Aug. 31, 1864, Washburne MSS., Lib. of Cong. On this subject of the movement to oust Lincoln and name another Republican candidate one finds an impressive set of documents (then newly published) in the New York *Sun*, June 30, 1889, p. 3.

81   10 The original correspondence between the three New York editors and the Republican governors is found among the manuscripts of the New York Historical Society. The letter from Andrew of Massachusetts, quoted in the text, is dated at Boston, September 3, 1864.

81   11 O. H. Browning to Edgar Cowan, Quincy, Ill., Sep. 6, 1864, MS., photostat in author's possession.

81   12 Charles R. Wilson, "New Light on the Lincoln-Blair-Frémont 'Bargain' of 1864," *Amer. Hist. Rev.*, XLII, 71–78 (1936). See also Allan Nevins, *Frémont, Pathmarker of the West* (1939); William E. Smith, *The Francis Preston Blair Family in Politics.*

81   13 *Works*, X, 203–204; Nicolay and Hay, *Abraham Lincoln: A History*, IX, 251. The cabinet signatures on this document (placed there by Lincoln's request in the days of August gloom) are those of William H. Seward, William P. Fessenden, Edwin M. Stanton, Gideon Welles, Edward Bates, Montgomery Blair, and John P. Usher. A photostat copy of Lincoln's memorandum with the signatures is among the Barton MSS., Univ. of Chicago.

82   1 *Dic. of Amer. Biog.*, II, 197.

Page
83   1 Nicolay and Hay, *Abraham Lincoln: A History*, IX, 40–41. Bright's use of the Cave of Adullam allusion occurred in a speech in the House of Commons in debate on the reform bill of Earl Russell's administration, on the motion to bring in the bill, March 13, 1866. James E. T. Rogers, ed., *Speeches on Questions of Public Policy of John Bright, M.P.*, II, 144. For the Biblical source, see 1 Samuel 22:1, 2.

87   1 Carl Sandburg, *Abraham Lincoln: The War Years*, III, 383.

IV. LINCOLN'S SUMTER DILEMMA

The article entitled "When War Came in 1861" appeared in the *Abraham Lincoln Quarterly*, 3–42 (1940) without notes. The subject of Sumter was treated with documentation in *Lincoln the President*, I, 311–350. In the present chapter there has been a good deal of rewriting, but the author's restudy has produced no essential variation in conclusion.

Page
89 ¹ For a series of interesting recent studies of Harriet Beecher Stowe, her writings and her influence, see *Lincoln Herald,* June 1946. From these pages one may quote the following estimates.

J. Winston Coleman, Jr.: "Despite the many criticisms . . . hurled against the immortal book . . . , it has stood up well and is today considered a very readable and popular novel" (p. 9).

Thomas D. Clark: "There was a desire for escape, and the American public was in a receptive mood for a social novel . . . . It was an age when a novelist with a good sentimental story, no matter how poorly . . . written, could have found omnivorous readers. . . . There are flaws on almost every page. The story is hacked to pieces by the side issues, and the eternal preaching of the author. She . . . actually used the very best traditions of the southern slave system to carry her story. If she had allowed George Shelby to arrive at the Red River plantation just two hours earlier to rescue Uncle Tom . . . and drive Simon Legree . . . back to his native New England, *Uncle Tom's Cabin* might have become one of the great pro-southern novels" (pp. 6, 28).

F. Lauriston Bullard: "The amazing success of her famous story lifted Mrs. Stowe to a plateau unscaled by any other American woman writer. The *Independent* . . . allotted her a first page column wherein she might set out her ideas on 'any subject from the Mayflower to Uncle Tom' " (p. 11).

92 ¹ In December 1860 a petition for compromise was signed by 22,313 citizens of Massachusetts. When Charles Sumner suggested that they signed in ignorance, there was indignant denial. C. N. Feamster, ed., *Calendar of the Papers of John Jordan Crittenden*, 248, 256, 261. One of the points in suggested compromise was the repeal of state laws to obstruct operation of the Federal fugitive slave act. Despite the severity of this act, leading citizens of Massachusetts urged such repeal. The paper in which this sentiment was expressed was phrased in terms of friendly conciliation with the South. *Lincoln the President*, I, 240.

93 ¹ For an excellent treatment of this crisis, see David M. Potter, *Lincoln and His Party in the Secession Crisis.*

94 ² Q. Busbee to Stephen A. Douglas, Raleigh, N.C., Mar. 11, 1861, Douglas MSS., Univ. of Chicago.

94 ³ Quoted in B. B. Munford, *Virginia's Attitude toward Slavery and Secession,* 266.

95 ¹ Randall, *Civil War and Reconstruction,* 344–345.

96 ² Potter, *Lincoln and His Party,* 234 n.

97 ³ For cabinet memoranda of advice concerning Sumter under dates of March

Page

15 and March 29, 1861, see *Works*, VI, 192 ff., 227 ff.

98   ⁴ For Lincoln's concept of the importance of holding Virginia, and for his
conference with John B. Baldwin of that state at the White House on April
4, 1861, see *Lincoln the President*, I, 324–328. Allan B. Magruder, who was
familiar with this incident, having served as messenger between Washington
and Richmond, considered that the best solution would have been withdrawal from Sumter, combined with "an earnest appeal to the country . . .
to stand by the Union . . . and stay the mad career of secession." There
is little doubt that this was the prevailing view of Virginia unionists. This
did not mean that Magruder considered Lincoln's course aggressive or deliberately provocative; he would have said rather that Lincoln made a mistake. He wrote: "It seems clear that Mr. Lincoln had fully resolved on the
policy of peace, and did not mean to permit the war to be inaugurated, if
it were possible . . . to avert that calamity. . . . All of the facts of the
case go to fortify this conclusion." *Atl. Mo.*, XXXV, 445 (1875).

98   ⁵ The missions of Lamon, Hurlbut, and Fox are treated in *Lincoln the
President*, I, 328–330.

99   ¹ Orders concerning Sumter and Pickens appear in *Official Records* (Navies),
1 ser., IV, 90, 107, 108, 227, 228, 232, 234, 235 ff.; *Official Records* (Armies),
1 ser., I, 235 ff. (*Official Records*, when cited in this book without further
designation, are to be understood as records of the Armies; for greater clear-
ness the word "Armies" is sometimes used.)

99   ² *Works*, VI, 302.

99   ³ *Official Records* (Navies), 1 ser., IV, 115.

99   ⁴ *Works*, VI, 301.

100   ⁵ *Ibid.*, VI, 302.

100   ⁶ *Ibid.*, VI, 226. The order of March 29 was that "an expedition . . . be got
ready to sail as early as the 6th of April . . . ."

100   ⁷ *Ibid.*, VI, 239–240.

100   ⁸ *Ibid.*, VI, 241.

101   ⁹ These matters as to Pickens and Sumter are treated, with documentation,
in *Lincoln the President*, I, 333 ff.

101   ¹⁰ *Official Records* (Navies), 1 ser., IV, 129, 138.

102   ¹¹ Lincoln's instruction to Chew is in his *Works*, VI, 241. Both this docu-
ment and an important instruction to Major Anderson were drafted by
Lincoln in his handwriting, though issued by the secretary of war. For Lin-
coln's close attention to these matters and his non-aggressive emphasis, see
Lincoln the President, I, 337 n. See also Nicolay and Hay, *Abraham Lincoln:
A History*, IV, 27–28, 34–35.

102   ¹² "General M. C. Meigs on the Conduct of the Civil War," *Amer. Hist. Rev.*,
XXVI, 285–303 (1921).

102   ¹³ For Seward's conduct, see *Lincoln the President*, I, 337 ff., II, 29–31.

103   ¹⁴ *Journal of the Congress of the Confederate States of America, 1861–1865*,
[U. S.] *Sen. Doc.* No. 234, 58 Cong., 2 sess., I, 60. The resolution referred to
the enforcement of "the existing revenue laws against all foreign countries,
except the State of Texas." In this and many other instances states of the
United States were considered foreign. Severance of the Union was treated
as if fully accomplished.

Page

103   15 J. F. Rhodes, *History of the United States* . . . , III, 350. One of the aides, A. R. Chisolm, wrote a journal in which he indicated that the aides, while under instruction from Beauregard, did exercise a certain amount of discretion. After noting that the three officers conferred with Anderson and found his answer unsatisfactory, he added that it was "discretionary" with the aides what to do next, and that "we informed him that in one hour . . . our Batteries would open fire." The Chisolm manuscript, a slightly known document, was made available to the author through the courtesy of Mr. Vernon Munroe of New York City.

103   16 Order of Leroy P. Walker, Confederate Secretary of War, April 11, 1861, *Official Records*, 1 ser., I, 301.

105   1 Charles W. Ramsdell, "Lincoln and Fort Sumter," *Jour. So. Hist.*, III, 259–288.

105   2 In addition to O'Sullivan and Ramsdell, other writers may be cited for a similar interpretation of Lincoln's Sumter policy. See Edgar Lee Masters, *Lincoln the Man;* Kenneth M. Stampp, "Lincoln and the Strategy of Defense in the Crisis of 1861," *Jour. So. Hist.*, XI, 297–323 (1945). A severely anti-Lincoln treatment is found in *Lincoln Takes Command*, by John Shipley Tilley.

105   3 Ramsdell, "Lincoln and Fort Sumter," as above cited, 272 and note.

105   4 *Ibid.*, 270–271.

106   5 Lincoln's attitude on specific points involving concessions is treated in *Lincoln the President*, I, 234–237.

107   6 For the full statement by Browning see p. 112.

108   7 *Official Records* (Armies), 1 ser., I, 235 ff.; *Official Records* (Navies), 1 ser., IV, 232 ff.

109   8 *Official Records* (Navies), 1 ser., IV, 235.

110   9 Ramsdell, as above cited, 272.

112   1 *Diary of O. H. Browning*, I, 476.

115   1 It is remarkable to note how far Lincoln qualified his pledge to enforce the laws. He said in his inaugural: ". . . to the extent of my ability I shall take care, as the Constitution itself expressly enjoins upon me, that the laws of the Union be faithfully executed in all the States. Doing this I deem to be only a simple duty on my part; and I shall perform it so far as practicable, unless my rightful masters, the American people, shall withhold the requisite means, or in some authoritative manner direct the contrary." *Works*, VI, 175.

115   2 *Ibid.*, VI, 176.

115   3 *Ibid.*

115   4 "The mails, unless repelled, will continue to be furnished in all parts of the Union. So far as possible, the people everywhere shall have that sense of perfect security which is most favorable to calm thought and reflection." *Ibid.*

115   5 David M. Potter, *Lincoln and His Party*, 329.

115   6 *Works*, VI, 299–300.

116   7 *Ibid.*, VI, 184.

116   8 *Ibid.*, VI, 176. In the same spirit Lincoln also spoke as follows: "Why should there not be a patient confidence in the ultimate justice of the people? Is there any better or equal hope in the world? In our present differ-

Page

ences is either party without faith of being in the right? If the Almighty
Ruler of Nations, with his eternal truth and justice, be on your side of
the North, or on yours of the South, that truth and that justice will surely
prevail by the judgment of this great tribunal of the American people."
Ibid., VI, 183. It is difficult to see how one can read Lincoln's inaugural address and fail to note its friendly, peaceful, and conciliatory tone.

116   [9] *Ibid.*, VI, 301. The context shows Lincoln's meaning to be that the abandonment of Sumter would be ruinous unless elsewhere there might be "a
clear indication of policy," which "would better enable the country to accept the evacuation of Fort Sumter as a military necessity."

116   [10] Pickett Papers, MSS., Lib. of Cong.

116   [11] *Atl. Mo.*, XXXV, 443; *House Report* No. 30, 39 Cong., 1 sess., 104.

116   [12] Remembering Lincoln's studious effort to make it clear that his Sumter
purpose was to land provisions, one can see that he was doing no more in
his holding of Sumter than Buchanan had done. Buchanan's ship, *The Star
of the West*, carried two hundred men, along with arms and ammunition.
The intention under Lincoln was to do even less in the matter of reënforcement than that which Buchanan attempted. See Rhodes, *Hist. of U. S.*, III,
245–251; *Official Records*, 1 ser., I, 9–10.

117   [13] Even if Lincoln had decided not to hold Sumter, there is evidence that
such a decision would have been criticized by secessionists. In the correspondence of Governor Francis W. Pickens of South Carolina one finds letters
and memoranda from John W. Lapsley of Selma, Alabama, purporting to
show that Lincoln was actually planning to announce the abandonment of
the Sumter garrison. Lapsley referred to such a course as "one of the foulest
and wickedest plots on record." He considered it a plot "to *cause the destruction of a brave and faithful garrison* . . . for the *sole purpose* of exciting
their whole people to a pitch of phrenzy so as to command their treasures,
for the support of the vast armies they expected . . . to rally under . . .
the same phrenzy, to be precipitated upon the South." John W. Lapsley to
Francis W. Pickens, June 4, 1861, and July 30, 1861; Lapsley to I. W. Hayne,
June 25, 1861, MSS., Duke University.

V. THE RULE OF LAW UNDER LINCOLN

This essay, with thorough and extended revision, is based upon "The 'Rule of Law' under the Lincoln Administration," *Historical Outlook*, XVII, 272–276 (1926).

Page

118   [1] Topics here presented have also been treated by the writer elsewhere. See *Constitutional Problems under Lincoln;* "The Government and the Citizen" (*The Civil War and Reconstruction,* chap. xv); "The Indemnity Act of 1863: A Study in the Wartime Immunity of Governmental Officers," *Mich. Law Rev.,* XX, 589–613 (1922); "Lincoln in the Rôle of Dictator," *So. Atl. Quar.,* XXVIII, 236–252 (1929); "Civil and Military Relationships under Lincoln," *Pa. Mag. of Hist. and Biog.,* LXIX, 199–206 (1945).

119   [2] Albert Venn Dicey, *Introduction to . . . the Law of the* [English] *Constitution,* ch. iv.

119   [3] On martial law in the United States, see: *The Military Laws of the United States* (8th ed., Wash., Gov't Ptg. Office, 1940); W. E. Birkhimer, *Military Government and Martial Law;* J. I. C. Hare, *American Constitutional Law,* chaps. 42, 43, 44; H. W. Ballantine, in *Yale Law Rev.,* XXIV, 189, and *Columbia Law Rev.,* XII, 529; *In re* Moyer, 85 Pac. 190; *Ex parte* Milligan, 71 U. S. 2; Dynes *vs.* Hoover, 61 U. S. 65; *Constitutional Problems Under Lincoln,* chap. viii. In certain states martial law has been used, especially in connection with labor troubles; on the Federal level its use has been less frequent.

120   [4] "Military necessity" is often a rather loose term. For public security—as at the time of a great fire to promote safety—military severity beyond established rules may be granted, but what about "necessity" for an aggressive attack, as upon Belgium in 1914? If such a dangerous power is used the commander should show that the object is justified, that the case is desperate, and that the means are not excessive but are conducive to order. If wrongly applied "military necessity" may be a fraud. At best the invoking of the principle is an admission that something irregular is being done. No reputable commander will do a deeply disreputable thing. Wanton criminality has no place in the procedures of a civilized nation, even when drawn into war. Looting, use of phony currency, mass killings, brutal collective reprisals, the rounding up of hostages, torture, slaughter of refugees, deportation, labor enslavement, annihilation of whole villages—for such practices the plea of military necessity is a lame excuse. The maxim "necessity knows no law" is by no means adequate as a statement of American doctrine. The Supreme Court held in Hilton *vs.* Guyot (159 U. S. 113, 163) that international law "is part of our law." For "General Orders 100" (the military code of the United States as codified by Francis Lieber) see Frank Burt Freidel, "General Orders 100 and Military Government," *Miss. Vall. Hist. Rev.,* XXXII, 541–556 (1946). See also *Constitutional Problems under Lincoln,* chap. ii.

120   [5] See special note at end of chap. v (pp. 133–134).

120   [1] An insurrection is an uprising which threatens governmental stability. An "insurgent" has been defined as "one who in combination with others takes part in active and forcible opposition to the constituted authorities, where

Page

there has been no recognition of belligerency." The term "insurrection" would be appropriate for a movement directed against the enforcement of particular laws, while in a "rebellion" an attempt is made to overthrow the government itself, at least in a part of the country. "War" has been legally understood to be a conflict between recognized belligerents. It has been defined as "that state in which a nation prosecutes its right by force." In traditional international law, or conventional jurisprudence, war has been considered a condition in which individual commanders and officers are relieved from responsibility if their conduct has been correct and regular under the rules. By the trial of war criminals, including high ranking Nazi leaders at Nuremberg, there has now been established the fundamentally important legal doctrine that aggressive war is a crime for which individuals are punishable and for which superior orders are no defense. A nation does not claim municipal powers over its enemies in a public war (temporary military occupation is a different matter); but it does assert that claim in the case of an insurrection or rebellion. U. S. *vs.* Fries, Fed. Cas. No. 5126; Prize Cases, 67 U. S. 635; U. S. *vs.* Smith, Fed. Cas. 16318; U. S. *vs.* 100 Barrels of Cement, *ibid.*, 15945.

120   2 From the standpoint of the government at Washington, the Civil War began as an "insurrection," though the word "rebellion" was also used with little attempt to maintain an accurate distinction between these two terms. The execution of the laws, as Lincoln proclaimed, was "obstructed by combinations too powerful to be suppressed by the ordinary course of judicial proceedings." But in the Prize Cases the Supreme Court held that the conflict was both a war and an insurrection (67 U. S. 670); and in Miller *vs.* United States the Court declared that "the United States sustained the double character of a belligerent and a sovereign, and had the rights of both." 78 U. S. 306–307. The existence side by side of two opposing legal principles is understandable if one remembers that the insurrectionary theory was not in fact applied as against Southern leaders and adherents of the Confederacy. They were not held personally liable as insurrectionists, as were the leaders of the Whiskey Insurrection. Certain phases of the legal nature of the Civil War have been dealt with by the writer in *Constitutional Problems Under Lincoln,* chaps. iii and v, and in *Amer. Hist. Rev.,* XVIII, 79–96 (1912).

121   3 Ford *vs.* Surget, 97 U. S. 605; Fifield *vs.* Ins. Co., of Pa., 47 Pa. 166, cited in 97 U. S. 620.

121   4 Thorington *vs.* Smith, 75 U. S. 1.

121   5 On disloyalty in the North; see Nicolay and Hay, *Abraham Lincoln: A History,* VIII, ch. 1; *Rep. of Judge Ad. Gen. on the Order of American Knights* (Wash., 1864); W. D. Foulke, *Life of O. P. Morton; Official Records,* 2 ser., II, 240 ff.; VII, 740 ff.; Rhodes, *Hist. of U. S.,* V, 317 ff.; Wood Gray, *The Hidden Civil War: The Story of the Copperheads;* George Fort Milton, *Abraham Lincoln and the Fifth Column.*

121   6 J. G. Randall, "The Interrelation of Social and Constitutional History," *Amer. Hist. Rev.,* XXXV, 1–13 (1929).

121   7 As this was a "pocket veto" Lincoln stated his objections in a public pronouncement, not in a veto message. *Works,* X, 153. In conversation with

Page

Senator Browning of Illinois, the President expressed his conviction that Congress had no power over slavery in the states. *Diary of O. H. Browning*, I, 555 (July 1, 1862).

121   8 *Works*, VIII, 31–32. At another time Lincoln qualified his statement of war powers as follows: "Civilized belligerents do all in their power to help themselves or hurt the enemy, except a few things regarded as barbarous or cruel. Among the exceptions are the massacre of vanquished foes and non-combatants, male and female" (*ibid.*, IX, 98).

122   9 On May 4, 1861, the President enlarged the army of the United States by his call for volunteers, an act which is to be distinguished from the earlier call, on April 15, for 75,000 militia. The May call was of the sort which usually follows congressional action authorizing an increase of the army. For Lincoln's comment, admitting lack of authority on this point, see *Works*, VI, 308.

122   10 On the following dates Lincoln issued orders for the suspension of the habeas corpus privilege: April 27, 1861; May 10, 1861; July 2, 1861; October 14, 1861; December 2, 1861; September 24, 1862. *Works*, VI, 258, 271–272, 295–296; VII, 8, 26–27; VIII, 41–42.

122   11 Certain ships had been seized for violation of the blockade proclaimed in April 1861 by the President. Congress had not declared war nor recognized the legal existence of civil war; thus the question arose as to the validity of the blockade. This involved the larger question whether the President acts legally when he takes measures against an enemy in the absence of congressional recognition of a state of war. Such, in brief, was the problem in the Prize Cases (67 U. S. 635) decided in 1863. Lincoln's conduct was sustained by a five-to-four decision. Judges of his own choosing supported him; so did Wayne of Georgia. Had any of the five decided the other way, which would not have been considered unlikely in the case of Wayne, the President would have been greatly embarrassed. Some were saying that the Court was deciding whether the whole war was illegal. This was an overstatement; Congress had given legal recognition to the existence of war in July 1861. The questionable part was before that.

122   12 *Works*, VI, 308.

123   13 Wilson's far reaching powers were mainly derived from statutes of Congress. C. A. Berdahl, *War Powers of the Executive in the United States* (Univ. of Ill. Studies in the Social Sciences, vol. IX), 268.

123   14 In the period of early presidential war measures (April to July 1861, Congress not being in session) Lincoln directed the expenditure of money from the treasury of the United States without that legislative appropriation which the Constitution requires (art. I, sec. 9). Though acting honestly in this matter in a time of great emergency, the President later admitted that he had acted without legal authority. Message to Congress, May 26, 1862, *Works*, VII, 189–194.

123   15 Much of what might be called presidential legislation consists of executive regulations or orders applying laws to given situations. Charles E. Hughes pointed out in 1917 that the war power of the President is greatly augmented outside his functions as Commander-in-Chief through legislation of Congress increasing his administrative authority. Charles E. Hughes, *War*

Page

Powers under the Constitution (Sen. Doc. No. 105, 65 Cong., 1 sess.), p. 9.

123 ¹⁶ *U. S. Stat. at Large*, XII, 597.

123 ¹⁷ General Orders, War. Dept., Nos. 94, 99, Aug. 4 and Aug. 9, 1862. *Official Records*, 3 ser., II, 291, 333–335.

123 ¹⁸ Judge Charles A. Peabody, "United States Provisional Court for . . . Louisiana, 1862–1865." *Annual Report*, Amer. Hist. Assoc., 1892, 199–210; *Appleton's Ann. Cyc.*, 1864, 480 ff.

124 ¹ *Lincoln the President*, II, 16 ff.

124 ² W. H. H. Terrell, *Rep. of the Adj. Gen. of Ind.*, vol. I, *passim;* W. D. Foulke, *Life of Oliver P. Morton;* H. G. Pearson, *Life of John A. Andrew.*

124 ³ State action in the raising of United States volunteer regiments was of great importance. See Fred A. Shannon, *Organization and Administration of the Union Army, 1861–1865*, I, chap. 1. Morton insisted on furnishing six regiments of Federal troops in 1861, though the call was for four. Foulke, *Morton*, I, 128. Cameron accepted only three of the ten regiments offered by Ohio, and a similar situation existed with regard to Massachusetts and other states. Pearson, *Andrew*, I, 224, 225. In the summer of 1861, Senator Browning of Illinois, after visiting the encampment of Federal volunteers from Rhode Island, located at Washington, wrote: ". . . the whole [is] . . . apparently under the direction of Gov. Sprague of R. I. who is with them in Camp." Browning, *Diary*, I, 480 (July 12, 1861). The Morton Papers in the state archives of Indiana reveal many interesting details concerning the activities of Robert Dale Owen who acted as "State Agent for Indiana" in procuring arms and military equipment, making war contracts (for which in the long run Federal money was used), and in general performing the sort of functions that would normally come within the province of the war department. See Richard William Leopold, *Robert Dale Owen, A Biography*, 346–350.

124 ⁴ *U. S. Stat. at Large*, XII, 591, sec. 9.

124 ⁵ Lincoln said concerning the second confiscation act: ". . . I cannot learn that this law has caused a single slave to come over to us." *Works*, VIII, 30 (Sep. 13, 1862). For the imperfectly understood question of confiscation in relation to emancipation of slaves, see *Constitutional Problems Under Lincoln*, 357–363.

124 ⁶ *U. S. Stat. at Large*, XII, 294 ff., 640.

125 ⁷ Report of Internal Revenue Bureau, in *Cong. Globe*, 42 Cong., 2 sess., 3387; McKee *vs.* U. S., 164 U. S. 292. By taking the amount of the direct tax of 1861 collected in the South, adding the forfeitures, and making allowance for the considerable undervaluation of millions of property taken over by the government, one reaches the conclusion that the people of the South, far from being deficient in their "quotas" for this United States levy, actually overpaid the tax. The matter came up in 1889 in connection with a bill of Congress to reimburse the states for amounts paid in fulfillment of this direct tax. In vetoing this bill President Cleveland stated that about $2,300,000 was credited to the "insurrectionary States." Obviously Cleveland was not including the amounts of the forfeitures nor allowances for undervaluation; had he included these factors he could have made his veto argument even more convincing. He did show, however, that reimbursement was unsound,

that there "should be a certainty and stability about the enforcement of
taxation." He also showed that the theory back of the reimbursing bill was
the notion that "nonpayment" "by the people of the rebellious States . . .
entitles the other States to a donation of . . . [their] share . . . [etc.]."
The reimbursement which Cleveland disapproved was provided by Congress
in 1891. It was for alleged non-payment of this Federal tax that Arlington,
stately home of Lee, was taken over by the United States government, to
become a national cemetery. In this case the Lee heirs were ultimately compensated by act of Congress in the amount of $150,000. Richardson, *Mes-
sages . . . of the Presidents*, VIII, 837 ff., esp. 839–841; *U. S. Stat. at Large*,
XXVI, 822; *Constitutional Problems Under Lincoln*, 317 ff., 423–424. For
Arlington, see *ibid.*, 320–322.

125   8 The eight were Arkansas, Tennessee, North Carolina, Louisiana, Alabama,
Georgia, Virginia (a special case), and South Carolina. In this enumeration
it seems logical to include the "restored government" of Virginia, since all
these remade governments of the seceded states, by December 1865, regarded
themselves as returning to the Union. Furthermore, there were certain legal
pronouncements of the period recognizing this restored government—that
of F. H. Pierpoint—as qualified to act for Virginia. *Constitution of the
United States, as amended to January 1, 1923* (Annotated), Sen. Doc. No.
96, 67 Cong., 2 sess., p. 28; *Constitutional Problems under Lincoln*, 396–401.

125   9 In the Thirty-Eighth Congress Virginia was denied representation in the
House of Representatives. One is speaking here of "restored Virginia"—i. e.,
not West Virginia, but the political body that adhered to the Union, claiming authority as the rightful government of Virginia. *Cong. Globe*, 38 Cong.,
1 sess., 2313 ff.; 2321 ff.; 2311, 2323.

125   10 James Harvey Robinson, *Mind in the Making*, 41.

125   1 Act of August 6, 1861, "to increase the Pay of the Privates in the Regular
Army . . . and for other Purposes," sec. 3. *U. S. Stat. at Large*, XII, 326.

125   2 *Ibid.*, XII, 755; G. C. Sellery, "Lincoln's Suspension of Habeas Corpus as
Viewed by Congress," *Bull. of the Univ. of Wis.*, Hist. Ser., vol. I, no. 3, pp.
213–286; *Constitutional Problems under Lincoln*, chap. vi, esp. pp. 130–131.
By act of March 3, 1863, it was declared that "during the present rebellion
the President . . . is authorized to suspend the privilege of the writ of
habeas corpus . . . [etc.]." There has been a famous controversy as to
where the power of suspension resides, whether in Congress or the President.
On this point the 1863 law was ambiguous and inconclusive. Some said Congress had the power and was now exercising it by conferring the authority
upon the President for the emergency; others argued that Congress (in saying the President "is authorized") was recognizing the existence of a presidential power.

125   3 "The Indemnity Act of 1863: A Study in the Wartime Immunity of Governmental Officers," *Mich. Law Rev.*, XX, 589–613 (1922).

126   4 Space is lacking for the presentation of all the evidence in the writer's
notes tending to show the lack of enforcement of the habeas corpus act, but
the following statement made by the clerk of the Federal district court at
Indianapolis in 1925 may be quoted: "I have personally gone through all of
the order books of both the Circuit Court of the United States and the Dis-

trict Court of the United States covering the entire period of the Civil War and I am unable to find that there was ever any list of prisoners filed by the Secretary of War or the Secretary of State, and there appears to be no order of Court ordering the release of any citizens held by military authority who were not indicted." Letter of William P. Kapper, Clerk of the District Court of the United States, Indianapolis, to the writer, June 15, 1925.

126 5 Though the penalty for treason was softened by the act of July 17, 1862 (*U. S. Stat. at Large*, XII, 589), even this milder penalty was not enforced; it is a striking fact that no life was forfeited and no sentence of fine and imprisonment carried out in any judicial prosecution for treason in connection with the Civil War. The unfortunate execution of Mumford under Butler's jurisdiction at New Orleans in 1862 was a military, not a judicial, case. Nicolay and Hay, *Lincoln*, V, 268–269, 278–279. Concerning certain treason and piracy cases that were being prosecuted in the Federal circuit court at Philadelphia in 1861, Justice Grier, of the United States Supreme Court, said: "I do not intend to try any more of these cases. . . . I have other business to attend to, and do not mean to be delayed . . . from day to day in trying . . . a few unfortunate men here out of a half a million that are in arms against the government." Statement of Justice Grier in U. S. Circuit Court, Philadelphia, Nov. 4, 1861 (enclosure in letter of J. H. Ashton to Attorney-General Bates, same date), Attorney General's Papers, MSS., National Archives. Referring to the same situation, Bates said: ". . . there are . . . political reasons, very operative on my mind, although prudently not proper for publication just now, which make it desirable to hold these cases up." Bates to Ashton, Nov. 10, 1861, *ibid.* The purpose of the Lincoln government was not to convict and punish any persons for treason, but to protect the nation against disloyalty. Arrest and detention of suspected persons was the method used; indictments for treason in the Federal courts, though rather numerous, were regularly "continued" from term to term and ultimately dropped.

126 6 The following bit of correspondence between Lincoln and Stanton throws light on the subject of the release of prisoners. Lincoln wrote to the secretary of war on Aug. 22, 1864: "I . . . wish to oblige [H. W.] Beecher by relieving Howard [imprisoned for complicity in the bogus proclamation published in the New York *World* on May 18, 1864] but I wish you to be satisfied . . . . What say you?" Stanton replied, "I have no objection if you think it right and this a proper time"; whereupon Lincoln gave the order: "Let Howard . . . be discharged." Stanton MSS., Lib. of Cong., XXII, no. 54446.

126 7 *Constitutional Problems under Lincoln*, 152 n.

127 8 J. G. Randall, "The Miners and the Laws of Treason," *No. Am. Rev.*, vol. 216, p. 312 ff. (1922).

127 9 *Constitutional Problems under Lincoln*, 103–117; Roy F. Nichols, "United States *vs.* Jefferson Davis, 1865–1869," *Amer. Hist. Rev.*, XXXI, 266–284 (1926).

127 10 Cramer *vs.* United States, 325 U. S. 1. In this case, described by the New York *Times* (April 24, 1945, p. 21, c. 1) as "the first test of the treason laws in its 150-year history," the Supreme Court by a five-to-four decision ruled that one Anthony Cramer, who conferred with two Nazi saboteurs in the New

York area, had not been proved guilty of an overt act of treason against the United States. ". . . Cramer furnished them no shelter, nothing that can be called sustenance or supplies, and there is no evidence that he gave them encouragement or counsel, or even paid for the drinks." Remarking the difficulty of securing testimony from two independent witnesses as to an overt act of treason, Justice Jackson, who delivered the Court's opinion, observed: ". . . the treason offense is not the only nor can it well serve as the principal legal weapon to vindicate our national cohesion and security." The opinion is significant not merely as it bears on the case of Cramer, but also because of its full historical summary of the crime of treason as legally treated in Britain and the United States.

127   11 *United States vs. McWilliams et al.*, 54 Fed. Supplement 791. Indictment was brought against thirty defendants, such as Gerald B. Winrod, William Dudley Pelley, George S. Viereck, and Elizabeth Dilling, who were accused of having "conspired . . . with one another and with officials of the German Reich and leaders and members of the Nazi party." The trial dragged out over seven long months. Though there was little doubt that the defendants had served the enemy's purpose, the unwieldy proceeding, with continual obstruction from defense lawyers and with all the safeguards which American courts afford for accused persons, ultimately broke down. Justice Eicher of the District Court of the United States for the District of Columbia imposed numerous fines on defense lawyers for repetitious tactics; in retaliation, the attorneys formed an "Eicher Contempt Club"; Mrs. Dilling demanded the presence of members of Congress to observe the trial; one defendant died; others had prolonged illnesses. When Justice Eicher died in the late fall of 1944, it was said that he had been literally "talked to death." The proceedings were thereupon declared a mistrial and with "practically no lamentations from any source" the government dropped (or suspended) the prosecution. New York *Times*, Dec. 10, 1944, sec. iv, p. 10, c. 5.

127   12 *Constitutional Problems under Lincoln*, 159–161. When a Federal marshal in Kansas, in 1859, maintained a large standing posse continuously in the field for a considerable period in order to suppress a band of desperadoes, his action was disapproved at Washington. It was made clear that no authority existed under which a quasi-military force could be maintained by a judicial officer. Attorney General's Papers, MSS., National Archives: Mar. 1, 1861; May 10, 1861; Sep. 10, 1868.

128   13 The attorney general's office under Bates in 1864 comprised eight persons (including clerks and messengers) and had not yet become an executive department. It took no significant part in dealing with disloyalty. Its yearly sum for salaries was $18,264. In 1940 the department of justice had an appropriation of $26,041,946 for salaries. *Ann. Rep. of Att. Gen., 1940*, 219.

128   14 C. A. Berdahl, *War Powers of the Executive in the United States*.

128   15 *Miller vs. U. S.*, 78 U. S. 268.

128   16 *Ex parte* Merryman, Fed. Cas. No. 9487.

128   17 "Confidential" letter of Bates to Stanton, January 31, 1863, Stanton MSS., Lib. of Cong., 52220.

128   18 8 U. S. 101.

128   19 71 U. S. 2 ff. Concerning the Milligan case, ex-Attorney-General Bates

Page

wrote: "If the S.[upreme] Court should decide that Military Commissions
are *lawful,* I predict that the judges who give opinion that way, will go down
to posterity with characters as black as that of L[or]d. Ch[ief] J.[ustice]
Saunders; and that their judgment will be far more odious to this nation,
than Saunders' judgment against the chartered rights and liberties of the
city of London, ever was to the English people." Howard K. Beale, ed., *The
Diary of Edward Bates, 1859–1866,* 547 (Feb. 16, 1866).

129   20 68 U. S. 243.

129   21 J. G. Randall, "The Indemnity Act of 1863," *Mich. Law Rev.,* XX, 589–
613.

130   1 *Constitutional Problems under Lincoln,* 176–179.

130   2 On the law of sedition, as well as on the broad subjects of freedom of speech
and of the press, see Zechariah Chafee, *Freedom of Speech.*

130   3 Elsewhere the writer has dealt with newspapers during the Lincoln administration. *Constitutional Problems under Lincoln,* chap. xix; "The Newspaper Problem . . . during the Civil War," *Amer. Hist. Rev.,* XXIII, 303–
323 (1918).

131   4 As to arbitrary arrests, only a few of the sources can be noted here. Arrests
conducted under Seward's authority early in the war are treated in Frederic
Bancroft, *Life of Seward,* II, chap. 34. J. A. Marshall's *American Bastile*
deals chiefly in abuse and adds little to the *Official Records.* One needs to
go through the voluminous material in the second series of these *Records*
for a comprehensive view of the subject. A table listing briefly the charges
against certain prisoners, and thus illustrating the reasons for arrests, is
found in 2 ser., II, 277–279. Material yet unpublished is to be found in the
National Archives.

131   5 *Official Records,* 1 ser., XXVII, pt. 3, pp. 437–438; 2 ser., I, 155.

132   6*Ibid.,* 2 ser., I, 282 ff.

133   7 Lincoln's reluctance to depart from established American principles, his
sympathy for the conscientious objector, his generosity in releasing political
prisoners, and his claim to the title of the "Great Conciliator" are effectively
set forth by Professor Arthur C. Cole in "Lincoln and the American Tradition of Civil Liberty," *Jour., Ill. State Hist. Soc.,* XIX, 102–114 (1926).

133   8 *Works,* VIII, 309–310.

133   9 ". . . often a limb must be amputated to save a life." *Ibid.,* X, 66.

134   10 New York *Times,* Oct. 5, 1946, p. 4.

VI. LINCOLN AND JOHN BRIGHT

This study first appeared in the *Yale Review*, XXXIV, 292–304 (Winter, 1945). In the present extended form there has been a considerable amount of rewriting as well as full annotation.

Page

135   [1] Edward L. Pierce to William H. Herndon, Milton, Mass., Sep. 15, 1889. Herndon-Weik Coll., Lib. of Cong. James Miller McKim, who related the incident to Pierce, was a prominent Pennsylvania abolitionist, one of the founders of the American Anti-Slavery Society, and later an intimate associate of Lucretia Mott and Theodore Dwight Weld. During the Civil War he was especially active in behalf of Southern freedmen and urged the enlistment of Negro troops in the Union army. The passage Lincoln quoted was probably the peroration of Bright's address at Birmingham, December 18, 1862, on "The War and the Supply of Cotton." Deploring the "measureless calamity" of the American Civil War and denouncing the "odious and . . . blasphemous" attempt of the Confederates to divide the United States, Bright concluded: "I have another and a far brighter vision before my gaze. It may be but a vision, but I will cherish it. I see one vast confederation stretching from the frozen North in unbroken line to the glowing South, and from the wild billows of the Atlantic westward to the calmer waters of the Pacific main,—and I see one people, and one language, and one law, and one faith, and, over all that wide continent, the home of freedom, and a refuge for the oppressed of every race and of every clime." James E. Thorold Rogers, ed., *Speeches on Questions of Public Policy by John Bright, M.P.*, I, 225.

136   [1] This was a marble bust of Bright, the work of a young sculptor named Mr. John Wood and described as "a singularly vigorous & life like representation of the honorable original." Mr. Thomas G. Blain of Manchester intended it as a gift to Lincoln. It came, however, after Lincoln's assassination and was offered as a present to the American nation to be placed in the White House. Thomas H. Dudley, United States consul at Liverpool, described Mr. Blain as "a warm friend of the United States and a great admirer of John Bright as well as of our late lamented President." Dudley to President Johnson, May 10, 1865, MS., National Archives, Wash., D. C. There are in the National Archives other documents on the subject: Blain to Dudley, Apr. 24, 1865, transmitting the bust; Dudley to Blain, May 1, 1865, inquiring as to what should be done now that Lincoln was dead; Blain to Dudley, May 2, 1865, asking that the bust be presented to the American nation; also communications from the state department and the commissioner of public buildings concerning acceptance and placement of the bust. "In June 1866 the bust [of Bright] was moved from the State Department to the Executive Mansion and 'placed in one of the alcoves of the lower Hall, corresponding with one in which the bust of Ex-President Fillmore stands' " P. M. Hamer (of the National Archives) to the author, Feb. 23, 1943.

136   [2] F. Lauriston Bullard, in *Amer. Bar Assoc. Jour.*, XXV, 219 (1939).

136   [3] "I take the liberty of enclosing three photographs of John Bright, one for

yourself, one for Governor Seward, the other for the President. Please present them to the Pres & Gov. Seward with my compliments. They are the best I have seen—indeed nothing can be more like the man." Thomas H. Dudley, Consul at Liverpool, to Congressman E. B. Washburne, Liverpool, Mar. 14, 1864, Washburne MSS., Lib. of Cong.

136 4 Shortly after Lincoln's death Henry Janney wrote from Washington to John Bright. Lincoln, he said, told him that he loved to read Bright's letters. Janney added that Bright's picture hung over the fireplace in one of the rooms of the White House, being the only portrait in the room. Henry Janney to John Bright, Wash., D. C., Apr. 24, 1865, Bright MSS., British Museum (Add. MSS. 43391). Schuyler Colfax, writing to Bright in 1866, told how he had often seen the British leader's portrait in Lincoln's reception room; he also told of Lincoln's expressions of high regard for Bright. Colfax to Bright, May 20, 1866, ibid. (Add. MSS. 43391).

136 5 The papers of Thomas H. Dudley, U. S. consul at Liverpool in Lincoln's day, contain two letters from Charles Wilson, written at Tunbridge Wells, which are of interest in this connection. On March 22, 1864, Wilson wrote: ". . . I last week sent to Mr Mybrea of Castle Street (or rather my brother-in-law Francis Frith of Reigate did) some copies of the large portrait of John Bright." He then referred to sending some of these portraits to the United States through Dudley's office. On March 28 Mr. Wilson wrote again to say that he had sent to Abraham Lincoln "a portrait of John Bright such as hangs in my Dining-room, the reception of which was very gratifying to him." He added: "He [Lincoln] sent me his most cordial thanks, & said that he should write to me as soon as he could find time from the cares of office." Thomas H. Dudley MSS., Henry E. Huntington Libr.

136 6 F. Lauriston Bullard, "Lincoln Pardons Conspirator on Plea of English Statesman," Amer. Bar Assoc. Jour., XXV, 215–220 (1939). See also Emanuel Hertz, ed., Abraham Lincoln: A New Portrait, II, 912.

137 7 Carl Sandburg, Abraham Lincoln: The War Years, III, 507.

138 1 Martin P. Claussen, The United States and Great Britain, 1861–1865: Peace Factors in International Relations (doctoral dissertation, Univ. of Ill., 1938).

139 2 Bartlett Woods to Schuyler Colfax, May 17, 1863, MS., Ill. State Hist. Lib. Woods (1818–1903) was born in Sussex, England, and came to America at the age of eighteen. Settling as a farmer in Lake County, Indiana, he kept a lively interest in civic affairs, was prominent in Indiana agricultural associations, helped organize the Republican party in Indiana, and served two terms in the state legislature. T. H. Ball, Lake County, Indiana, from 1834 to 1872, 298–299; Sam B. Woods, The First Hundred Years of Lake County, Indiana.

140 1 F. L. Owsley, King Cotton Diplomacy, chap. xv. In this chapter Mr. Owsley treats "The Diplomatic Break with England in 1863: Withdrawal of Mason and Expulsion of the British Consuls." James M. Mason, Confederate envoy to London, was never accredited by the British government; instead he was treated with such "offensive arrogance" and "rude incivility" by Earl Russell that the Confederate authorities by August 1863 gave up all hope of recognition and ordered Mason's withdrawal. Official Records

Page

       (Navies), 2 ser. III, 581, 852. See also Randall, *Civil War and Reconstruction*, 646–664.

141   [1] Among the significant titles on Bright are the following: R. A. J. Walling, ed., *The Diaries of John Bright* (foreword by Philip Bright, son of John); George Macaulay Trevelyan, *The Life of John Bright;* R. Barry O'Brien, *John Bright: A Monograph;* George Barnett Smith, *The Life and Speeches of the Right Hon. John Bright, M. P.* (2 vols.); James E. Thorold Rogers, *Speeches on Questions of Public Policy by John Bright, M. P.* (2 vols.).

142   [2] R. Barry O'Brien, *John Bright*, preface, xi.

142   [3] Trevelyan, *Bright*, 88.

142   [4] *Ibid.*, 3, 9.

142   [5] Speaking in the House of Commons on March 13, 1866, Bright referred to the spokesman of a small dissentient group as having "retired into what may be called his political *Cave of Adullam* . . . [etc.]. *Ibid.*, 355–356. For Lincoln's earlier use of the same Biblical allusion, see pp. 83, 224.

142   [6] Trevelyan, *Bright*, 429.

143   [7] *Ibid.*, 309.

143   [8] Martin P. Claussen, as above cited.

143   [1] Mass. Hist. Soc. *Proceedings*, XLV, 151 (1911–12).

143   [2] *Ibid.*, 152.

143   [3] *Ibid.*, 153.

144   [4] Bright's speech at Rochdale, Dec. 4, 1861, quoted in Trevelyan, *Bright*, 313. Three days later Bright wrote to Sumner: "My speech has been published very widely, in all the chief London and many influential county papers. It may do some good here." Mass. Hist. Soc. *Proceedings*, XLV, 153.

144   [5] *Ibid.*, 151.

144   [6] *Ibid.*, 158.

144   [7] *Ibid.*, 154.

144   [8] *Ibid.*, 150.

144   [9] Quoted in Trevelyan, *Bright*, 321.

146   [10] *Lincoln the President*, II, 48–49. For a readable account of the *Trent* affair see Jay Monaghan, *Diplomat in Carpet Slippers: Abraham Lincoln Deals With Foreign Affairs*, 155–193. Monaghan's pages give a full and vivid treatment of international matters under Lincoln; naturally much of his attention is devoted to England.

147   [1] Among the useful guides to English political history during the Victorian era are E. L. Woodward, *The Age of Reform, 1815–1870* (G. N. Clark, ed., *The Oxford History of England*): J. A. R. Marriott, *England since Waterloo* (Charles Oman, ed., *A History of England*, VII); and Sidney Low and Lloyd C. Sanders, *The History of England during the Reign of Victoria (1837–1901)* (William Hunt and Reginald L. Poole, eds., *The Political History of England*, XII). Other significant titles are Herbert W. Paul, *A History of Modern England;* Spencer Walpole, *The History of Twenty-five Years;* Theodore Martin, *The Life of His Royal Highness the Prince Consort;* John Morley, *The Life of William Ewart Gladstone;* and John Morley, *The Life of Richard Cobden.*

148   [2] There is no adequate biography of the Earl of Derby. In addition to the general works mentioned in the preceding note, one should consult George

240 NOTES

Saintsbury, *The Earl of Derby* and Thomas Edward Kebbel, *Life of the Earl of Derby, K. G.* There is also material on Derby in Kebbel's *A History of Toryism: From the Accession of Mr. Pitt . . . to the Death of Lord Beaconsfield . . . .*

148 ³ Frank L. Owsley, *King Cotton Diplomacy*, 463.

148 ⁴ Trevelyan, *Bright*, 322.

148 ⁵ *The Times* (London), July 14, 1863, p. 8, c. 4.

149 ⁶ Trevelyan, *Bright*, 322–323.

149 ⁷ For numerous reports of resolutions adopted at these meetings see *House Exec. Doc.* No. 1, 38 Cong., 1 sess., 117–123, 142–147, and *passim*. Paul Gaylord Hubbard's "Lincoln in Relation to Liberal Sentiment in Great Britain" (MS. master's thesis, Univ. of Ill.) is a competent study.

149 ⁸ O'Brien, *John Bright*, 152–153. For a photograph of the resolution in Lincoln's handwriting, see Trevelyan, *Bright,* facing p. 303.

150 ⁹ MS., Dep. of State, National Archives.

VII. LINCOLN'S PEACE AND WILSON'S

A paper with the above title was read before the Mississippi Valley Historical Association at Cedar Rapids, Iowa, on April 22, 1943. It was published unannotated in the *South Atlantic Quarterly* in July 1943 (XLII, 225–242). Conclusions presented in 1943 have not been withdrawn, but have been considerably expanded and strengthened in the light of later developments. The author, having made a special study of the Wilson administration, realizes that topics here opened up are much too important and complicated for treatment in one essay. In such a situation annotations will not meet the case fully, but the following notes are intended to give citations to sources, to suggest further reading, and at a few points—e. g., Lodge's round robin—to explain matters barely mentioned in the text.

Page
152   [1] The writer has treated Lincoln's reconstruction policy in *Lincoln and the South*, 117–161. See also Charles H. McCarthy, *Lincoln's Plan of Reconstruction*.

152   [2] *Memoirs of Gen. W. T. Sherman* (1891 ed.), II, 326–327.

152   [3] Horace Porter, in R. U. Johnson and C. C. Buel, eds., *Battles and Leaders of the Civil War*, IV, 739. Grant's pencil draft of surrender terms, with deletions and interlineations (facsimile in *Personal Memoirs of U. S. Grant*, II, 496), differs slightly in wording from the text in *Battles and Leaders*.

152   [4] "In my opinion the officers and men paroled at Appomattox Court House . . . cannot be tried for treason so long as they observe the terms of their parole," wrote Grant on June 16, 1865. On August 26, 1867, he strongly urged the attorney general "to quash all indictments found against paroled prisoners of war and to desist from further prosecution of them." Enclosure in letter of Acting Attorney General Binckley to U. S. attorney for middle dist., Tenn., Aug. 28, 1867, Attorney General's Papers, MSS., National Archives. See also *Constitutional Problems under Lincoln*, 101–102.

153   [5] *Diary of O. H. Browning*, II, 216; *Lincoln and the South*, 135–137.

153   [6] "Then recalling the conversation of Mr. Lincoln, at City Point, I sat down at the table, and wrote off the terms . . . ." *Memoirs of Gen. W. T. Sherman*, II, 353.

153   [7] Gideon Welles, "Lincoln and Johnson. Their Plan of Reconstruction and the Resumption of National Authority," *Galaxy*, XIII, 526–527 (April 1872); Frederick W. Seward, *Reminiscences of a War-Time Statesman and Diplomat, 1830–1915*, 254–257. After the war Secretary Seward stated that the plan of reconstruction later announced by Johnson "grew during the administration of Mr. Lincoln." *House Report No. 7*, 40 Cong., 1 sess., 79 (first pagination).

153   [8] *Works*, VIII, 79.

153   [9] Jonathan T. Dorris, "President Lincoln's Clemency," *Jour., Ill. St. Hist. Soc.*, XX, 547–568 (1928).

153   [1] *The Civil War and Reconstruction*, 731–813.

154   [2] New York *Times*, Nov. 11, 1923, p. 1, cc. 2–3.

242

NOTES

Page

154   **3** "The Unpopular Mr. Lincoln," above pp. 65–87; citations, pp. 220–224.

154   **4** To treat this anti-Wilson *cliché* in full is impracticable here. A few points may be briefly noted.

(1) Wilson's policy as to submarine warfare was all of a piece; it was not one thing before the election and another thing afterward. That policy was stated in vigorous diplomatic notes to Germany; it was agreed to by Germany on September 1, 1915. *Diplomatic Correspondence Between the United States and Belligerent Governments Relating to Neutral Rights and Commerce* (Supplement to *American Journal of International Law*,) X, 166. When in March 1916 the sinking of the *Sussex* indicated a departure from this pledge, Wilson sent a sharp note (April 18, 1916), indicating that unless similar sinkings were abandoned, the United States would sever relations with Germany. *Ibid.*, 186–190. When the German government announced on January 31, 1917, that unrestricted submarine warfare would be resumed, Wilson's answer was a breach of relations (February 3).

(2) Wilson's various efforts toward peace, as in his attempts to clarify war aims in December–January, 1916–17, were never inconsistent with his policy of holding Germany to "strict accountability" in the matter of international rights at sea. These, however, were genuine peace efforts following the election of 1916. Wilson worked toward a peaceable solution if possible; he also stated the American position vigorously; he did not, however, change his policy either as to peace or as to submarine warfare after the election.

(3) Wilson spoke and worked toward preparedness in 1916. Various measures of preparedness were passed that year, as to the army and navy, shipping, control of railroads, economic readiness (as in creating the Council of National Defense), etc. Never before in a peacetime year had so much been done in the United States in preparedness for defense.

(4) In a series of speeches Wilson presented the matter of preparedness to the American people, making it clear that the time might come when peace would, in his view, be no longer possible. Ray Stannard Baker and William E. Dodd, eds., *The New Democracy: Presidential Messages, Addresses, and Other Papers (1913–1917) by Woodrow Wilson*, II, 1–121.

(5) One need not belabor the argument that the President does not make war; sometimes presidential policy may lead to war. It is, however, a matter of obvious history that the instrument by which the United States entered the war against Germany was a joint resolution passed by an overwhelming majority in Congress. Before that, Congress approved the breach with Germany.

(6) Wilson did not get the pro-German vote in 1916. It is well known that the pro-German element in the United States worked against him in the years of American neutrality. He made no such appeal, for keeping the country out of war, as to please the Germans. See Clifton James Child, *The German-Americans in Politics, 1914–1917*, 111–153.

(7) The American policy as to submarine warfare that would have pleased the German government was embodied in the McLemore resolution in the House of Representatives, presented in February 1916. Wilson used his influence against that resolution and it was tabled. So also the similar Gore resolution in the Senate. (Some pacifically minded people honestly differed

with Wilson. The point here is that the President's policy was not a shifting thing, changing its tune after the election.) *Congressional Record*, 64 Cong., 1 sess., LIII, pt. 4, pp. 3465, 3720.

(8) One of the outstanding factors in the Wilson administration was the difference between his policy and that of Bryan. It was Bryan who—sincerely, of course—advocated an alteration in American policy so as to "keep us out of war."

(9) Was Wilson neutral? It is at least true that he sought to mediate, and that he explored the resources of neutrality. When belligerent spokesmen urged Wilson to be neutral, they really meant that they wanted help for their side. Bernstorff is authority for the statement that Germany missed a great chance in not accepting Wilson's "peace without victory" and that it was German militarism that prevented such a German decision. Wilson did uphold American rights, but he was never antagonistic to the German people.

(10) As the war progressed, and as peace efforts (including reasonable proposals put forth by Wilson) failed, he came to the point where he believed that Allied victory—not in itself, but integrated with a constructive postwar program—would produce a less war-bent world than German victory. Transition from neutrality to war, a most complicated subject, can be historically explained without the unjust implication that Wilson made a promise to the people and then violated the promise after the election.

155   5 Frederick Logan Paxson, *American Democracy and the World War: Pre-War Years, 1913–1917*, 1–100, gives an excellent treatment of the domestic achievements of the first Wilson administration.

155   6 This episode is briefly summarized in William E. Dodd, *Woodrow Wilson and His Work*, 257–265. It has also been treated in Ruth Cleworth Young, "The War Ministry and Overman Act, 1918" (MS., master's thesis, Univ. of Ill., 1930).

156   7 *Congressional Record*, 66 Cong., 2 sess., LIX, pt. 5, p. 4599 (Mar. 19, 1920).

156   8 Thomas A. Bailey, *Woodrow Wilson and the Great Betrayal*.

156   9 The round robin, drafted by Philander C. Knox, was made known on the night of March 3, 1919, when Lodge arose in the Senate and offered a resolution that "the constitution of the league of nations in the form now proposed . . . should not be accepted by the United States." Further language of the resolution favored prompt negotiation of peace with Germany, after which "the proposal for a league of nations" was to be considered. Lodge admitted that consideration of his resolution was "clearly out of order"; to take it up would have required unanimous consent. Swanson objected, whereupon Lodge said: "I merely wish to add . . . the following"—then he read a paper in which members of the new Senate put it on record that they "would have voted" for the resolution if they had had the opportunity. Thirty-seven senators or senators elect, all Republicans, had signed the statement. This was more than a third of the new Senate, and a third can kill a treaty which the majority favors. In treating this senatorial "ultimatum" D. F. Fleming has shown that the purpose of the signers was not to suggest revisions in the covenant; if such suggestions had been made the evidence is that the President would have given them due consideration. Here was a so-

called "resolution," on one of the most important questions in American
history, presented to the United States Senate, a body well known for elaborate debate and long delay, shortly before midnight on the last day of the
session. Of course it was not intended to be taken seriously as a resolution.
Fleming shows that a majority vote of the Senate to pass the resolution was
"most improbable," that it was "doubtful whether the fathers of the declaration would have permitted a vote on it," and that the proposal for later
action by the Peace Conference on the question of a League was lacking in
sincerity. After peace had been made Wilson "would have then no leverage"
at Paris, and the senators knew that. "The publication of the Round Robin
[writes Fleming] was a highly significant move . . . . It was to lay its orig-
inators open . . . to the charge of attempting to strengthen the hands of
reactionary forces abroad against the supreme effort of an American President to achieve international security at the close of fratricidal warfare that
had all but extinguished civilization." *The United States and the League of
Nations*, 153 ff. On the day after these proceedings, the New York *Sun*
(March 4, 1919) declared: "Woodrow Wilson's League of Nations died in
the Senate tonight." See also Lodge. *The Senate and the League of Nations*,
118 ff.

156   10 A poll of American newspapers, presented in the *Literary Digest* on April
5, 1919, showed prevailing support for the League; in the same period the
League was endorsed by thirty-two state legislatures and thirty-three governors. Among Republican and independent papers much of the approval
was "conditional." If one counts only half of this conditional approval on
the affirmative side, together with the large element of unconditional approval, it appears that support for the League was overwhelming. Fleming,
218–220.

156   11 At a time when preliminary steps were being taken in shaping Republican
strategy in the Senate, Lodge, who was chiefly responsible for such strategy,
conferred (in late April 1919) with William E. Borah. Organization of the
incoming Senate was the subject of discussion. Lodge wrote: ". . . it seemed
. . . obvious to me that any attempt to defeat the treaty . . . with the
League by a straight vote in the Senate, if taken immediately, would be
hopeless . . . . I told him . . . there was only one thing to do and that
was to proceed . . . by way of amendment and reservation. He [Borah]
told me that he agreed entirely . . . , that he did not believe the treaty
could possibly be beaten at that time by a direct vote . . . ." Borah went
on to say that he would support amendments and reservations, and then "on
the final vote he would vote against the acceptance of the treaty . . . ."

    The whole passage needs to be read in order to show how Lodge was satis-
fying men who, like Borah, were "against the treaty in any form whatever,"
while also, as Lodge blandly wrote, keeping "the support of those who . . .
were anxious to adopt the treaty if it could be done with safety to the United
States." Lodge thus prevented pro-League Republicans from breaking away
from control, but in the outcome, the result was in the Borah sense. The Republicans had the tiniest majority (two) in the Senate, and the Borah type
of irreconcilables was very far from a majority even of the Republicans. To
think of the proceedings of the whole Senate being so manipulated as to

satisfy only the few "die hard" enemies of the League is one of the amazing aspects of the subject. Lodge, *The Senate and the League of Nations*, 146–148. See also D. F. Fleming, *The United States and the League of Nations*, 206–208.

156 [12] In the period following Lodge's round robin Senator Knox, though opposing the League, was willing to give a pledge that in case of threatened future aggression the United States would "consult" with other nations as to means of removing the menace. "Even that indefinite commitment was too much for Borah. Lodge and Borah understood one another." The Senate committee on foreign relations refused to support so mild an obligation as the Knox pledge. (Fleming, 222–223.) It was under these circumstances that Taft expressed deep regret that the foreign relations committee was constructed "by a careful selection of Republicans . . . whose opposition to the treaty has been pronounced." Taft added: "Senator Kellogg would naturally have been taken before Senator Moses, a new Senator . . . . Senator Kellogg, however, had ventured to make a speech in favor of a league of nations . . . and had refused to sign the 'round robin.' " (*Ibid.*, 223).

157 [13] Lodge, *Senate and the League*, 210–211.

157 [14] In October 1920 thirty-one eminent people, to whom an additional twenty-five were later added, appealed for support of Harding as the best way to assure the adherence of the United States to the League of Nations. This group, described as "the brains and conscience of the Republican party," included Root, Hughes, Hoover, and others of great distinction and prominence. Bailey, *Woodrow Wilson and the Great Betrayal*, 329 ff.

158 [15] Wilson's alleged "betrayal" of Germany is refuted by Charles Seymour in "America's Responsibility to Germany," *Atl. Mo.*, vol. 133, pp. 824–832 (June 1924).

158 [16] Maurice Léon, *How Many World Wars? The Warning of Foch.*

159 [17] *The Memoirs of Count Bernstorff*, 104–105, 108.

159 [1] See, for example, Lloyd George's statement of war aims of Jan. 5, 1918, which closely parallels Wilson's Fourteen Points. James Brown Scott, ed., *Official Statements of War Aims and Peace Proposals, December 1916 to November 1918*, 225–233.

160 [2] Ray Stannard Baker and William E. Dodd, eds., *War and Peace: Presidential Messages, Addresses, and Public Papers (1917–1924), by Woodrow Wilson*, I, 254–255.

160 [3] *Ibid.*, I, 233–234.

161 [4] The text of the American treaty with Germany in 1921 is given in *Sen. Doc. No. 70*, 67 Cong., 1 sess. Germany agreed to accord "all the rights and advantages stipulated for the benefit of the United States in the Treaty of Versailles . . . notwithstanding the fact that such Treaty has not been ratified by the United States."

162 [1] New York *Times*, Feb. 26, 1936, p. 11, c. 2.

163 [2] Traditional ideas as to the harshness of the Treaty of Versailles upon Germany have been partly due to the book, *Economic Consequences of the Peace*, by J. M. Keynes, but in a recent book, *The Carthaginian Peace*, Etienne Mantoux has retrospectively and factually analyzed the situation concerning which Keynes was making broad predictions. According to Man-

toux, if Germany's partial payments on reparations account are balanced by loans to Germany from Allied countries—loans which were defaulted—the Allied contribution to Germany in the post-Versailles period exceeded payments by Germany to the extent of billions of dollars. In the net balance it was as if the Allies were paying huge reparations to Germany. Mantoux shows that Germany was better off in 1929 than in 1913 in coal and steel production and in real national income, while its merchant marine had been to a large extent restored. Taking the post-Wilson period it is but stating the obvious to recognize (1) that fear of a new wave of German military aggression was not baseless, and (2) that Germany did build up its economic structure with Allied consent and huge financial support. In this picture it is significant to remember the shattering terms that Germany was imposing upon Russia in the Treaty of Brest-Litovsk.

165　　¹ After the United Nations was established in 1942 Norman Angell said: "We are united because we are at war. The tragedy is that if we had been united in time of peace there would have been no war." In contrast to this concept of international solidarity to prevent war from breaking out, the theory of statutory neutrality was that a nation would seek only to isolate itself from involvement. In time of peace, a law for future neutrality would be passed. It would already be on the books; special legislation for a particular war would be unnecessary; the generalized law would be so wise and so all-embracing that it would fit whatever war situation might yet arise.

　　To accomplish this purpose the main formula was the embargo; then it was found that as to Spain, and as to Japan, some of the sponsors of the embargo did not want it applied. It was realized that the embargo helped the fascist cause of Franco, as also of Hitler and Mussolini. Senator Nye himself, in the spring of 1938, offered a resolution to lift the embargo against Loyalist Spain. The resolution was not adopted, but the New York *Times* stated that if it had been, even if the cash-and-carry provisions had been retained, it would have been "regarded as the end of the experiment in statutory neutrality" (May 5, 1938).

　　At no point did the neutrality legislation cause the United States to be isolated from foreign imbroglios. As to Japan's war against China the very idea of any embargo was highly provocative; its application would have inflamed the Japanese militarists. It was not applied against Japan, nor would its sponsors have wished it applied. The embargo was their instrument of "neutrality"; yet they considered that the embargo would lead to war. Finally, as to Hitler the policy of statutory neutrality served both as an encouragement for aggression and an utterly misleading prediction of American indifference.

　　The neutrality legislation was an example of the unstable and misleading substitute to which a nation resorts when it gives up, or has previously helped to tear down, the basic principle of international solidarity. The main problem of this whole period was to prevent war by discouraging the aggressor, especially in the case of Hitler and Japan. Hitler could not have gone ahead against a solid international front. He wanted only a one-front war, knocking off one nation at a time. The non-international program in the United States—framed on the theory that the nation should prospec-

Page

tively try for its own insulating solution—had the effect of showing un-realistic apathy where deep international concern was the unmistakable fact.

166 [1] Harold Dwight Lasswell, *Propaganda Technique in the World War.*

166 [2] George G. Bruntz, *Allied Propaganda and the Collapse of the German Empire in 1918.*

166 [3] George Creel, *How We Advertised America* . . . .

166 [4] James Robert Mock and Cedric Larson, *Words That Won the War: The Story of the Committee on Public Information, 1917-1919.*

166 [5] George Sylvester Viereck, *Spreading Germs of Hate.*

166 [6] *Ibid.*, 207.

166 [7] Lasswell, *Propaganda Technique,* 216-217.

166 [8] J. G. de Roulhac Hamilton, *The Correspondence of Jonathan Worth,* I, 289, 297.

166 [9] *Works,* XI, 85.

167 [10] *Ibid.,* XI, 88.

168 [11] *Congressional Record,* 68 Cong., 2 sess., LXVI, pt. 5, 5413 (Mar. 3, 1925). See also Denna Frank Fleming, *The United States and the World Court.*

168 [12] *Congressional Record,* 69 Cong., 1 sess., LXVII, pt. 3, 2825 (Jan. 27, 1926).

168 [13] Bailey, *Woodrow Wilson and the Great Betrayal,* ch. xx.

169 [1] Howard K. Beale, *The Critical Year: A Study of Andrew Johnson and Reconstruction.*

169 [2] In Louisiana the Warmoth (anti-Grant) faction of Republicans supported McEnery for governor (1872). Louisiana Democrats also supported him and the state returning board certified the election of the McEnery ticket. The Grant faction of radical Republicans, however, declared their candidate, Kellogg, to be elected; thus the state had two organizations, both claiming to be the government of Louisiana. According to Warmoth, the Kellogg group, failing to capture the returning board, made up their own board which, "without having a single return from any poll in the State, proceeded to fabricate . . . what they claimed to be the result of the State election." H. C. Warmoth, *War, Politics and Reconstruction: Stormy Days in Louisiana,* 206. See also Rhodes, *Hist. of the U. S.,* VII, 110. The Louisiana case is one example to show how radical machines in the South worked. The collapse of such machines was complete with Hayes's withdrawal of Federal troops from the South in 1877. It is in contrast to such conditions of the Grant period that one should judge Lincoln's plan as to Louisiana.

171 [3] See above, pp. 156, 243-244.

171 [4] On Henry White, Lodge, and the League, see Allan Nevins, *Henry White: Thirty Years of American Diplomacy,* 387-416; Fleming, *United States and the League,* 180-181.

173 [5] In this passage the quoted portions are taken from Arthur B. Tourtellot, ed., *Woodrow Wilson: Selections for Today,* 135, 161, 169. The whole of the Tourtellot volume, however, being an excellent selection, is worthy of careful reading for the distinguished eloquence of Wilson's statements and for an understanding of his program. For Wilson's speeches in his tour of the country in September 1919, see *Addresses of President Wilson . . . on his Western Tour . . .* [etc.], Sen. Doc. No. 120, 66 Cong., 1 sess. (1919).

NOTES

Page
173   6 *The Federalist* (Everyman's Library ed.), No. XLI, p. 204.
174   7 Herbert Agar's *A Time for Greatness* is a stimulating study of peace making with special reference to World War II.
174   8 Baker and Dodd, eds., *War and Peace*, I, 234.
174   9 *Works*, XI, 47.

VIII. LINCOLN THE LIBERAL STATESMAN

Page
175   [1] Stanley Pargellis, "Lincoln's Political Philosophy," *Abr. Lincoln Quar.*, III, 275–290 (1945).

177   [2] Richard Nelson Current, *Old Thad Stevens: A Story of Ambition*, 53, 226.

178   [3] *Works*, VI, 126.

178   [4] *Lincoln the President*, I, 281–282. See also Reinhard H. Luthin, "Abraham Lincoln and the Tariff," *Amer. Hist. Rev.*, XLIX, 609–629 (1944).

179   [5] William H. Herndon to Truman H. Bartlett, July 19, 1887, MS., Mass. Hist. Soc.

179   [1] *Works*, V, 249.

181   [2] For Lincoln on internal improvements, see speech in House of Representatives, June 20, 1848, *Works*, II, 28–48. Quoted passages are from this speech.

181   [3] Fragment on government [July 1, 1854 ?], *Works*, II, 182–183.

182   [1] *Works*, VI, 312–313.

182   [2] *Ibid.*, I, 151–152.

182   [3] *Ibid.*, I, 197–198.

184   [4] Ray Allen Billington, *The Protestant Crusade, 1800–1860: A Study of the Origins of American Nativism.*

184   [5] New York *Evening Post*, Feb. 3, 1855, article headed "Albany [Correspondence of the Evening Post]."

184   [6] *Ibid.*

184   [7] *Dic. of Amer. Biog.*, VII, 142.

185   [8] "Its [the Knownothing party's] candidate for Governor was Henry J. Gardner, a very skilful political organizer. He had a book in which he had the names of men in every town in the Commonwealth whom he attached to his personal fortunes by promises, or flattery, or because in some cases of their sincere belief in the doctrine. He understood better than any other man I ever knew the value of getting the united support of men who were without special influence, even the men who were odious or ridiculous among their own neighbors, but who united might be a very formidable force. He organized with great skill and success the knave-power and the donkey-power of the Commonwealth." George F. Hoar, *Autobiography of Seventy Years*, I, 189.

185   [9] *Works*, II, 287.

185   [10] *Ibid.*, VI, 45.

185   [11] *Lincoln the President*, I, 161 n.

185   [12] *Works*, V, 130.

186   [13] *Ibid.*, VIII, 200. Explanation of the revocation is here given in a letter from Halleck to Grant, Jan. 21, 1863. The quoted words may well have been Lincoln's own. (When the Lincoln papers in the Library of Congress are opened in 1947 we will probably know the reason why this Halleck communication is included in Lincoln's works. At times Lincoln would himself draft an order or communication to be issued in the name of the secretary of war or the general in chief.)

186   [14] Current, *Old Thad Stevens*, 103–104.

187   [15] *Works*, I, 199.

Page
187   16 *Ibid.*, I, 206.
187   17 *Ibid.*
187   1 *Ibid.*, VI, 26.
187   2 *Ibid.*, I, 262.
187   3 *Ibid.*, V, 361.
188   4 *Ibid.*, V, 247–248.
188   5 For quoted portions in this paragraph, see *Works*, VII, 56–59.
188   6 *Ibid.*, V, 360.
188   7 *Ibid.*, V, 361.
189   8 *Ibid.*
189   9 *Ibid.*, VI, 321.
189   10 *Ibid.*, VIII, 194–197.
189   11 *Ibid.*, X, 53–54.
189   1 *Ibid.*, VI, 177.
190   2 *Ibid.*, II, 229.
190   3 *Ibid.*, I, 35.
190   4 *Ibid.*, I, 49–50.
191   5 In this passage (on Lincoln's warnings as to unfavorable tendencies in American democracy) the quoted portions are from his address before the Young Men's Lyceum of Springfield, Illinois, Jan. 27, 1838 (misdated 1837 by Nicolay and Hay). *Works*, I, 35–50.
191   6 *Ibid.*, I, 38.
191   7 *Ibid.*, I, 44.
192   8 *Ibid.*, I, 43.
193   1 *Ibid.*, X, 39.
193   2 *Ibid.*, II, 227–228.
194   3 *Ibid.*, II, 327–328.
194   4 *Ibid.*, II, 229.
194   5 *Ibid.*, II, 226.
195   1 Lincoln's attention to domestic economy in the South, and his wish that emancipation should proceed by easy transition rather than by serious disruption, appear in his letter to General N. P. Banks, Aug. 5, 1863. Referring to Louisiana he thought "it would not be objectionable for her to adopt some practical system by which the two races could gradually live themselves out of the old relation to each other, and both come out better prepared for the new." (This is but one example; there were others.) *Works*, IX, 56.
195   2 Various factors which enabled Lincoln to understand Southern viewpoints have been briefly presented by the author in *Lincoln and the South.*
196   3 "If all earthly power were given me, I should not know what to do as to the existing institution." Speech at Peoria, Oct. 16, 1854, *Works*, II, 206.
196   4 *Works*, II, 279–280.
196   5 For Lincoln's explanation of his house-divided declaration, and his regret that the famous slogan was misinterpreted, see *Lincoln the President*, I, 117–118.
196   6 *Works*, II, 205.
196   7 *Ibid.*, V, 345.
197   8 *Ibid.*, V, 345–348.
197   9 *Ibid.*, V, 351–352.

Page
197 10 *Ibid.*, V, 356–357.
198 1 For quoted portions of the Mexican War speech, see *Works*, I, 340–341.
198 2 *Ibid.*, VI, 322.
199 1 *Ibid.*, II, 127–128.
200 2 *Ibid.*, II, 164–165, 171.
200 3 *Ibid.*, I, 207–208.
201 4 *Ibid.*, I, 208–209.
201 5 Tyler Dennett, ed., *Lincoln and the Civil War in the Diaries and Letters of John Hay*, 19–20.
201 6 *Works*, VI, 304.
201 7 *Ibid.*, VIII, 131.
202 1 Allen Thorndike Rice, ed., *Reminiscences of Abraham Lincoln by Distinguished Men of His Time*, 379. The newspaper correspondent Noah Brooks, an intimate friend of the President, doubted that Lincoln made the remark. Brooks, *Washington in Lincoln's Time*, 29.
202 2 Well treated in T. Harry Williams, *Lincoln and the Radicals*.
203 3 *Lincoln the President*, II, 229–232. In A. K. McClure, *Abraham Lincoln and Men of War-Times*, 268 ff., the conference is treated with what would now be called window-dressing, or after-the-event publicizing. One needs to go behind the more obvious record to discover the difference between the conference as planned, in which lack of confidence in Lincoln was a prominent motive, and the public understanding of the conference as held, and as managed by the President. For a fuller treatment see William B. Hesseltine, "Lincoln's War Governors," *Abr. Lincoln Quar.*, IV, 153–200 (Dec. 1946).
203 4 *Lincoln the President*, II, 241–249.
204 5 F. B. Carpenter, *The Inner Life of Abraham Lincoln: Six Months at the White House*, 217.
204 6 Diary of Salmon P. Chase, in *Annual Report*, Amer. Hist. Assoc., 1902, II, 87.
205 7 Carl Sandburg, *Abraham Lincoln: The War Years*, III, 300.
205 8 In the month after his Mexican War speech Lincoln sent a notable letter to his partner Herndon, concerning the contention that "if it shall become necessary to repel invasion, the President may . . . invade the territory of another country," the President being the judge as to whether the necessity exists. Vigorously refuting this contention, Lincoln wrote: "Allow the President to invade a neighboring nation whenever he shall deem it necessary to repel an invasion, and you allow him to do so whenever he may choose to say he deems it necessary for such purpose, and you allow him to make war at pleasure. Study to see if you can fix any limit to his power in this respect, after having given him so much as you propose. If to-day he should choose to say he thinks it necessary to invade Canada to prevent the British from invading us, how could you stop him?" Lincoln to Herndon, Washington, D. C., Feb. 15, 1848, *Works*, II, 1–3. See also *Herndon's Lincoln* (Angle ed.), 224–226.

INDEX

Godwin, Parke, and move to displace Lincoln, 80.

Gould, Jay, 40.

Governors. *See* war governors.

Grant, U. S., compared to McClellan, 85; abused by war correspondents, 130; confers with Lincoln at City Point, Va., 152; urges Lee to confer with Lincoln, 153; order concerning Jews revoked, 185-186; considers surrender terms inconsistent with postwar prosecution, 241; administration of, in relation to reconstruction in Louisiana, 247.

Great Britain, and War of 1812, 1-2; American relations with, 51; Union propaganda in, 63; "rule of law" in, 119; attitudes toward American Civil War, 137-141, 149; reaction to emancipation proclamation, 144; Liberals and Tories, 147-148; meetings in favor of Lincoln and emancipation, 149-150.

Greeley, Horace, questionnaire to Republican governors in 1864, 80-81; policy of letting erring states go in peace, 96.

Grier, Justice, on treason indictments, 234.

Grimké, Sarah M., 212.

Gurney, Mrs. Eliza P., Lincoln's letter to, 59.

Gurowski, Adam, Count, denunciations of Lincoln cited, 220, 221.

Habeas corpus, suspension of, 122, 131-132; dates of suspension, 231; act of 1863, 126, 233-234; not ruled on by Supreme Court, 128; who is authorized to suspend, 233.

Hague Conference, 168.

Hahn, Michael, Lincoln's letter to, 193.

Hall, Christopher Newman, 146.

Halleck, Henry W., revokes order on Jews in Lincoln's name, 249.

Hamilton, Alexander, 179.

Hanks, Nancy, 30.

Harding, W. G., President, campaign for in 1920 in relation to League of Nations, 245.

Hawley, Joseph R., General, quoted, 221.

Hay, John, and Bixby letter, 32; and Lincoln's central idea of Civil War, 201; questionable attitude toward McClellan, 214. *See also* Nicolay and Hay.

Hayes, Rutherford B., 169.

Helper, Hinton R., *Impending Crisis* 61, 89.

Henry, Patrick, Caesar and Tarquin speech, 2.

Hergesheimer, Joseph, quoted, 36-37.

Herndon, William H., and Mrs. Lincoln, 7-9; theory of Mrs. Lincoln's "revenge," 7-9; comment on Lincoln, 68; letter of Pierce to, 135; describes Lincoln defending liberty, 179; Lincoln's letter to (1848) concerning "preventive war," 205, 251; quoted, 208.

Hesseltine, William B., quoted, 60.

Hill, Benjamin H., 91.

Hilton *vs.* Guyot, 229.

Historical revision or restoration, 2-3.

History of American Life, 217.

Hitler, Adolf, 151; and notion that Wilson betrayed Germany, 158; Allied bargaining with, 162; in relation to American neutrality, 246.

Hoar, George F., praises Republican party, 17-18, 210; humane purity of, 26; characterizes Henry Joseph Gardner, 184-185; quoted on Knownothing party, 249.

Homestead act of 1862, signed by Lincoln, 181.

Hoover, Herbert, 245.

House of Representatives, favors World Court (1925), 168; dominated by Stevens, 176, 186.

House-divided speech, 196.

Howard, Joseph, Jr., forger of presidential proclamation, his imprisonment and release, 234.

Hughes, Charles Evans, on presidential legislation, 231-232; supports League, 245.

Hughes, John Joseph, Archbishop, promotes Union cause in Europe, 63.

Hungary. *See* Kossuth.

Hurlbut, Stephen A., 98.

Illinois, and "internal improvements," 180; Lincoln desires no slavery in, 196. *See also* Lincoln-Douglas debates.

Inaugural address of 1861, 94; peaceable character of Lincoln's statements, 227-228.

Indemnity act of 1863, 129.

Indiana, Robert Dale Owen as state agent, 232; Bartlett Woods in, 238.

Insurgent, defined, 229-230.

Insurrection, defined, 229-230.

Isolationists, 58, 163-165; valued by Nazis, 164; produce entanglement in foreign affairs, 167-168, 172.

72; and abolition issue, 72; anti-liberal
and anti-Lincoln, 73; dominant in Lincoln's party, 75; attempt to clip Lincoln's
authority, 77; their opposition to Lincoln's renomination, 78-79; profit from
election of 1864, 82; denounce Milligan
decision, 176; and reconstruction in
Louisiana, 247.
Ramsdell, Charles W., quoted, 24; interpretation of Sumter episode, 105 ff.
Raymond, Henry J., journalist and chairman of Republican national committee,
63; gloomy regarding Lincoln's prospects
of reëlection, 79, 222.
Rebellion, defined, 230.
Reconstruction, Lincoln's plan, 152-153;
harshness due to defeat of Lincoln's principles, 85-86; collapse of Republican program, 169.
Reid, Whitelaw, letter to Anna E. Dickinson, 79-80.
Reparations, dropped by Allies, 163.
Republican party, and Free Soil party, 17;
relation to Whig party, 18; and territorial laws, 19; its members in Congress
avoid prohibition of slavery in territories
in 1861, 19-20, 93-94; restricted antislavery program, 48-49, 89; use of the
name "Union" party, 62, 219; Republican senators worry Lincoln, 77-78; discouragement in 1864, 79-80; movement to
oust Lincoln after nomination, 80-81; in
relation to Sumter question, 105, 108;
Illinois convention of 1860 at Decatur,
207; praised by George F. Hoar, 210; its
varying appeals in different states, 210-
211; "alliance" with Buchanan proslavery
Democrats, 211; criticized by Stanton,
214; and Senate round robin, 243; and
organization of Senate (April 1919), 244;
October 1920 declaration of leading Republicans in support of the League, 245;
and reconstruction in Louisiana, 247;
"Black Republicans," 89; and tariff, 178.
See also radical Republicans.
Retaliation, Lincoln's cautious attitude, 60-
61.
Rhett, Robert Barnwell, 46; distrustful of
Southern coöperative action, 48.
Rhineland, Allies allow Hitler to invade,
162; remilitarized, 163.
Rhode Island, volunteer regiments, 232.
Ricardo, British economist, 145.
Richmond, Convention of 1861, 46.

Robinson, James Harvey, quoted, 125.
Roebuck, John Arthur, favors recognition
of Confederacy, 148.
Roosevelt, Franklin D., war powers granted
by Congress, 123; prosecutions for disloyalty under, 127; avoids suspension of
habeas corpus privilege, 131.
Roosevelt, Theodore, President, support of
Second Hague Conference, 168.
Root, Elihu, offers formula for adherence
to World Court, 168; possible appointment on Peace Commission, 170; mentioned, 171; joins in pro-League appeal
for Republican votes (October 1920),
245.
Round Robin of March 1919 (Republican
anti-League maneuver in Senate), 156-
157, 243-244.
Rubery, Alfred, pardoned by Lincoln, 136-
137.
"Rule of law," British and American concepts, 119; during Civil War, 118-134.
Russell, Earl, British foreign secretary, 147;
policy of non-intervention toward American Civil War, 148; favors unbroken
harmony with United States, 149; does
not receive Confederate envoy, 238-239.
Rutledge, Ann, 5-6.

Saar, reclaimed by Germany, 163.
Sandburg, Carl, 52, 87, 137, 204-205, 208-
209, 215, 217.
Sanitary Commission, 38.
Saunders, Lord Chief Justice, 235.
Schlesinger, Arthur M., Sr., cited, 217.
Scott, Dred. See Dred Scott.
Scott, Winfield, advises evacuation of Sumter, 97.
Secession, its relation to war causation,
45 ff.; resisted by Convention at Richmond, 46; leaders unwilling for Southern
state coöperation, 47; cultural factor (and
secession per se), 88-89; unilateral action
of states, 90, 93; relation to Lincoln's
election, 92; of lower South, 93; regarded
by some as temporary, 96. See also Confederate States of America.
Sedition trial (1944-45), 127, 235.
Senate of the United States, discourteous
toward Seward, 54-55; and World Court,
168; Lodge's round robin, 243-244; and
League of Nations, 156 ff.; Republican
organization of, 1919, 244.

Swartwout. *See* Bollman and Swartwout case.

Swett, Leonard, defeated Republican candidate for Congress, 77, 222.

Taft, William H., President, 170; approves League to Enforce Peace, 168; supports League of Nations, 171.

Tammany Hall, 62.

Taney, Roger B., Chief Justice, 21; Dred Scott decision, 11 ff.; holds presidential suspension of habeas corpus unconstitutional, 128.

Tappan, Arthur, 212.

Tappan, Lewis, 212.

Tariff, 177-178, 214; collection of duties in the South, 115; under Wilson, 155.

Taxation, levied on South by United States during Civil War, 232-233.

Taylor. *See* Fort Taylor.

Taylor, Zachary, President, 22.

Tennessee, ratifies thirteenth amendment, 233.

Territories, slavery in, 13, 19; Republican attitude toward, 93-94; Lincoln's declaration, 196. *See also* Dred Scott decision, Douglas, Kansas-Nebraska act, Republican party.

Texas, 226.

Thirteenth amendment, ratification of, 125.

Thompson, George, 146.

Tilden, Samuel J., 105.

Tilton, Theodore, and questionnaire to Republican governors in 1864, 80-81.

Times, The (London), 138-139, 144.

Toombs, Robert A., 45, 103.

Tourtellot, Arthur B., editor of Wilson's selected speeches and writings, 247.

Treason, indictments not pushed, 126, 234; negative United States record in prosecuting, 127. *See also* Cramer *vs.* United States.

Treaty of Versailles. *See* Versailles, Treaty of.

Trent affair, 140, 146; and Bright's wish to avoid war, 143-144; Lincoln's policy, 198.

Trevelyan, George Macaulay, quoted, 142, 143, 148-149.

Tribune, Chicago. *See* Medill, Joseph.

Trumbull, Lyman, 75.

Tunbridge Wells, England, 238.

Turner, Frederick Jackson, 217.

Twain, Mark, quoted, 6.

Tyler, Mrs. Alice Felt, cited, 215.

Uncle Tom's Cabin, 89, 225.

Underwood tariff, 155.

Union, and slavery, 221-222. *See also* secession.

Union League, 62.

Union party. *See* Republican party.

United Nations, 198.

United States, intellectual aspects in Lincoln's day, 52 ff.; racial backgrounds, 53; social attitudes, 53; military policy, 118-119; "rule of law" in, 119; relation to Confederate States (legal aspects), 213; treaty with Germany (1921), 245.

United States *vs.* Jefferson Davis, 127.

United States *vs.* McWilliams *et al. See* sedition trial.

Vallandigham, Clement L., arrested in 1863 for speech denouncing Lincoln administration, 57, 132; case summarized, 129-130; Supreme Court declines to overrule military commission, 129; unmolested after return to Ohio, 130.

Vallandigham group, demands cessation of hostilities, 81.

Van Buren, Martin, President, 22.

Versailles, Treaty of, 161, 162, 163; relation to German-American Treaty of 1921, 161, 170; revisionist study by Mantoux as to economic effect upon Germany, 245-246.

Viereck, George Sylvester, on Wilson's speeches as propaganda, 166; and sedition trial of 1944, 235.

Vineyard, Mrs. Jesse. *See* Owens, Mary.

Virginia, 45, 49; Peace Convention and attitude toward Union, 46 ff.; no prewar grievance, 47, 217; in relation to Sumter question, 97-98; Unionist government, legal status of, 125; efforts to prevent secession of, 226; ratifies thirteenth amendment, 233; "restored Virginia" denied representation in Thirty-Eighth Congress, 233. *See also* Peace Convention.

Vogdes, Captain Israel, 100.

Wade, Benjamin F., 171; dislike of Lincoln, 70; anti-liberal policy, 176.

Wade-Davis bill (1864), 79; disapproved by Lincoln, 121.

Walker, Robert J., 63.

Wallas, Graham, quoted, 47, 50.

War, realistic treatment, 37-40; explanations (cultural, economic, etc.), 41 ff.;

APOLLO EDITIONS

Fairleigh Dickinson University
Florham-Madison Campus Library
Madison, NJ